Class and
the British Electorate

Class and
the British Electorate

DAVID ROBERTSON

Basil Blackwell

First published in 1984 by Basil Blackwell Limited,
108 Cowley Road, Oxford OX4 1JF

British Library Cataloguing in Publication Data

Robertson, David, 1946 –
  Class and the British electorate.
  1. Elections – Great Britain   2. Social
  structure – Great Britain   3. Great Britain
  – Social conditions – 20th century
  I. Title
  324.2'0941   JN956
  ISBN 0-85220-606-3

Typeset by Margaret Helps and Associates, Norwich
Printed and bound in Great Britain by
The Camelot Press, Southampton

To Bill Aughterson, Tony Fox and Deborah Quare

Contents

Preface

This book, like the recently published work by Bo Sarlvik and Ivor Crewe, *Decade of Dealignment* (1983, Cambridge University Press), is one of the many products of the British Election Study. This project, though not originally conceived under that name, has effectively been running since 1963, and still goes on. In the sixties David Butler and Donald Stokes carried out a number of surveys before and after the elections of 1964, 1966, and 1970. From these appeared the first major survey-based study of British electoral behaviour, *Political Change in Britain*. Just before the first 1974 election, responsibility for these surveys, by then financed by the Social Science Research Council, was transferred to a team at Essex University, headed by Crewe and Sarlvik, with James E. Alt as Chief Research Officer. Two surveys were carried out then, after each of the general elections of 1974. In 1975 I joined Crewe and Sarlvik as the third co-director, initially to help carry out a survey of the 1975 referendum on membership of the European Community. The three of us were collectively responsible for the final wave of research at Essex, the post-election survey of the 1979 election. So many people have been involved in these surveys, and in research arising from them, that it is impossible either to mention them all, or to list the resulting publications. As the project goes on, back now in Oxford under the directorship of Anthony Heath, who has carried out a survey of the 1983 election, a quite unique, sustained collaborative venture continues.

This book, like Sarlvik and Crewe's, is principally concerned with the elections of the seventies, though both draw heavily on data and research from earlier waves of the project, and would be impossible but for that backlog of information and expertise. Far more than most works in the social sciences, none of us can be sure where to claim credit, or try to dodge blame. In particular this book might be seen, as was originally intended, as a companion to *Decade of Dealignment*, concentrating more heavily on the social background of voters. Much of the work for both books was carried out by the same team of research assistants, for example, and I am no more solely responsible for those parts of the questionnaires from which I draw my data than are Sarlvik and Crewe for what they study. I must publicly say that I regard them effectively as my co-authors though they are entitled to the usual disclaimer of responsibility for error. In the end only I can be blamed for the design and execution of the study. It is one that does not necessarily fit completely with the thesis of *Decade of Dealignment*, but the two books are in no sense competitors — they are intended to be complementary, if at times they are not mutually complimentary.

This particular book has two purposes. First, it reports on the current state of social background effects, principally various forms of social class effect, as they were in the elections of the seventies, and especially 1979. In so doing part I intentionally replicates much other work, and especially the pioneering work of David Butler and Donald Stokes. As such it originally formed part of the joint project.

The second purpose of the book, mainly carried out in part II, is to challenge the conventional two-class model of voting studies, and, to some extent, to challenge the preoccupation with vote, rather than with voters' thoughts. Throughout I am concerned with the idea that class has become much less important than it used to be in British politics. As readers will discover, my own argument is that it has not become less important, but that the nature of class cultures, and their linkage to the vote or to public opinion, has become much more complicated — not only more complicated, but complicated in such a way as to give a superficial appearance of a classless and volatile electorate. I argue against the unimportance of class, and against the view of volatility that has often been pejorative to the voter. The more time I have spent on this book, the more it has come to seem the second half of a project in defence of the rational and aware voter that I started seven years ago with my book *A Theory of Party Competition*. That dealt with parties, and with more formal theory. This deals with voters and, to the extent that it has a theory, it is more one of *verstehen*, but for me anyway, they fit together.

Far more people have helped with this than can be named, including many students in Oxford. With them I filled many tutorials meant for some other subject by my fascination with the British class system. For the record I would associate myself with Professors Crewe and Sarlvik in thanking those they mention on our joint project. My two most important helpers have been the two Senior Research Officers on the project to whom this book is dedicated. Many other people will see their impact in the arguments and analyses. I am grateful to all of them. I acknowledge permission of Oxford University Press to quote from Halsey *et al.* (1980), pp. 108-9 of this book. Finally, I wish to record my deep gratitude to the members of the Senior Common Room of St Hugh's College for their support, help and friendship. I promise to talk about some other topic now, at least for a year or two.

David Robertson
Oxford, September 1983

PART I

The Two-Class Voting Model

1

Classes and Electorates: An Introduction

1.1 PROBLEMS OF THEORY AND MEASUREMENT

There are two propositions which would be accepted by most who observe the British electorate, whether as academics and pollsters, or as practising politicians. The first proposition is that British politics, both in terms of electoral choice and public opinion, and in the nature of the major parties and their public appeals, is structured by the underlying class divisions of society. The second proposition is that the degree and intensity of this structuring has declined in the last decade, may have changed its nature, and that the change and decline may be continuing. If the decline and change is actual, and if it does continue, major consequences will result for British political life. Part I of this book explores these two propositions, especially with reference to the election of 1979, and mainly in terms of actual voting choice. Part II offers an alternative model of class and partisanship, concentrating more on public opinion than the vote, in order to cope with the change and decline in the class structuring of our political life that has seemed so obvious and so inevitable for so long.

This chapter prefaces the detailed discussion in two ways. First, I try to sketch some sort of understanding about what classes actually are, why they should be expected to have any impact on voting, and why and how they are measured in the way they are by political sociologists. There are no very satisfactory answers to any of those questions, but the assumptions about the importance of classes are so deeply held, and the crude facts so stark, that some attempt must be made to penetrate this obscure phenomenon. The other role of the chapter is to set the scene by giving an outline of the relations between voting and social structure, and by putting the British experience into at least a rough comparative and historical context.

3

What classes does Britain have?

In 1979, when asked whether they thought of themselves as belonging to a social class, 50 per cent of the respondents to a survey said they did, and on being asked, with no prompting, what class that was, all but 2 per cent of that group answered either 'working class' or 'middle class'. After prompting by the interviewer by suggesting that many people think of themselves as belonging to one or another of these two classes, the vast majority of the rest of the sample were prepared to put themselves into one or other category. So ultimately 95 per cent of the sample admitted to seeing itself as belonging to one or other of two social classes. Furthermore the proportions acceding to the rival labels correspond well to the standard breakdown by political scientists and pollsters, who would, as a rule of thumb, accept a 30 per cent middle class, 70 per cent working class division as characterizing modern British society. In fact the very high figure of those who will not spontaneously offer a class label is most important, and I argue at length about it later in the book. For the moment I cite these figures to show how easily the British population accepts a class distinction, and what a simple model of the class structure it is that they accept.[1]

Most contemporary readers will find little strange in this — we are so used to precisely this dichotomous class model, with these labels attached, that it might in fact seen odd even to comment on their ease of use in the population. Not long ago, in 1954, John Bonham published the first really serious study of class voting in Britain, entitled *The Middle Class Vote* (Bonham, 1954). What strikes a contemporary reader of this book, from the Preface onward, is the uphill struggle Bonham feels he engages in even to persuade the reader that any such thing as the middle class exists. In defending the existence of his research object, Bonham uses popular mentions of the middle class in the newspapers, by politicians in speeches, and so forth. As he admits, the examples he can find from days before the Second World War are very few indeed, and the post-war references have an aura of mentioning a newly-discovered social animal.[2] Exactly how accurate Bonham's researches are is not particularly to the point; other sources would certainly support the general idea that a 'middle' class, of any size or political significance, was not frequently seen to exist much before 1945. This is not to say that any particularly great change in objective social structure occurred at this period. Rather nothing so cohesive, identifiable, and capable of bearing political or economic common interest as a class was thought of as occupying that social location until the post-war world. In fact Bonham is probably correct in arguing that it was effectively the election of the 1945 Labour government with a huge majority and a massive programme of social and economic reform that helped give a concrete status to those who now easily think of themselves, or, perhaps, are easily thought of, as middle class. The Labour Party represented the working class, and about that notion no-one seems to have been in doubt, nor did they trouble over much about any problems in defining it. Throughout the inter-war years, the 20 years or so of Labour's infancy, there was no problem of seeing who the working class were. They were the poor, urban, industrialized, manual workers, and the class enemy were equally simply identified, the rich, the owners and bosses, who came close enough to making up a marxist ruling class. The rest could be ignored, or certainly were ignored politically, though of course their votes were needed and were gained principally by the Conservatives.

However inaccurate such a model was to reality before 1945, it became too evidently so after the great working class victory, because the 'true' working class was not big enough to win that victory by itself. Even more to the point, the policy measures — especially in the area of taxation — which the Labour government needed to help the base they recognized did not hurt only, or even perhaps particularly, the old class enemy. Slowly it dawned on Labour politicians, and on political journalists, that there existed a large proportion of the population outside these rival camps. They were neither a traditional ruling, nor a proletarian, class, but had to be seen as having a class interest.[3] These are the people Bonham studies; they are the people who are now seen as forming the principal political opposition to the working class. Little or no concern is any longer addressed to the previous opposition class. Either in reality, or certainly in perception, the small, rich, 'owning', ruling 'upper' class has vanished. This gives us, with not too much problem, a two-class system of the sort that commentators and ordinary voters seem to think of so naturally. Analytically, however, there are numerous problems, problems which Bonham studied, and to which many others have paid some empirical attention ever since. We do not appear to have much in the way of a theoretical justification for treating all of those who are 'not working class' (the title, incidentally, of one of Bonham's chapters) as particularly alike, as being, in fact, a 'class' at all. This might not matter too much if the other end of the bi-polar class model was steadier, if we could be sure that there was, at least, a clearly identifiable, theoretically explicable, and politically coherent working class.

Bonham's book had been out for only five years when the Labour Party that seems to have caused the visibility of the middle class by winning in 1945, lost the third election in a row to the Conservatives, with the third successive drop in votes. Just as the potential solidity of the middle class was highlighted by the fact that Labour must have got a lot of their votes to win in 1945, a potential insubstantiality in the working class was suggested by the fact that the Tories must have gained, and kept, the votes of rather a lot of relatively poor urban industrial unskilled workers. Books with titles like *Must Labour Lose?*,[4] the 1960 edition of the monumental Nuffield Election Studies (already becoming an institution), and a series of sociological articles and studies now started showing how the class solidarity of the workers was diminishing, or at least could not be relied on. Most subsequent studies have, in fact, found the industrial working class to be more clearly cohesive and more 'class like' than the middle class, but not by that much, and not without major problems in explaining away the one third of clearly working class people who regularly vote Conservative (McKenzie and Silver, 1968; Nordlinger, 1967).

One line of enquiry suggested that the increasing affluence of some industrial workers, especially skilled workers in high technology industries, was producing an 'embourgeoisement', a 'middle class' orientation in sectors of the working class, so that a Labour Party which appealed to traditional class interests and class conscious partisan loyalty would be increasingly out of tune with sectors of the class. This thesis certainly gained some backing from an extensive study by John Goldthorpe and David Lockwood into the attitudes of affluent workers in the early sixties (Goldthorpe *et al.*, 1968). They found that such workers, whose personal socio-economic interests could be seen as crossing the division between the classes were more 'instrumental' in their political choices. By 'instrumental' the researchers largely meant that such voters were likely to weigh up the relative advantages to them of the two major parties, and vote accordingly, instead of supporting the Labour Party automatically from class loyalty. Rather later some supporting evidence of a different sort for this was provided by comparing swings in constituencies with 'traditional' working class industrial bases, such as mining constituencies, with swings in constituencies more characterized by 'affluent worker' style industry (Crewe, 1973).

An alternative approach to Labour's rather varied electoral popularity with the working class tended instead to focus on political generations and socialization patterns. Thus David Butler and Donald

Stokes, rather than suggesting that the working class was becoming less cohesive and capable of bearing a class interest, instead argued that much of the support for the parties other than Labour arose because the party was only just starting to come into its full inheritance of political loyalty from the working class.[5] Those who had come of voting age before the Party had much experience of government, perhaps before the Labour Party was even much present to vote for, could not be expected to have developed the class political loyalty that later generations seemed to have.

All of these analyses and assumptions have some part to play, but I am not concerned here with whether one can explain variance in working class vote by differing attitudinal patterns, economic experiences, or political inheritances inside the class. My immediate point is that both the voting performance of the class, and the reasons adduced for it themselves suggest that the working class is no more clearly a real social entity than is the middle class, however much more cohesive it might once have been. One should also note that the different explanations of why not all the working class voters supported the Labour Party themselves revolved around different, though often unspoken, assumptions about what the logical connection between class identity and voting choice was supposed to be. That, the question of why classes and parties go together, as well as the question of what constitutes a class I have already listed as needing some sort of answer. I shall discuss these two questions before turning to general evidence for class politics.

What is a class?

There is, of course, a series of class theories one might borrow from, especially those deriving from either Marx or Max Weber. There are even more working definitions used by social scientists, with no particular class theory to back them. Marxist theory is in some ways the simplest, and has been touched on already, when I discussed the absence of concern for a 'middle' class before 1945. In that context one could adopt a marxist notion in which only two classes did, or could, exist: those who owned and controlled the means of production, the 'boss' class, and those forced to sell their labour to the bosses, largely on the bosses' own terms. To apply such a class model to modern voting data, even were one otherwise content to accept a marxist theory, would get one nowhere. In an electoral democracy the ruling class in this sense is trivially small, and unless one restricted the working class by some further criterion, it would become co-extensive with 95 per cent of the electorate, and would therefore not be capable of any explanatory role *vis à vis* the party division of the vote.[6] Naturally no intelligent marxist would proceed with such a model, and various alternatives exist in the marxist litera-ture for dealing with the classification of those who are neither bosses nor obviously members of the industrial proletariat (Miliband, 1969; Poulantzas, 1973). The interesting point is that, for the marxists, the problem is only partially different from that facing non-marxist analysts — it is the problem, again, of the 'middle' class. The advan-tage of the marxist model is that it is, at least, linked to a general social theory as far as the two clearly identifiable polar classes are concerned. The theory may not be acceptable, and hardly fits empirical data, but it gives a reason for identifying classes, and for expecting them to have political consequences. To a marxist, classes are defined round the central driving force of social change, the means and modes of production. Ownership or non-ownership of means of production not only defines two logically consistent classes, but also requires them to be in conflict, because of the link-age of the class theory to a wider theory of the nature of economic change.

In fact a marxist would require a further element before arguing that we could identify the inevitably conflicting classes — this element is the presence of class consciousness, an awareness on the part of the individual (a) that he belongs to a particular class, (b) that others belong either to his or the rival class, and (c) that the members of the other class are natural enemies. Classes take on their full political role only when self-aware, and the self-awareness itself comes partly from conflict. The role of class consciousness is clearly vital, but it can hardly be a definitional element of a social class, unless we intend to take a largely social–psychological approach to the relation between class and politics. As my general orientation in this book is towards structural, sociological explanations of political belief and electoral choice, I prefer to treat consciousness as a factor affecting the nature of the class–vote relationship, rather than part of the definition of class (Butler and Stokes, 1971; Gerth and Wright Mills, 1963).

The marxist tradition, though intellectually much alive in Western universities, has not been adopted by many empirical political socio-logists, and, in particular, there are no electoral behaviour studies carried out using a marxist definition of class. As I shall shortly argue, however, many modern marxist theories of class come very close, when dealing with the problem of 'the middle class', to the same sort of definition as has most typically been used in empirical studies of class and politics. Outside the marxist tradition there are two main approaches to social stratification. One, perhaps of decreasing importance, is largely of American inspiration and usage. It arose from studies of small communities in the USA, often influenced by social anthropology, and is based really on denying that there is a class structure *per se*. Instead of any single hierarchical ordering in society, the tradition claims that there are a large number of dimensions of social and economic status, and that social stratification is a matter of average positioning on all of these. Thus educational attainment, wealth, power and authority, occupational prestige and so on can take varying values for the same person, producing an inchoate and multi-valued set of statuses. Such varied status groups are unlikely candidates for basic political formations towards which parties could direct their appeal, and lack the solidity that might engender class loyalty or consciousness (Marwick, 1980). Whether or not the description of the United States as classless and characterized by multi-dimensional status stratifications is empirically accurate need not concern us here. What is of interest is that even in America all these dimensions are shown to be highly correlated with one particular variable, occupational ranking.[7]

It is this idea of defining classes around occupational hierarchy that has characterized most non-marxist European approaches to social stratification. While such an approach is logically distinct from marxist models, which take property relations as class differentiations, it is still securely located within an economic perspective. As Frank Parkin, probably the leading contemporary theorist of class in Britain. says (1971), this form of stratification centres on the division of labour, rather than property as that aspect of economic life that gives shape to our social structure.

There are several alternative, but compatible reasons one can give for using this thesis of class structure, and they are reasons that do retain a sense to calling the resultant groups classes, rather than merely status aggregates. At the simplest empirical level, it happens to be true that most alternatives for producing stratification models, at least in Britain, are not only highly correlated with occupational prestige rankings, but arguably determined by an individual's, and his family's, occupational rank. Candidates for aspects of class are multiple; obvious ones are wealth, income, social prestige, access to authority and power positions, and so on. These all seem to depend very highly on occupational level; several studies of social status, based on asking interviewees to rank job descriptions, have shown a very clear patterning of prestige along lines of occupational ranking, for example (Hope, 1972). Furthermore, access to state-provided benefits, especially education, which function, as it were, as 'social capital' to determine occupational status over generations is itself largely influenced by occupational status itself. Indeed the very fact that occupational status is to a very large extent inherited, despite an increase in social mobility since 1945, is one of the best reasons to take class as emanating from this hierarchical aspect of the division of labour (Goldthorpe, 1980).

Alongside these purely empirical considerations are various social theories which lead to roughly the same 'operationalizations' of classes. One of the most powerful of modern alternatives to marxist class analysis comes from the German social theorist Ralph Dahrendorf (1959). He seeks to replace property relations with authority relations to produce a dichotomous class model, also based, as with marxists, on inevitable conflict, but truer to reality in industrialized society. This theory, ultimately derived from Marx's main rival as a theorist of modern industrial society, Max Weber, is entirely compatible with a division-of-labour-based occupational ranking, because the usual ranking of occupations coincides with authority hierarchies in industrial contexts. Both would put senior management above young executives, them above supervisors and foremen, all of them above industrial workers. Weber's (1947) principal definition of a class is neutral, based on the probability of people in similar social contexts having similar chances and experiences. For him a class exists when 'a number of people have in common a specific causal component of their life-chances in so far as this component is represented exclusively by economic interests in the possession of goods and opportunities for income, and is represented under the conditions of the commodity or labour markets'. This leaves the question of how one actually identifies class membership as entirely empirical; in my context, if occupational position satisfies Weber's criteria, then it is perfectly adequate to stand as a basis of class.

Other sociologists have, quite properly, pointed out that, whatever its basis, class is not in practice purely an economic relation, but must also take some account of social relations and general social properties. The best statement may come from David Lockwood, in a study of a group likely always to produce difficulty in classification, the non-manual, but low status and low-pay workers in occupations akin to clerking. In his study *The Black Coated Worker* Lockwood (1958) defines class partly on Weberian lines, but with two components. One is what he calls, as above, 'market situation'; 'that is to say, the economic position narrowly conceived, consisting of source and size of income, degree of job security, and opportunity for upward occupational mobility'. His second criterion is 'work situation'; 'the set of social relationships in which the individual is involved at work by virtue of his position in the division of labour'. Much of the time it is precisely these two situations which enter into occupational hierarchy codings, producing largely consistent status levels along a continuum for the two situations, although there can be differences. Clearly the first of his situations, the market situation, replicates Weber's definition. The second has a good deal to do with Dahrendorf's authority dimension.

We have then a series of independent but reinforcing reasons to take occupational categories, and their ordering into a hierarchy from unskilled manual worker, via gradations of manual skill into levels of supervisory rank and ultimately managerial authority as the building blocks of social class. Where certain categories do not exactly fit the theoretical justifications in terms of one 'situation', they can usually be placed analogically by virtue of the other. Thus, for example, many professions, especially if self-employed, as, say, a solicitor, or in a somewhat unhierarchical environment like a university teacher, probably have no manual underlings to command at all, but can nonetheless easily be equated with the senior ranks of line management. This is not only because the social prestige scales and income coincide, but more generally because the elements in the 'work situation' that Lockwood defines are closely similar, and because, though not perhaps directly endued with institutional authority, a general social authority spills over to them.

So far there is little problem then in producing a stratification, or in seeing that, in general, this stratification can be cut at one or more points to produce classes. The trick, and the trouble, comes in deciding the cutting points. The fashion has very much been, until recently, to make one cut, the cut that produces for us the familiar working class versus middle class division, and to make it at very roughly the same point. This has been to divide the stratification continuum between manual and non-manual jobs. This results in a 'working class' consisting of two categories, skilled and semi-skilled workers on the one hand, and unskilled workers on the other (the advertising and market research labelling for these has by now become almost common knowledge, and I use it from time to time hereafter — the two working class groups are, respectively, C2 and D). The middle class then consists of all the remaining categories, A and B, the higher and lower ranks of management and the professions, and C1, the supervisory and routine non-manual jobs. Effectively we are back, by a very roundabout route, to Bonham's 'working class' and 'not working class' distinction, and back with a very broad and non-cohesive middle class. Nonetheless this scheme has been used, with notable success, in hundreds of studies by now. It is the one I use for part I of this book, mainly so as to be able to replicate and compare crucial findings from the existing research tradition. Later, briefly in chapters 2 and 3, I suggest problems in this particular division, and in part II of the book I argue for, and adopt, a rather different class trichotomy. But such arguments are better left until needed. For the moment the better reasons for making this traditional cut need to be considered. Politically the best reason, as future chapters will show, is that a cut at that point fits voting data best, in the sense that there is a sharp change in the probability of Conservative and Labour voting at that point. Secondly, much of the social prestige variance appears at that point — the distinction between the 'blue-collar' or 'boiler suit' jobs and the 'white-collar' or 'going to work in a suit' statuses is much greater than variances inside such jobs, just as attitudes to life seem to change at that point. It is worth noting that of Lockwood's (1958, p. 16) two 'situations', he describes the 'work' situation as 'the most important social condition shaping the psychology of the individual'. This led the author of a rather neglected but vital political sociology investigation in the sixties, Nordlinger, in *The Working Class Tories*, to exclude from his sample of 'the working class' some occupations 'sometimes found in the C2 category in public opinion studies, (such as) office workers like calculating machine operators, even though their work is essentially the same as that of many factory workers, and shop assistants, notwithstanding the fact that in terms of skill and wages they oftentimes rank lower than many factory workers' (Nordlinger, p. 57). He says he excludes them because 'they do not wear blue collars at work; wearing white shirt and suits they find themselves in a different work-place environment and tend to hold different conceptions of themselves in class terms than do blue collar workers'. Other modifications are made from time to time, and the exact breakdown used in part I of the book, copied exactly from the classic work by Butler and Stokes, is given later in this chapter.

Such modifications seldom have either theoretical justifications or strong empirical evidence to back them, but reflect intuitive senses of tidying up marginal cases on the part of the authors. No-one can deny the margins are likely always to be awkward, but the fact that the cutting points used to, at least in broad outline, reflect an understanding of classes in economic terms of life chances, co-ordinated with other status hierarchies and co-extensive with social experience and, to some extent, self-image, makes the non-manual versus manual distinction a real class distinction, and not an arbitrary division into aggregate status scores.

Returning briefly to marxist thinkers, we find that most leading revisers of the original marxist class spectrum opt for a very similar distinction. Poulantzas, one of the foremost marxist sociologists in Europe, uses a combination of several distinctions culled from earlier writings of Marx, especially the distinction between 'productive' and 'unproductive' labour, and the distinction between 'manual' and 'mental' labour. The latter, at least, is largely a translation of our manual and non-manual distinctions, whilst the former tends to coincide for different reasons with a 'professional and self-employed' versus a 'manual employee' contrast. The two criteria, together with the traditional 'property owner' versus 'proletarian' dichotomy, in fact very largely reintroduce the two classes I adopt in following the non-marxist tradition (Goldthorpe, 1980, ch. 2). Other simpler neo-marxist approaches also replicate our division, in ways very close to Dahrendorf's, by arguing that anyone 'implicated' in running the capitalist economy (like a foreman or supervisor), or anyone whose income and position depends on the state apparatus in certain ways (a national health service doctor or an academic), is tied up with the ruling capitalist system, and all of them belong to one class, opposed by the working class (Giddens, 1973). So for whatever reason, we end up with the two familiar classes, but hopefully now with some grounds other than empirical convenience for using them.

Why should electoral behaviour be based on classes?

In case this question seems absurdly obvious, I might point out immediately, as section 1.2 will show, that class politics do not happen to be crucially important everywhere, even when classes clearly exist. One simple answer to the query posed by this question is, in fact, that classes matter electorally in Britain because nothing else does. In an international perspective, class politics ranks only equally with religious, linguistic, ethnic, rural versus urban, and other bases for political choice. But in Britain most of the other potential or actual cleavages have declined in importance (like religion, discussed elsewhere), or are highly localized (as with national identity politics in Scotland and Wales), or have been combined into class-based politics as with the rural/agricultural versus urban/industrial patterns.[8]

At its most obvious, the connection between class structure and party system is one of economic interests. The working class are generally held to have different economic policy interests from the middle class, especially if one adds welfare and social service provision to economic interests. One political party, the Labour Party, was created by working class institutions, the trade unions, directly and deliberately to represent these working class economic interests. On the other side of the party division, the Conservative Party is descended from a party which originally represented not its current constituency of the middle class, but particular economic interests which were opposed by the Whig and later Liberal Parties, inside the 'not working class' population that formed then the whole of the electorate. Indeed, at risk of extreme simplification, the middle class, such as it has a historical antecedent before the rise of the Labour Party, was represented by the Liberals, and the Conservative Party stood for the real ruling class of rural landowners and their allies amongst the really major industrial families. But such a history tells us very little about why the contemporary Conservative Party should be seen as automatically that of the middle class, and the Labour Party still commands the loyalty of the working class.

Problems in this simple economic interest connection between class and party arise for several reasons, and from both empirical and theoretical perspectives. The first, an empirical point, I have touched on earlier — it is that the actual proportions voting according to the 'natural' class interest are not high enough for us to dismiss deviant cases as not calling for explanation. After all, as I later show in detail, only about four working class voters in every ten did in fact bother to go to the polls in 1979, and, when there, vote for the Labour Party. One senior Conservative minister and thinker once actually suggested the working class Tory vote was proof that the country did not have a class voting system.

Faced with this, the assertion that class and party are linked by economic interests requires us either to believe that a very large minority of the electorate cannot tell what is in their own interest, or that the interests are extremely complex and subtle and not easily identified, or that we have the definition of social class wrong. There is almost certainly no re-definition of the working class that would remedy the situation, so we must consider other alternatives. The best way to look at the matter is to raise the question of whether or not economic interests are necessarily the only matter of modern politics. They clearly are not, because many other issues are touched on in any campaign, and, furthermore, class differences exist on many non-economic issues, whilst policies are often ranked as highly important by interviewees in surveys which have no economic connection to classes. This whole area is studied at length in part II of the book, but I may as well point out that issues like law and order or racial integration are often seen as vital, and do indeed amount to elements in class ideologies, without having any surface connection to class economic interests. Then there are issues which are clearly economic, but only tangentially connected to the problems of a particular class. One of the most obvious here is the problem of inflation, regularly seen as being of crucial importance by all voters, regardless of class.[9] It is important to avoid the mistake of assuming that because ideologically motivated politicians or economists may see an issue like inflation, or perhaps Britain's membership of the EEC, as differentially affecting the social classes, so do voters.

At the least one probably needs to distinguish three types of issue or policy. There are those, to start with, which do have a clear class connection; levels of welfare provision, costing policies for council housing or tax relief on mortgages, are good, but relatively rare, examples. Associated with these are some policy areas which, because they relate to equality of opportunity have a definite class interest relevance even if, on the surface, they are about some more general principle. The best example is the question of the conversion of grammar schools to comprehensives. For two decades this has been the attitude question that best discriminated between Conservative and Labour voting along class lines.[10] But one needs also to subtract from this type of policy some which might appear *prima facie* to have a class relevance, but do not necessarily do so. Here, probably, attitude to the power of trade unions is a good example of an issue that one might expect to have a clear class relevance, most trade unionists in TUC unions being working class, but where public opinion is fairly constant across class lines.

The second area of policies, and the most important now and for some years in the past refers to overall macroeconomic policy, and its lack of success. Problems of unemployment, inflation, economic growth and wage control have been crucial, and seen as crucial for most of the sixties and all of the seventies. Yet these are issues where success or failure by governments, though it may in fact have a differential effect on the classes, is largely a cause of national response in elections. It seems unlikely that failure to control inflation is responded to very differently by members of different social classes. As these are so important in determining the vote, and are handled by voters more or less in terms of rewarding successful governments and punishing failures, the actual class-to-party linkage is at least weakened (Goodhart and Bhansali, 1970; Alt and Turner, 1982).

Finally comes the area of policies that have no direct, and certainly no direct *economic*, connection to social classes. Yet many of these, basically social issues of the nature of the society in which we wish to live, do in fact relate to broad ideological positions which often are the product of class culture. For, and part II of this book concentrates on this issue, classes are not simply collections of people with similar economic interests, even if they are defined originally in this way. If classes really exist, and are deeply rooted in British history and experience, they are, or have become, ideological and cultural entities as well as consumption and production units. All these types of policy and issue occur in all elections, and they all call for a different logic of connection between class and party. The decline in the importance of class, if, as seems to be the case, there has been such a development, may well come from the decline in the extent to which parties have offered class-oriented policies of the first and third types (or, rather, a decline in the disparity between the offerings of the parties), and an increase in the salience of the middle category, issues of macro policy success. It is a truism, but a vital one, that there are two sets of partners to any class structure–party system relationship. The most coherent, conscious, and conflicting of polarized classes cannot produce high levels of class voting if the political parties resolutely refuse to align themselves in accordance with issue opinion between the classes. Part of the argument in part II of this book is indeed that this has been to some extent what has happened, whilst there can be little doubt that 'success or failure' issues have been increasingly important, and that no party has succeeded for a long time. If both of these propositions about class opinion and party policy are true, one would expect declining levels of class voting even without a decline in the importance or reality of social classes themselves.

A final area must be touched on in this consideration of why a class might be expected to vote for any particular party. I have said little, but assumed a good deal, about the nature of the voting act itself. That is, I have assumed that when people vote, they do so out of fairly well-considered motives, after some process of thought, whatever their actual beliefs, and that more or less immediate and specific policy issues are the material for this cogitation. Although that is a position which, on the whole, I intend to maintain, it is only one of a series of rival view on how voting decisions are arrived at (Barry, 1970). Which process of decision making one chooses to believe in affects the nature of the class/party tie, and the reasons for changes in this tie one will expect. Crudely one can imagine three different vote decision processes underlying a class vote. One, which (though they seldom spell it out) most previous analysts of class voting have probably accepted, is that the tie between class and party is more or less immediate to the voter. This position is supported, for example, by the analysis in Butler and Stokes' *Political Change in Britain*. A working class voter supports the Labour Party out of an immediate sense that Labour is 'for the likes of us'. He does not identify any specific problems, and decide that the Labour Party has the right policies, or even think they will, in general, adopt the correct solution for him, given the problems he is aware of. That something like this is the process by which many people in both classes operate cannot be denied, though how important it is, and how its importance may be changing is another matter. In this case though, a decline in class voting must come about by a decrease in class identity, or a pervasive doubt that a party does indeed, in general, stand for one's own class. It is, in other words, largely a problem of socialization and consciousness.

The logic of the connection between fairly policy-oriented ratiocination and class voting I have already sketched. There is a slightly fuzzy area between these extreme models of the logic of class voting that I touch on from time to time, especially in part II of this book. This is to suggest that, while detailed policy reflection and comparison between parties is probably fairly rare, values and opinions may still be the connection between party and class. I suggest there may exist in the electorate rather broad and general ideological persuasions (though not necessarily in the terms of academic understanding of socialism and conservatism).[11] These would be fairly permanent and stable value positions, themselves to a large extent the result of a socializing and learning process highly influenced by class and class-related factors. In this case one would see class as not a direct (though certainly not a spurious) cause of voting, but as the underpinning of a general ideological preference which would lead to party choice. A decline in class voting under these assumptions could come about either because of a lack of fit between party position and class-related ideology, or because of a decline in the influence of class on general ideological position. Most probably both factors would have a role to play, and all three models have some degree of empirical reality. The teasing out of these matters, to the extent that it can be done at all, is the work of the rest of this book. For now, having argued for the existence and nature of classes in British politics, and suggested reasons for their political role, I turn to setting the scene for the detailed discussions in subsequent chapters. The first thing to do is to get some impression of how important class is in Britain nowadays, compared with the electorates of other countries.

1.2 CONTEMPORARY BRITAIN IN CONTEXT: CLASS VOTING ABROAD AND IN THE PAST

Whenever a discussion occurs of class voting in a comparative perspective, the number of potential methodological and definitional problems is huge. For this reason the simplest possible approach is much to be desired, and I turn immediately to the classic study of voting in the Anglo-American democracies, where class voting is most likely, and the definitional problems minimized (though by no means precluded altogether). This is the 1963 publication of Robert Alford's *Party and Society*, which is principally a study of the level of class-related voting in Britain, Australia, Canada and the United States. Alford's work is a particularly useful starting point for several reasons; it is, for one thing, quite old now and portrays class voting at what may well have been the heyday, in the immediate post-war decades. Secondly, he produces a whole mass of data, deliberately arranged in the most easily comparable form. Most importantly, Alford designed a powerful but very simple arithmetical measure of the extent of class voting, which I use, as do many analysts, throughout this book in different contexts.

Clearly, if we are sensibly to compare levels of class voting, either between periods in one country, or between countries, some form of standardized index needs to be used, some single number that summarizes the complexity of voting patterns so that we can see at a glance how much class voting any set of data portrays. The Alford index, as it is known, does this without recourse to subtle statistics that often beggar interpretation (Alford, 1963, ch. 4). His index works by setting up a hypothesis, defensible only on substantive grounds, for what would constitute class voting in any society. This step is unavoidably the job for the individual analysts — no index can make up for inadequate sociological insight, or over simplification. Usually in his own work Alford argues the hypothesis that, however many parties there may be in a society, there are one or more that are clearly more left-wing than the others. In his usage, left-wing means a party which stands, overall, for the social and economic interests of the working class, as that is understood in the society in question. Thus in his four countries, the left-wing party is: for the USA, the Democratic Party; for Canada, either the Liberal Party, or what has become the New Democratic Party; for Australia, the Australian Labour Party; and, for Britain, naturally, the Labour Party. All the other parties in the system are taken as collectively non-left. (The European usage of 'bourgeois' party for all those who do not specifically espouse left-wing policies or working class interests is useful here, as it avoids necessarily labelling them 'Conservative', which might well not be true. But the usage also, of course, implies what is to be demonstrated, that they are predominantly supported by the middle class.) The question for which the index is used as an answer is, How much of the vote for the left-wing party can be attributed to class orientations?

This is not as easy as it might seem to measure, because, and this is another great virtue of the index, class voting must imply class conflict, at least to some extent. Thus a political system in which all the working class voted for the left-wing party might not, in fact, be highly class-ridden, if a large proportion of the middle class also voted in that way. Analogously, the total absence of middle class support for a left-wing party would not mean much were that party so generally unpopular that only a small percentage of the working class supported it. Thus the mere fact (were it true, which it is not) that only unskilled workers voted for the various British far-left splinter parties like the Revolutionary Workers Party would not mean anything much about the British political system. Instead the Alford index works by comparing the proportions of each class that supports the left-wing party. The thesis is that a system in which exactly the same proportion of each social class votes for the Left has, effectively, zero class voting. By contrast the most extreme case would be one in which all of the working class, and none of the middle class, supported the Left. The arithmetic of the index is therefore very simple: we will call the index, here and later, A. The equation is calculated over all the voters (or all those in an opinion poll who support any party), but excludes non-voters or those of no preference.

$$A = \text{(per cent of working class voting Left)}$$
$$- \text{(per cent of middle class voting Left)}$$

Thus in table 1.1, which records the class and party distribution of the vote in Britain in the 1979 election, the index is:

$$A = 51 \text{ per cent} - 22 \text{ per cent} = 29 \text{ per cent}$$

TABLE 1.1 Vote by class in Britain, May 1979 (%)

Class	Party			
	Con.	Lib.	Lab.	Total
Middle class	63	15	22	100
Working class	36	14	51	100

Theoretically the index actually takes the values from –100, via 0 to 100, but a negative score would only come about in a situation where more of the middle class than the working class voted for the Left. There are a few mistakes that can be made in interpreting these index figures, against which one must take care. For example, a negative index, as mentioned above, would not be an equally good test in the opposite direction because one would not necessarily have justified the collection of parties thrown into the 'non left-wing' category as being actually 'right'-wing. One might, in the British example, want to claim that a test of class voting could be designed in which the middle class percentage voting for the Conservative Party, minus the percentage of the working class voting for the Conservative Party, would be a good index. So it might, but it would not be the reciprocal of the index calculated above, because the Liberal Party would be treated differently. A more general warning is that the index has meaning only in terms of the hypothesis offered about what class voting means. As an example here one could reduce the A for Britain in 1979 to only 22 per cent, were one to calculate the figures on the basis of the electorate as a whole, not on the basis of those voting for the major parties. Only 42 per cent of the working class voted Labour, as compared with the 51 per cent shown in table 1.1 – the difference is made up by non-voters. In fact such measures may well be more significant, and I often later calculate in this way. Alford, however, often used opinion poll figures taken between elections, rather than survey reports of actual election results. As there is no proper equivalent to non-voting in such cases, he calculates measures for all those who express views, and, for the sake of comparability, my figures in this section involve only those who actually claim to have voted. Finally, class voting is measured by these indexes only inasmuch as the choice of party is correct. Given that I concentrate in a later part of the book precisely on issues where there is no obvious logical reason to associate one class with a particular party, this means that I see the index as capturing only part of what is true about the extent of class voting. Probably the party with the purest working class support, and the least middle class votes in the country is the very right-wing National Front, yet this form of class voting would never be caught by an index where Labour voting is taken as the essence of class support (Schoen, 1977).

We can now look immediately at Alford's own evidence of class voting in the four countries he chooses for comparison as having similar political cultures and class systems. One must bear in mind that Alford's definition of class, and mine in part I, and for similar reasons, is that to be middle class is to have a non-manual job, to be manually employed is to be working class. Table 1.2 is my recalculation of his detailed summary tables in the appendix to *Party and Society*. I have chosen to take results from around 1955, the mid-point of his time period. This is a quarter of a century earlier than the earliest suitable British data, but long enough after the war for politics to have shaken down and stabilized in the four countries.

TABLE 1.2 Class voting in the mid-fifties, four Anglo-Saxon democracies (%)

	UK (1955)	USA (1956)	Canada (1954)	Australia (1955)
Middle class	23	39	61	34
Working class	62	52	69	69
Alford index	39	13	8	35
Average index for post-war period	41	16	8	34

Note: The entries are the percentage of the class voting for the 'left-wing' party in the system, by Alford's definition. This table is derived from tables 1–4 in appendix B of his book, pp. 347–55.

The particular date I have chosen is shown, by the bottom row in the table, to be a fair comparison point, because the figures chosen for the mid-fifties correspond very closely to the averages I calculate from Alford's data for all the time points he reports from 1951 onwards. Unsurprisingly for those committed to the notion that British society is, or was then, class-ridden, Britain stands out as having clearly the highest level of class voting of all four countries. The British level was five times higher than in one of its own Dominions, Canada, and three times higher than in the United States at a comparable date. Only Australia, at this period probably the most 'British' of the Dominions, comes anywhere close. The Australian example is perhaps the hardest to be sure of, because such indexes, measured on very varied samples and subject to differences in detailed occupational coding, can hardly be reliable to a small number of percentage points. However, according to Alford's tables, there was no time from the mid-fifties on when the British figure was not at least slightly higher than the comparable Australian one.

Any lengthy explanation of this pattern is beyond my scope here. The simplest explanation, though, is a very obvious one. In both Canada and Australia, as well — very obviously — as in America, other divisions in society cut across class lines. In Australia an important division then, and still (though to a lesser extent today) was religion. This led most Catholics to vote for the Australian Labour Party, to some extent because it was less associated with loyalty to the (Protestant) 'mother country'. As most Catholic immigrants at this time and in the past were, in any case, from Ireland, the attraction of the ALP was reinforced, and capable of overcoming class divisions (Aitken and Kahan, 1974). In Canada the provincial identity and provincial interests of voters often reduced class voting, even when the whole question of Quebec was set aside. But that question cannot be set aside, and forms a major reason for the lack of class import-ance. In the United States the historical voting patterns developed from the New Deal at least, and, in the case of the Southern Whites, from the Civil War, completely transcend class lines. Apart from these historical factors, geographical diversity leading to highly decentralized political loyalties have tended to mean that even where class motivates voting, it cannot produce a national level class/party split of any great salience.

Although all these factors, and more, exist and truly reduce class impacts, or obfuscate them, one may be dodging the real issue. This is that social class may either not exist to the same extent, or may matter much less, outside Britain. In one sense that suggestion is clearly wrong. Class exists in all these four countries, if only because we have defined it in such a way that it must exist, by objective occupational measurement. Yet, as I argued at length in the first half of this chapter, the manual/non-manual distinction is only an opera-tionalization of, a measurable surrogate for, a more full-blooded measure of class. Alford puts an aspect of this well in asking why Australian voting should be less class related than Britain's:

> Class politics is not infused with the sharp status differentiation which is embedded in British society, and probably the level of class voting in Australia reflects the actual structural cleavages of the society in as bare a form as possible.

He cites an Australian emigré to Britain, saying that though the

Australian worker is aware that 'other people own the country . . . and this makes him a worker, he knows nothing of the emotional and psychological implications of belonging to a subject class, which has so restricted the outlook of the British proletariat' (Alford, p. 173).

Whether or not the British proletariat actually has this awareness, or 'should' do, is far from clear nowadays, but may well have been more plausible 20 years ago. It is impossible to investigate this properly even in one country, but one is left with the sense that class voting in Britain is higher than elsewhere for reasons other than that voters in other countries have other divisions to face.

Although Alford was obviously wise to choose four countries sharing, in part, a common political culture, we cannot truly estimate the degree, the possible uniqueness of the British class voting record without some comparison from much less similar countries. One can make estimates on less secure foundations to draw some rough comparisons between Britain and other European societies. In these cases I choose a later date, roughly in the late sixties. This is largely because data sources are less reliable until such a time for most non Anglo-American societies. The data here are extracted from an invaluable comparative study of voting behaviour edited in 1974 by Richard Rose, *Electoral Behaviour: A Comparative Handbook*, and cover West Germany, Italy and the Netherlands.

The relevant comparison figure for Britain in this case is drawn from the 1970 General Election, as studied through a survey taken by David Butler and Donald Stokes. This sample, immediately after the 1970 election, revealed that 59 per cent of the working class had voted Labour, and only 27 per cent of the middle class had done so, giving an Alford index of 32, notably down from the 1955 figure. Once again it is vital to remember that I am citing figures as a percentage of all those who voted for major parties, and do not include the non-voters in the calculations. As non-voters are usually disproportionately working class and Labour voting, this method raises the index level in most cases. The Italian case is perhaps the one where we would least expect to find high levels of class voting, at least as demonstrated by these indexes. The only major left-wing party was, and still is, the Communist Party. Its principal opposition, the Christian Democrats, were still, in the late sixties, widely regarded as a catch-all party, a party appealing to all sectors in the cause of constitutional and democratic government.[12] As it had, in addition, the strongest support from the Roman Catholic Church in an officially Catholic country, the imposition of the religious cleavage is unavoidable. This does indeed show in the data, as where the 1968 index is at much the same level as that of the United States a decade earlier, with A = 16. It is, though, worth noting that, compared to the British figures also given in that table, the Italian index rate is lower because *both* classes deviate more from their class interest. Only 50 per cent of working class Italians vote for the left-wing party; that this is 9 per cent less than in Britain is no doubt due to the special factors I have suggested. But, at the same time, and despite these apparently awesome barriers to voting for the PCI, more of the Italian middle class manage to support the Left than did the British middle class in 1979. Yet there was need for no fear of communism, and no religious barrier for the British non-manual groups to overcome. This would suggest (and it is not a data arti-fact – the phenomenon of middle class non-Catholics voting PCI is well attested) (Penniman, 1978) that our class system may be, in a deep sense, more politically influential, and not only because of the absence of other salient cleavages.

The Netherlands provides another good test, being, at this time, divided by religion to such an extent that there were two opposed Protestant parties as well as a Catholic party antagonistic to both of them. On top of this historically crucial religious divide was a class cleavage in politics with a lengthy history. Using the PvdA (the Dutch Labour Party) as the left-wing party, and combining all the others together for the purpose of calculation, the Alford index stands at A = 17 per cent for 1967, half the British level. The final comparison is with West Germany. Here we have perhaps the fairest compari-son in Europe, because, despite their names, the coalesced non-left governing parties, CSU–CDU (Christian Social Union, Christian Democratic Union), the actual religious base had largely vanished by the sixties. The SPD, the socialist opposition (although in 1968 it was actually part of an all-party coalition, it was soon to break off and rule Germany, along with the liberal FDP for the next 13 years) had only fairly recently moderated its semi-marxist position, and was definitely the most 'left-wing' party with any electoral success in the Federal system. As a result we do indeed get a much higher level of class voting in the German figures, with an index of 28 per cent. Even Germany, however, cannot manage to reach the level Britain attained two years later. As German politics developed, the class base of the SPD declined rapidly, with the onset of a more ideological, but also less traditional, political style, especially amongst the younger 'professional' middle class, and a direct correspondence between Britain and Germany in the early seventies would most probably show a greater differential with Britain being more class oriented (Hildebrandt and Dalton, 1978). Where one can push aside non-class cleavages, however, class voting figures are prone to rise. An alternative way of looking at the Netherlands case, for example, is to accept that for a large part of the electorate political conflict is about something else altogether. If we look instead only at the portion of the electorate who vote for secular parties, the index does indeed go up. Amongst this sector, A = 34 per cent; but this figure might be much higher, given that 79 per cent of the working class vote for the Labour Party in this restricted electorate, were it not that over a third of the middle class also do so. As a contrast it is worth noting how intense cleavages can be. The equivalent index for religious based politics in the Netherlands can be calculated by dividing the sample into those who regularly practise a religion (Protestant *or* Catholic), and those who do not. If we then combine the three religious parties and look at the proportion of the religious who vote for them, minus the proportion of non-religious who do so, the index hits 64 per cent. It is perhaps a useful corrective to taking as enormously class based a society where the class index only reaches 40 odd per cent. Other countries would largely replicate these findings. Only in the Scandinavian countries, where there are known to be problems about applying the index, would Britain be beaten.

As far as international comparisons go then, we are safe in saying that, at the least, Britain is one of the most class oriented societies, in voting terms, or at least was so. A stronger version would be that throughout the post-war world, at least until the early seventies, Britain was very probably the country with the highest levels of class voting outside the generally exceptional Scandinavian nations. But we might also wish to ask about the degree of change that has happened. The 1955 figure in table 1.2 was, after all, higher than the most recent figure, given in table 1.1, for 1979. Does this mean that there has been a steady decline in class voting? One important thesis, originating with Ivor Crewe and his colleagues who ran the 1974 election studies from the University of Essex, would suggest so. This argument, known as the 'partisan dealignment thesis', I shall come back to on several occasions later (Crewe, 1977). At the moment it is enough to say that Crewe argues, from data mainly collected from 1963 to 1974, that British politics have experienced an unfreezing of fixed patterns of loyalty to the major parties since the fifties. Not only have decreasing percentages of the electorate voted at all, but the Liberals, nationalists, and minor parties have steadily eroded the huge share that Labour and the Conservatives used to get. Whilst over 80 per cent of the total vote, representing perhaps around 60 to 65 per cent of the whole electorate voted for one or other of these parties, by 1974 perhaps only half of the electorate, or less, had voted Labour or Conservative. Crewe's main thesis would link this change to decline in what is usually known as 'party identification', an American notion of close, but non-rational, psychological linkage to political parties (Campbell *et al.*, 1960; Budge *et al.*, 1976). Once, the argument goes, nearly everyone had such a psychological predisposition, usually inherited from parents, and likened by Butler and Stokes to support for a local football team (Butler and Stokes, 1971, p. 47). Such identification led to a crystallized electoral structure, with very little net change. For our purposes the thesis, which cannot entirely be doubted, has some implications. As class has so much been a guide to voting in the past, party identification was closely, though by no means perfectly, correlated with class. If, therefore, voters are more 'mobile', less loyal to their previous party affection, or perhaps lacking one altogether, it must to some extent mean that they will be less likely to vote on class lines. Crewe himself offers some evidence for a decline both in actual class congruent voting, and in the extent of class identity as a subjective quality of voters. He links this to a generational model of decline in class and partisan alignment, of which I am less convinced. This argument I take up later, but we need first to see if there has been a decline in crude class voting.

The next table, table 1.3, combines data reported by Alford for Britain from the mid-fifties to 1962 with data drawn from election studies for the elections from 1964 to 1979. The following table, table 1.4, gives rather more detail for the 1964–79 period, but it is important to note one crucial difference between them. The second table is based on the whole of each sample, and not just those voting for the three major parties, and the resulting Alford indexes are not comparable between the tables.

TABLE 1.3 Alford indexes for Britain, 1955–79 (%)

Year	1955	1957	1958	1959	1962	1964	1966	1970	1974	1979
Percentage of working class voting Labour	62	67	64	57	57	64	66	59	59	51
Percentage of middle class voting Labour	23	24	22	21	22	23	25	27	26	23
Alford index	39	43	42	36	35	41	41	32	33	28

The pattern in table 1.3 does seem to suggest a decline in class voting, though not too much reliability can be attached to any particular result before 1964, as all the data in the earlier period comes from public opinion poll figures rather than academic samples. This does not in any way detract from the overall trend, but leads one to be cautious about the timing. 1964, for example, appears to be suddenly higher than the two preceding figures. But these latter were not taken immediately after elections, and may not as well represent what people would have actually done had they really just voted. It seems safer to assume that until some time after 1964 the average level of class voting was such as to give an index of around 40 per cent, give or take, say, 2 per cent. After that period there would seem to have been a fairly sudden decline to a level between 28 and 32 per cent, which may, or may not, be part of an overall continued decline. It might have been attractive to add a later figure from opinion polls or the 1983 election. This has been resisted because, with the advent of the SDP–Liberal Alliance, and the arguably temporary internal strife of the Labour Party, it would be very difficult to know how to assess these figures. Indeed, until we know more about the real political nature of the SDP, and the strength of its bond to the Liberals, it is hard even to decide what should count as the 'left-wing' party for the construction of such an index. The whole question of how the Alliance is likely to benefit from, and affect, any dealignment or decline in class voting is left, instead, to the last chapter.

The figures from the last three elections, where the decline in class voting is most clear, are difficult of interpretation, because they actually represent two different modes via which a decline in class voting can come about. In both 1970 and 1974, elections won alternately by the two major parties, the percentage of the working class voting for the Labour Party remained at its general post-war level, with only the 67 per cent working class Labour vote of the period around 1957 significantly higher; it was a shift leftward in the middle class that depressed the index. But in 1979, an election where the whole country seems (as later chapters argue) to have lurched rightwards, the working class Labour vote dropped massively for the first time, by enough to make up for the return of the middle class to their typical post-war levels. For this reason, we actually do not have a substantial trend. Until another election can give some confirmation, any definite argument about a decline in class politics overall is suspect. What seems less suspect, from these figures, would be the thesis that a volatility existed in the seventies that had the effect of making any one of the elections less predictable along class lines than the past few years. This is hardly the same thing. A rather clearer picture of what may have been happening appears from the next table, table 1.4. Here I have given the percentage of the whole electorate (as estimated by post-election surveys) who actually came out and voted for the two major parties, and have broken it down into the two main party votes for each class.

TABLE 1.4

Social class voting for the Conservative and Labour Parties since 1964 (%)

| | Elections | | | | | |
	1964	1966	1970	1974(1)	1974(2)	1979
Middle class voting Conservative	56	52	54	48	44	55
Middle class voting Labour	20	22	22	20	21	20
Working class voting Conservative	24	21	26	21	20	29
Working class voting Labour	55	57	46	49	47	42
Alford index	35	35	24	29	28	22

Note: This table refers to the percentage of the whole sample voting in a certain way, and is not restricted to percentages of those who actually voted. The class definition is as in tables 1.1 and 1.2, middle class being defined as the non-manual grades (A–C1 B), working class as the manual grades (C2 and D).

With this presentation, which allows the impact of changing, and possibly differentially changing, turnout to show, the Alford indexes can definitely be seen to take a fairly abrupt change after the 1966 election. (The figures of 35 per cent for A in 1964 and 1966 are probably very close to the 40 per cent level of the earlier years, given the change in basis of calculation.) Two patterns stand out, only one of which really involves a decline in class voting in a full sense. This decline must surely be evident in the fact that in no election after 1966 has as much as 50 per cent of the working class actually voted for the Labour Party. If class is to be a basis for politics, it cannot be restricted only as measured by the choice of those who bother to vote – not bothering to vote for a party which is supposed to represent your interests, when you are a member of a social class supposedly disadvantaged by a ruling class party is nearly, if not quite, as strong a reason to doubt that very class analysis as voting *for* that ruling party or one of its 'bourgeois' allies. In contrast, the other element in the Alford index, the percentage of the middle class voting for the Labour Party is totally static, varying only between 20 and 22 per cent, well within the expected error margins for such sample based figures.

Much more detailed analyses are made in the next chapter of how the two major parties have fared, across differential social groups, in the seventies. Thus far one can tentatively suggest two things. One is that there is some, though indecisive, evidence for a decline in the levels of class voting after 1966. The second is that this has mainly come about by Labour losing the active support of the working class, but not by gaining any corresponding support from the opposite class. For, although the Conservative share of the middle class vote has not been constant, its middle class supporters have stayed on the same side of the class line, largely by voting for the Liberal Party, in the two elections where they have deserted at all. Trends on such small numbers of points are not easy to establish, of course; but in the four post-1966 elections, the Conservative Party share of its natural class has twice kept up to the earlier levels, whilst the Labour share of the working class vote has never got back to the 1964-6 level. So far, in this introductory chapter, we can say this much only – class has in the past been more important in Britain than in almost any country, and it may be getting less important.

I finish this chapter by completing the description of the context of class by comparing class with other social background variables that might be seen as rival explanations, or as sociological associates. In this I also make a preliminary foray into the notion of class consciousness which crops up in most consequent chapters at some stage, before being dealt with properly in chapter 4.

Objective social class and voting – other similar variables

Earlier I discussed the measurement of subjective class images. Another way of considering the potential decline of class politics is to consider the connection between party choice and the voters' private perceptions of the social class to which they belong. Some, especially Crewe as part of the dealignment thesis, have suggested that a decreased willingness to give oneself a class label at all is part of the general decline in the stability of voting behaviour, and of the fixed class connection in particular. In fact there is very little evidence that there has been a decline in subjective class identification. In the 1964 election study, the data suggest that about

50 per cent of the population would not say that they thought of themselves as 'belonging to a particular class'. Although it is true that this figure dropped even further in the 1966 and 1969 surveys, it rose to 43 per cent in 1970, and was back to the 50 per cent level in 1979. (Most disagreements on this matter are, in fact, a result of measurement problems and question wording.)[13] But even if awareness of class has not really declined, the correlation between subjective class and voting might have declined, as it has marginally with occupationally defined class. It is, in any case, part of any introduction to the political role of class to consider the impact of class consciousness, a logically necessary element of which is the assumption that voters do in fact have private understandings of their social location. Table 1.5 read along with table 1.1 gives the basic comparison between Conservative and Labour voting in 1979, according to objectively defined, and according to subjective, social class.

TABLE 1.5 1979 voting according to subjective class (%)

| Subjective class | Party | | | |
identification	Con.	Lib.	Lab.	Total
Middle class	61	16	23	100
Working class	28	14	58	100
Alford index: 58 – 23 = 35				

The results are interesting, and fit quite well with the implications that seemed to follow from the time comparisons on table 1.4. There I suggested that any decline there was in class voting was largely a matter of working class desertion from Labour loyalty. When one compares objective and subjective measures, as there, one must remember that merely giving oneself a class label, not more common than 50:50 on probability, is to mark oneself out as unusually aware of social class. Thus to find a very sharp decline in working class Labour loyalty amongst those whom we externally judge to be working class, compared with those for whom being working class is a private perception, does suggest that the mere fact of class placement is perhaps not, of itself, all that important. When, as here, the middle class have identical voting profiles, regardless of whether they are so ascribed themselves, or by the analyst, makes sense of the apparent reduction in the working class base for the Labour Party. So, in fact, does a time series. Compared with 1964 there is a drop in the Alford index when based on subjective class from 47 per cent to 35 per cent in 1979, based almost entirely on a reduction in Labour working class support, rather than any change amongst the subjectively identified middle class. Later chapters will considerably broaden the argument here, which is, essentially, that class consciousness is necessary to bring the full benefit of class politics for the Labour Party, and that the Conservatives get the support of the middle class, however it is defined, that class having shown no tendency to weaken its class loyalty. There is some evidence to suggest that in this particular respect there may have been a general decline in the class consciousness which is needed by Labour, which is overwhelmingly for those who are objectively working class to see themselves in that light. In 1964, 44 per cent of the manual workers had spontaneous working class identities, while the figure averaged less than 40 per cent for the elections of the seventies. The percentage of the middle class who see themselves as middle class has remained constant at around a quarter, but the Conservatives, as I have said, seem not to need class consciousness.

To complete this survey of the general impact of class on voting, it is worth looking briefly at a series of other variables that form parts of the whole social background of voters, and which are involved, along with class, in shaping electoral politics.

Both age and sex show the general sort of distribution that previous studies have led us to expect, inasmuch as women and the elderly are slightly more prone to vote Conservative than are men and the young. As is usually the case, younger people were less likely to vote at all. In 1979 nearly 30 per cent of those under 24 admitted to abstaining — the actual rate could well have been nearer 40 per cent. Unusually in this election, the Labour Party did not get a disproportionate share of the young, a factor that not only hurt them in 1979, but which may well continue to damage their chances later in the century, given that vote so often still remains constant throughout life. The political generation effect suggested by analysts like Butler and Stokes might well mean that we have here an age cohort permanently advantageous to the Conservatives.[14] The youngest age group seems also, unsurprisingly, to have been more attracted to the Liberals than any other major sector of the electorate, although the political leanings of 1979 Liberals can only be treated with caution now the Social Democrats have come on the scene.

Religion is another variable that requires more subtle treatment than the rather crude data presented in table 1.6 allows, but its impact is now so slight in Britain that it can nonetheless be treated quickly. Here though, there is certainly a change, again one in which traditional voting cleavages seem to be eroding, and in a way that particularly hurts the Labour Party. Because of its historical linkage to establishment politics, religion has had a long-term connection with the vote in Britain. Whilst the Anglican Church could be described as 'the Tory Party at prayer', nonconformism was for a long time a basis for Liberal Party support, especially in the Celtic fringes. Indeed of all the divisions of all the variables summarized in table 1.6, 'other Protestants' have the highest single Liberal voting strength at 17 per cent. The nonconformists also used to support the Labour Party quite strongly, however, as did the Catholics, in the latter case because of the relatively low social and economic status many of them enjoyed, especially if they were Irish immigrants. These patterns, as I shall show later, are rapidly dying away.

Education as a variable is doubtless of importance in British politics, but it is so closely tied to other structural aspects, especially class and sex, that its direct effect on voting behaviour is hard to disentangle from the overall social background of a voter. Although the effect of education is mentioned from time to time elsewhere in this book, I do not have the data to examine it at length. It is particularly difficult to deal with it at this stage in British political history, because the generations have a much more varied educational experience than would be the case, for example, in either America or France, where the state school system has remained much the same throughout the century. In Butler and Stokes' classic voting study the principal tables dealing with education pertain to the old grammar school versus secondary modern school distinction, which is of rapidly decreasing relevance in British politics (though not necessarily as an issue, as opinion data in part II of this book testifies) (Butler and Stokes, 1974, ch. 5).

The three remaining structural variables in the table do, however, show marked political cleavages so as to suggest that even if class in certain respects is losing its direct political relevance, class related economic phenomena are still vitally important. Housing is a good example of this. The economics of housing have never since the war ceased to be of prime political interest — not only Mrs Thatcher's promise to cut mortgage rates in 1974, but Harold Macmillan's pride in his housebuilding drive in the fifties, square with the Tory emphasis on the sale of council houses in 1979. How exactly that issue may have affected Conservative votes is not my job at this point to analyse. Table 1.6 shows clearly, though, a sharp contrast between the politics of those who are property owning and those who rent

TABLE 1.6 Selected social structure measures and the 1979 vote (%)

	1979 vote					Number of respondents
Variable	Con.	Lib.	Lab.	Did not vote	Total	
Age						
18–29	29	15	29	24	100	361
30–44	39	11	30	16	100	569
45–64	41	12	35	8	100	607
65+	46	8	29	12	100	340
Sex						
male	37	12	31	15	100	913
female	40	11	31	14	100	978
Education						
high	53	17	20	10	100	291
medium	44	14	26	16	100	276
low	36	11	36	16	100	1054
Religion						
Roman Catholic	43	7	37	10	100	184
Church of England	48	13	27	11	100	578
other Protestant	36	17	26	15	100	270
none	33	10	34	18	100	784
Housing						
owner occupancy (mortgage)	46	14	25	11	100	625
owner occupancy (owned outright)	53	13	20	10	100	412
council house	22	9	48	17	100	569
privately rented	34	11	48	22	100	211
Trade union membership						
member	24	13	42	14	100	580
non-member	45	11	27	15	100	1277
Region						
Scotland	31	9	32	13	100	149
Wales	18	12	56	9	100	103
North	38	11	35	13	100	513
Midlands	37	10	34	17	100	328
South	48	14	22	13	100	586
Greater London	35	8	30	21	100	214

Notes:
    Some of the rows do not add up to 100%. This is because those voting for minor parties have been left out. Except in Scotland and Wales these are very small percentages of the electorate.
    Education levels are defined in terms of qualifications gained. 'High' education means the respondent has gained either one or more 'A' levels or any qualification above. 'Medium' education implies passing one or more subjects at CSE or 'O' level, but no higher qualification. 'Low' education means that no qualification at CSE/O level or above has been gained.

their homes. The large proportion of the population who rent from local authorities are less Conservative than any socially defined sector of the population. Even more interesting in some ways is the sheer 'owning' versus non-owning aspect of the table, with the six-point difference between mortgage holders and those who own a house outright. Housing is, of course, so good an indicator both of relative wealth and local socio-political milieu that one cannot take it as a simple single variable in its own right.[15] Butler and Stokes also show a strong council house versus owner distinction, with 76 per cent of owner occupiers in the middle class (non-manual) sector voting Conservative, but only 28 per cent of the manual workers who lived in council houses doing so in 1970, a figure for Conservative voting actually higher than in 1979, even though the 1979 figure refers to all social grades in such housing. The way housing is a measure of wealth and social milieu is perhaps best indicated by the fact that other data from the 1979 survey gives those living in detached houses a three times greater chance of voting Conservative than the inhabitants of terraces, with semi-detached dwellers in between. These and other data on wealth and expenditure patterns and income are discussed more extensively later.

In an election when the power of the trade unions was so much at issue, it is hardly surprising that much less than a third of union members should vote for the Conservatives, while nearly half of all who are not members do so. These figures could be made much more stark if one were to take note (as I do later) of the fact that non-membership often reflects non-employment, and that being in a union family rather than actually being a member is the more important measure. Unionization principally reflects a structured orientation to economic trends, as does the question of a voter's region. Immediately after the 1979 election the clear regional differences in electoral fortune of the parties was noted, Mrs Williams, the defeated Labour Cabinet member (as she then was) describing it as an election fought between the 'haves' and the 'have nots'. She was thinking of the fact that the still affluent South gave the Conservatives nearly half of their vote and Labour barely a fifth, while Labour led the Conservatives in Scotland and Wales. Though the Celtic fringes have always been more pro-Labour (rather few English seats were won by the Labour Party in the thirties, for example), a decade ago the vote through the English areas was held to be very uniform. In 1979 the North and Midlands lagged some 10 per cent behind the South in terms of Conservative support. The London results would most probably have been more like the rest of the

South but for its usual low turnout and a Liberal showing worse than anywhere outside Scotland.

We can see then that, in general, the 1979 election shows the continued importance of those structural aspects that can clearly be related to economic and financial experiences, but shows an over-all decline in the direct relevance of more generalized social and demographic matters. Naturally, these other factors like age, sex and class, more broadly conceived, link back to immediately economic considerations, as much of the rest of this book will argue.

2

Class, Demography and Work

2.1 CLASS AND DEMOGRAPHY

No-one would ever claim that social class, especially when measured only with a few socio-economic status grades, was all that counted about a voter. What is crucial about class is that it is, at least relatively, an external and fixed fact about a person unlike, say, his attitudes and views. It is, again only perhaps relatively, outside his choice, unlike (for example) marital status. But there are plenty enough other such fixed attitudes. Two of these, age and sex, have often been thought to have an important impact on people's political preferences. The old, as a matter almost of folklore, are supposed to be more Conservative than the young. Much of this is summed up in the cultural dogma that 'a man ought to be radical when young, or what will he be like when old?' Similarly there has been a belief, held particularly profoundly amongst those on the Left, that women are innately more Conservative than men. Here the folk axiom is that Britain would have had a Labour government permanently since the thirties but for the 1928 Voting Act that granted the suffrage to all women on the same terms as men, the (in)famous 'Flappers' Act. Even without the folklore expectations, it is reasonable to expect that policies which attract or turn away the middle class do not have the same blanket effect on an 18-year old girl and a 70-year old man just because they are both middle class. The evidence that has been cited for such age and sex effects in the past, however, has usually not been very strong, and seldom been clear cut in its interpretation. Women do tend to show up as more Conservative than men if survey research samples are looked at casually.

This is by no means restricted to Britain — Giscard d'Estaing in 1981 had more women supporters than should have been the case statistically, and the Christian Democrats in both Germany and Italy draw heavily on women for their support (Rose, 1974). There are usually intervening factors which throw doubt on the simple idea that women are inherently more Conservative than men. In Britain, for example, the greater life expectancy of women leads to more women than men being older, and being older itself is correlated with Conservative support. In France, Germany and Italy, strong adherents of Christian churches tend to be Conservative, and it is well known that church attendance is very much higher in those countries amongst women than men.

As far as age goes, the problem is not so much a spurious correlation, as with sex, but a question of two ways of looking at the relation between age and political leanings. There is a large and sophisticated research literature on this matter, which I need only touch on here (Converse, 1964). Basically one needs to distinguish between a straightforward ageing process, and a 'generational' phenomenon. The ageing process would treat the correlation between age and conservatism as tantamount to that between age and arthritis, a natural causal consequence of experience and merely living, that unfolded in a unidirectional manner. Conservatism, like death and taxes, would be inevitable. A generational effect, however, postulates that people born in a certain period are likely to adopt a political faith, because of the stimuli of the events in their socializing phase. This faith will stay with the generation as it grows older. Thus it might be entirely accidental that those currently oldest are most Conservative, because they grew up largely before the Labour Party was well established. A younger generation might be equally Conservative, having grown up under a later period of Conservative dominance, with a more left-wing intermediate generation. One could thus see both age and sex impacts on politics as entirely explicable *ad hoc* patterns, with no suggestion of a genuine causal link between gender or maturity and conservatism. Certainly this is the position about the age–vote correlation one finds in such works as Butler and Stokes' (1967, ch. 3) *Political Change in Britain*, and whilst there cannot be a final decision between the generational model and the ageing model, the former seems the more plausible.

Either way the supposed impacts of sex and age would be different in kind from the impact of class. But I have been at pains to stress the need to understand rationally the class–vote connection, rather than accepting it as a sociological given. There is no reason why age and sex should not be relevant to a person's voting decision, in the same way, based on self-interest and cultural perspective, that class is relevant. As our political parties are not, however, organized

TABLE 2.1 Age, sex, class and voting in two elections (%)

Age (years)	Sex	Class	1979 Vote				1974 Vote				Left-right score		Swing to Con. between	
			Con.	Lab.	Lib.	Total	Con.	Lab.	Lib.	Total	1979	1974	1974-9	1970-9
23-35	M	MC	49	23	28	100	36	41	23	100	16.5	14.7	15.5	12.5
	M	WC	31	52	17	100	16	64	20	100	13.9	12.2	13.5	7.5
	F	MC	70	19	11	100	42	27	31	100	15.8	14.5	18.0	19.5
	F	WC	34	53	13	100	24	55	21	100	14.3	13.3	6.0	9.5
36-55	M	MC	67	21	12	100	53	23	24	100	17.5	15.7	8.0	1.0
	M	WC	34	53	13	100	22	70	8	100	14.1	12.6	14.5	10.0
	F	MC	57	24	19	100	48	25	27	100	16.3	15.6	4.0	-2.0
	F	WC	32	53	15	100	22	59	19	100	14.0	13.3	8.0	2.0
56+	M	MC	59	31	10	100	60	27	13	100	16.1	16.0	1.5	-1.5
	M	WC	41	46	13	100	29	55	16	100	14.7	13.5	10.5	6.5
	F	MC	72	19	9	100	62	22	16	100	16.9	16.1	6.5	8.5
	F	WC	42	47	11	100	29	52	19	100	15.2	14.5	9.0	9.0

expressly in terms of age group interest or sexual ideology, any gender/age patterning ought to be flexible, and relatively easily alterable between elections. As socio-economic conditions and party policy change, those interests of an individual that relate to age and sex should give different answers to the question of whom to vote for, whilst class differences are likely to be less fluid, simply because parties should, being organized on class lines, be more stable in their attraction. Thus it is in change between elections that sex and class groups ought to be predictively important. In 1979 anyway, the evidence for direct vote differentials in terms of age and sex groups is slim, though not insignificant. Table 2.1 gives age group and sex vote profiles for both 1979 and 1974, subdivided by class grouping.

One thing the table does show is how confusing the question is of whether or not women and the older voters are more Conservative. In both years there is a slightly greater Conservative vote amongst women (though ignoring class the difference in 1974 is a mere 1 per cent). Yet 1974 is actually the year when such age/gender differences are generally higher. The answer, of course, is in the fluctuations of the Liberal vote; the Liberals lost a good deal of their early seventies support between the two elections, and this dampened all the contrasts in table 2.1. This is notably true of age: whilst there is clear evidence of an age difference in 1979, it is neither so marked, nor so linear, as in 1974, when there was a 16 per cent point difference between the youngest and oldest age groups. The trouble is that the general thesis that women are more Conservative than men is unclearly specified. Is it meant to be a statement about a sex difference in political belief, hence capable of expression through voting for either the Conservative or Labour Parties? Or is it simply a statement about tendency to vote specifically for the Conservative Party? Either way it seems that the difference, not great in 1974, was further attenuated by the end of the decade. A good check on this are the columns in table 2.1 where positions on a simple but effective left–right political dimension are given. (Details of its construction appear in chapter 6.) It is clear from these that no real difference can be detected in general ideology between the sexes by 1979, and that only a marginal difference existed earlier. As I shall show shortly, there is, in fact, no longer any good reason to believe in a general sexual difference in political leanings, though this does not mean that gender cannot be one of the personal characteristics that goes to direct a party choice under the conditions of a particular election, or that influences partisan change between pairs of elections.

With age the picture remains closer to the one long-term trends would suggest. There was in 1974, and remained five years later, an age difference, whether measured by percentage voting Conservative, percentage voting non-Socialist, or ideological score. A factor that may come to be of greater importance in the future, with the arrival of the SDP and Alliance on the scene, is the relative attraction to the young of the third-party option; the considerable lead the Conservatives have amongst the most elderly part of the population is in large measure the result of their lack of interest in the Liberals in both elections. If the 26 per cent of the population who voted for the Alliance in 1983 turns out to be younger on average than that voting for either of the major parties, which seems likely from polling during the 1983 campaign, age could come to be a more important aspect of politics than it has been. If this is so, and the data in table 2.1 suggest that this is so, it would most probably be a generation effect, amongst those whose age cohort for many reasons has been less fully socialized into the two-party strong allegiance system. This would conform, for example, to the USA pattern where the younger cohorts show weaker partisanship and a much greater tendency to identify as 'independents' than their elders (Hill and Luttbeg, 1980).

In fact, however, my preference for social background analysis is to treat age and sex, as much as class, as characteristics which interact together to form the basis on which consumer choices in the political market are made. If this is so, there is no good reason to expect either sex or age *per se* to show correlations of any strength with party choice. The real evidence should come from considering the voting profiles of groups defined by all three aspects, as they are presented in table 2.1. Here I show the vote for all three parties in the two elections for the 12 natural socio-demographic groupings that arise from combining three age groups, two classes and two sexes.

This table gives a mass of information. The crucial points are threefold. First, sex and age differences vary very considerably if one 'holds class constant', that is, abandoning the notion that there should be one sex effect or one age effect, and allowing that voting profiles will vary as these three variables intersect. For example, women and men do, in some cases, vote very differently: young middle class women were 21 per cent more likely to vote Conservative in 1979 than were men in the same age and class group; a smaller, though large, gap of 13 per cent separates men and women on the over 55-year old middle class bracket. But, in contrast, middle class

women between 36 and 55 were 10 per cent less likely to vote Conservative than men. Age, too, shows distinct patterning when one
looks inside sex and class groups, though in no especially linear way
that might support the simple age-cycle, rather than generational
thesis. Secondly, the 1979 and 1974 data do not, on the whole, show
the same details of pattern. If nothing else, the swings between 1974
and 1979 vary far too much for this to be true — the events of the
five years, and especially the fluctuating fortunes of the Liberal Party,
produce very considerable differences for the 12 groups. Finally,
both sex and age are far more important in shaping voting amongst
middle class people than amongst the working class. A very effective
way of showing this, and summarizing the mass of information in the
table, is presented in figure 2.1. This gives a spatial display of the
similarity of the 12 groups. The technique used is multi-dimensional
analysis. With this one can take a matrix of scores representing the
similarity of each pair of socio-demographic groups, treat the scores
as though they were measures of physical distance, and reproduce
each group as a point in a two-dimensional 'map'. In this case I have
taken the voting profiles of the 12 groups for each of the three
major parties in all three elections reported in table 2.1, and derived
a simple score for likeness of each pair of profiles. The resulting two-
dimensional display (which satisfies very well the relevant statistical
measure of goodness of fit to the original data, i.e. the 'stress' coefficient) shows all the six working class groups closely together. For
them, it mattered very little over the decade whether the voters in
question were 50-year old men or 19-year old women — they were
working class, and that seems to have sufficed to give them a rough
identity of reaction.

The middle class groups are spread out in a much larger area,
however, as age, sex, and the interaction between the two lead to
different levels of party support, and different rates of change
between elections. More precisely, amongst the working class the
age groups divide neatly, presenting us with three pairs of points,
each consisting of the two sex divisions. There is no such neat
patterning amongst the middle class, though the positioning of the
women in both the youngest and oldest age groups, and the way
that young men are much out of line, shows the interaction of sex
and age inside this class. This is borne out by a more straightforward
application of a statistical test on the vote percentages in each
category for 1979 and 1974.

This approach, testing directly for the explanatory power of each
of the three main variables, and their combinations, uses the sort

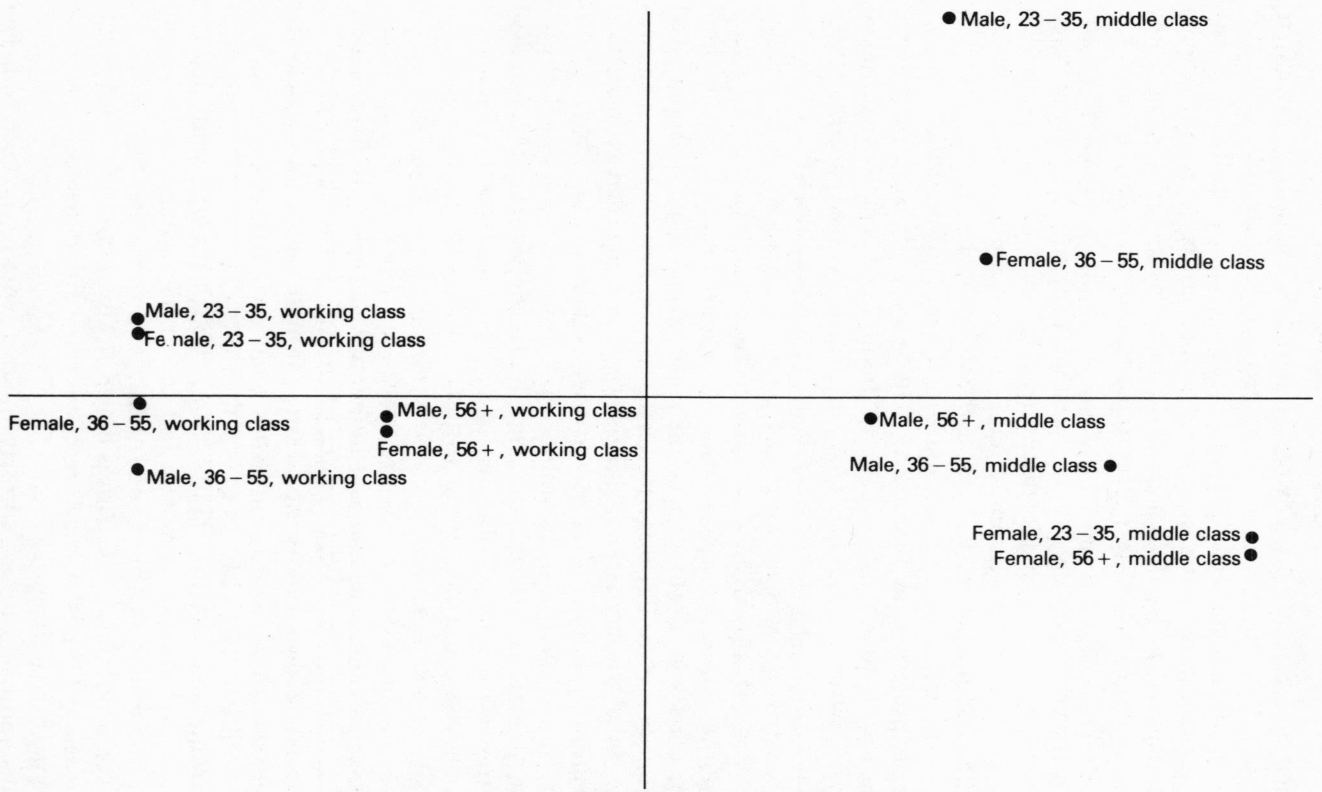

● Male, 23 – 35, middle class

● Female, 36 – 55, middle class

● Male, 56 +, middle class

Male, 36 – 55, middle class ●

Female, 23 – 35, middle class ●
Female, 56 +, middle class ●

● Male, 23 – 35, working class
● Fe.nale, 23 – 35, working class

● Male, 56 +, working class
● Female, 56 +, working class

Female, 36 – 55, working class
●
● Male, 36 – 55, working class

Figure 2.1 A spatial representation of similarities between
12 socio-demographic groups in terms of voting profiles over three elections

of log-linear model used extensively in part II of this book. I leave explanation until then. In order to find a statistical model that satisfactorily predicts the distribution of vote across the three parties at the elections of 1979 and 1974, one has to take notice of the individual's class, age, and his or her sex. But, in addition, to get a decent statistical fit, one has to know which intersection group of sex and age a voter is in. This means, in simple language, that one does not just get so many extra probability points for Conservative voting from being, say, male, and another amount from being, for example, over 55. Rather, the effect of age varies with sex and *vice versa*. The political cues to subgroups are highly differentiated.

Thus my general thesis, that such background factors as basic demographic attributes do not have a fixed sociological or psychological impact of their own, seems to be borne out. Instead they are, as it were, external tokens of how interests and ideologies will guide a choice in terms of the political context. They are, as one would expect, and as I have argued, less important as predictors than class. For the working class, they are of very little importance at all; why this might be so we shall see later. It remains to point out that one of the best predictors of how a group will vote is what it believes. Table 2.2 gives the 'left-right' attitude scores for the groups as measured in both elections. It is notable how right-wing all groups have become. There is, in fact, a very good statistical correlation of 0.85 or higher between the average score of the group and the proportion of its vote going to the Conservatives in each election. More important, at this stage, is that the correlation between the size of the rightward *shift* in attitude between the two elections is also highly correlated (0.74) with the size of the swing towards the Conservative Party. An immediate example is that the group with the smallest swing to the Conservatives, old middle class men, has the smallest ideological change. The actual levels and the rate of change in attitude vary considerably over the groups, as do the raw voting figures, of course. But again, this is what one would expect from a universe populated with people for whom fixed background factors were vital but intervening matters.

2.2 CLASS AND WORK

I have stressed at length the idea that factors like age and sex cannot be expected to have simple and universal impacts. Why then, following this logic, should social class have such an effect? The quick answer is that it does not. Just as the impact of being a woman varies with her class and age, the impact of being an unskilled worker or a white-collar professional varies with the more precise details of that industrial location. Again, this should be expected if class is to be seen as a guide to calculative voting, rather than a fixed social fact of direct explanatory power in itself.

There are a series of possibly important dimensions to social class. Only two relatively simple ones can be examined here. I suggest, as a useful simplification, the following two-dimensional model of a class. We need to take account of the sort of hierarchical location a worker is in, and the sort of industrial sector he is in. The hierarchical situation is, of course, meant to be modelled into the six-point scale already used to build the non-manual/manual class model, but repays rather closer attention. Because part II of this book, and chapter 5 especially, offers an alternative to the two-class model, I shall not take up time here with a theoretical discussion of problems with the six-point scale. This part of the book is intended to portray the class effect on the 1979 electorate within the conventional framework of previous voting studies, however, and therefore some detailed comment is necessary. The best starting point is to look again at the vote profiles of each of the six standard classifications as used by Butler and Stokes and most subsequent researchers. These are presented in table 2.2.

TABLE 2.2 1979 Vote by social grade (%)

Grade		Con.	Lib.	Lab.	Did not vote	Total	Number of respondents
A	Higher managerial and professional	57	17	16	7	100	145
B	Lower managerial	55	12	21	8	100	233
C1A	Skilled non-manual	53	13	14	13	100	176
C1B	Lower non-manual	45	11	25	15	100	202
C2	Skilled manual	29	11	40	17	100	664
D	Semi-skilled and unskilled manual	29	11	42	17	100	294

Notes:
1. This table is based on the social grade of the head of the household, not necessarily on a social grade coding for the voter actually interviewed, although, of course, the vote recorded is that of the person interviewed.
2. The letter grades are directly equivalent to the numerical grades I to VI used by Butler and Stokes, who also use the letter grades at times.

The key to why the standard six-point scale is problematic has been known since Butler and Stokes' own work on data from the early sixties, and is still unresolved. It is the problem of the lack of homogeneity of the non-manual group in terms of one pivotal social grade, the C1B group. These are those with lower non-manual posts, mainly untrained clerks and unskilled white-collar workers whose jobs have a minimal manual content. As far as percentage voting Conservative goes, it is clear that the C1B group does not belong with the three higher groups, and yet its Conservative vote is 17 per cent greater than the clear-cut working class, and it casts 16 per cent less votes for Labour. But, at the same time, the Conservative lead in the group is exactly half that of the higher non-manual group. Then one might note the 'did not vote' column. This is a variable of some interest because, regardless of actual political commitment, the fulfilling of the democratic citizen's role as a voter has always seemed, empirically and through eons of political thought, something that distinguishes classes in political terms. Yet here the division would be between B and C1A, not between C1B and either the group immediately above or below it.

Whatever else may commend itself to analysts, it is apparent from the table that a division into non-manual/manual or, inside those two categories, between the more or less skilled or talented, is not very revealing. What *is* revealed is enough to show that hierarchy, whether it be one of skill, talent or reward, is clearly related to voting. There appear to be no differences inside either of the huge ranges 'higher managerial' to 'skilled non-manual' on the one hand, or 'skilled' to 'unskilled manual' on the other — except for this oddly idiosyncratic group in C1B. Such a situation would hardly be credible given the huge known disparity of life and job styles enjoyed in a modern economy, unless class was a conscious community. Chapter 4 argues that it is not. Hence the need for the more detailed analysis in table 2.3, where I pick out certain aspects of skill and authority that divide workers inside any institution. Here I deliberately concatenate some of the hierarchical distinctions of the previous table. For example, the A/B distinction between higher and lower management will often relate more to the stage a voter has reached in his career, not to any politically relevant division. At the same time it introduces other distinctions, especially the 'foreman' category in both non-manual and manual occupations below the clearly 'upper' A/B grades.[1]

Effectively the table gives us back a version of the intermediate non-manual group as a hinge for class-based voting. But it does so

TABLE 2.3 1979 Vote by socio-economic group (%)

Socio-economic group	1979 Vote					Conservative percentage minus *Labour* percentage	Number of respondents
	Con.	*Lib.*	*Lab.*	Did not vote	*Total*		
Managers	58	13	21	7	100	+37	189
Employed professionals	54	20	19	7	100	+35	85
Non-manual foremen	54	22	17	7	100	+37	41
Other manual	48	13	25	14	100	+23	266
Manual foremen	33	7	42	17	100	− 9	151
Skilled manual	22	12	46	17	100	− 24	414
Semi-skilled manual	28	15	44	13	100	− 16	177
Unskilled manual	23	8	51	19	100	− 28	65
Owners of small enterprises and self-employed professionals	63	10	10	17	100	+53	71
Own account workers	60	5	18	18	100	+42	74
Farm managers, owners, and own account farmers	81	8	8	4	100	+73	26
Agricultural workers	46	4	23	27	100	+23	26

Note: The categories in this table are formed by collapsing certain more refined categories used in coding. With a larger sample no such concatenation would have been necessary, but no point in this chapter would have been affected. Certain other categories, with very small sample size, and which are ambiguous in class location, have been omitted.

with some chance of comprehension. We can now see a virtual identity of voting (and, just as important, non-voting) profiles in the first three groups. The first and second relate to what one might call the 'unarguably middle' class, the managerial and professional elites in modern institutions, commercial and otherwise. The third group, which joins this profile with a Conservative lead as great as the clear 'managerial' category, is from the C1 sector. It is a group consisting of non-manual foremen. They all share a characteristic which social theorists from Weber to Dahrendorf have seen as vital, the exercise of authority. When one passes the authority threshold, one is talking of those whose working life, however well rewarded, consists of obeying orders rather than giving them.

Inside the 'objective middle class', the non-manual workers comprise the biggest single group, at least 45 per cent of the whole class. We find immediately a sharp drop in voting for *either* of what a European would call the 'bourgeois' parties, the Conservatives and the Liberals. Non-voting in this group is much the same as that of the working class, and the Conservative lead is reduced compared with the rest of the non-manual sector. Nonetheless it is still predominantly Conservative. The economic rewards, especially in terms of job security and conditions, if not pay, mark them out from manual workers. But the gap between them and the rest of the 'command' structure of British society is clear in sociological and voting terms.

The importance of this authority dimension is surely underlined by the behaviour of the next group down the list, the manual workers who also exercise authority, as foremen. To be sure, as 'working class voters', they favour the Labour Party. But their support for it, and the lead they give Labour over Conservatives, differs from the rest of the manual group as clearly as the gap between the 'other non-manual' group and the rest of the middle class. What this table shows is the existence of a basic political orientation that does indeed distinguish between those whose conditions of economic life are manual or non-manual, with all that means in terms of respect, money and security. But superimposed on that, and producing two ambiguous sectors inside each 'class' is the authority question. This marks out in each class a special group. One has authority when the class as a whole does not (manual foremen) and the other does not wield authority when the rest of its class often does, non-manual 'other' jobs.

Of the other points to be picked up from such a detailed analysis, the most important for the future refer to the Liberal Party. The Liberals must stand as surrogates here for the Alliance of the eighties. In tables that distinguish voters on class (or nearly any other terms) they usually show no variation at all, being so thoroughly an 'unsectoral' party. Here, though, there are three particular entries where the Liberals do much less well than amongst comparable groups. One is the managerial sector of the middle class, where they get 7 per cent less of the vote than amongst the professional workers. The manual working foremen are less Liberal and so are those at the bottom of any class table, the unskilled manual workers. Though the Liberal vote fluctuates elsewhere, it is always within a fairly narrow margin, at least within broad class lines. For two of these groups, the managerial middle class and the quite unskilled working class, one might well suggest that orthodox class politics is quite adequate. There is evidence throughout this book that the Liberals' major appeal may be principally as a classless party. Thus they have no real hope of gaining in these extreme sectors. Such an argument may also apply to the manual working foreman. If his manual worker status does not make him Labour (as it does for 42 per cent of the category), there is no reason why he, someone marked out from the rest of his class precisely by being an authority holder, should vote Liberal. There are other points of interest in the table which suggest that all groups in which the Liberals do badly share the characteristic that the conflicts of a straightforward dichotomous class system fit their situation well. Not only clearly 'elite' managers and clearly *'lumpen-proletariat'* unskilled workers, but foremen for whom either the 'authority bearer' or the working class role is likely to be convincing fail to support the political centre. There are also the non-employed and the agricultural economy groups. These, all of them, pay very little courtesy to the Liberals.

Those who are not related to an authority hierarchy at all need to be fitted into a class model of politics, and they pose real problems. In some countries, notably Germany, voting analysts have tended to consider the middle class vote as divided between the 'new' and the 'old' middle classes (Kaase and von Beyme, 1978). Here the self-employed constitute much of the 'traditional' or 'old' middle class, and others, managers, professionals, white-collar foremen, etc. are a separate group, the 'new' middle class. For these the traditional class/party divisions are unfitted. So it has been possible to show convincingly that what we have been happily dealing with as, perhaps tricky, but unquestionably, middle class employments, are much more left-wing than the traditional middle class. Sometimes, as in Germany, they are more radical than the working class, especially in terms of 'green' socialism. In Britain we now have so small a self-employed or actually 'employing' sector as to make them at most peripheral to the mainline middle class. Nonetheless, they exist, and are very Conservative. The biggest Conservative lead over Labour of any group for whom our sample is large enough to speak with any reliability at all, are those who are either self-employed as professionals or fit a marxist notion of owning and controlling the means of production. This group is notable for several reasons. It has the highest Conservative vote at 63 per cent (but if one excludes non-

voting, over 80 per cent!). It gives only 10 per cent of its vote to
the Liberals, and it has a very low turn-out, much more like the
manual workers than the non-manual employed. Here is the real class
conflict, perhaps. Certainly, it is a group for whom there are no
possible politics but those of the Conservative Party, though even
conservatism holds little attraction. This is understandable because,
in terms of welfare, the semi-socialized tax and benefit policies of
the post-war state offer them nothing. The new Thatcher brand of
conservatism may be more to their liking than that practised since
'Butskellism' — the consensual practice of Keynesian demand management from 1950 to the early seventies.

The next line in the table is for the self-employed who have
working class status jobs, probably with no more than working class
level incomes, described in official terms as 'own account workers'.
They rely on themselves, without the prop of institutions, for their
security just as much as the higher class equivalents previously
discussed. They, too, are entirely Tory in their politics. More of
them vote Conservative than any group but the 'old' middle class.
They are even less Liberal. Added to one or other of the two groups
just mentioned should be the penultimate line in the table, those who
make their living through agriculture, either as managers or owners of
farms large enough to have a labour force, or as agricultural equivalents of 'own account' working class voters. As a separate subgroup
they are far too small to allow of any significant conclusion. Unfortunately, the structure of occupational coding makes it very difficult
to know to which group to allot them. It hardly matters, for any
allocation could do nothing but confirm the strong picture that all
those in Britain who are detached from an organizational job, or who
otherwise rely entirely on their own energies and talents, are solidly
Conservative, and very far from the Liberal Party. This itself is not
unremarkable because one might otherwise have rather expected
the Liberals in this country, as in others, to pick up the support of
the 'individualist' worker. Instead the Liberal Party seems to do
particularly well amongst those who are entirely inside the organized
economy, but for one reason or another, are unhappy with the
prevailing class structure. I return to this suggestion in chapter 4.

If the nature of the position inside an industrial hierarchy can
act so strongly to shape voting profiles, we would do well to look
at further differentiation. The most obvious is the question of which
sector of the economy a voter works in. A full analysis beyond
my scope here, would presumably show considerable variation between primary, secondary and tertiary sectors, for example. The

distinction that has caught most attention in the professional literature is between the public and private sector, however, rather than
between product sectors (see Dunleavy, 1980; Alt and Turner, 1982).
Table 2.4 presents a very simple version of the public sector/private
sector distinction over some of the social grades I have just discussed.

TABLE 2.4　1979 Vote by socio-economic group and economic sector (%)

Economic sector socio-economic group	1979 Vote					Conservative percentage minus *Labour* percentage	Number of respondents
	Con.	Lib.	Lab.	Did not vote	Total		
Private sector							
managerial and professional	60	13	18	9	100	+42	193
lower non-manual	51	14	21	15	100	+30	171
manual foremen	31	8	43	18	100	-12	97
skilled manual	25	13	43	18	100	-18	285
other manual	31	13	38	18	100	-7	165
Public sector							
managerial and professional	51	21	26	3	199	+25	81
lower non-manual	46	15	28	12	100	+18	136
manual foremen	37	6	41	17	100	-4	54
skilled manual	21	12	53	15	100	-32	129
other manual	18	12	62	8	100	-48	77

Note: This table covers only those in employment. Public sector is defined as anyone working in a nationalized industry or for central and local government in any capacity other than
the military.

It contrasts the whole of the private enterprise sector with the whole
public sector, whether industrial, as with nationalized industries, or
administrative and service oriented. Even this distinction, however,
shows up important contrasts. The recent debate has combined
pragmatic with more theoretical arguments, the former being of
main interest here. Public sector workers of all grades are prone to
experience a different political rationale in their voting compared
with private sector equivalents. On the one hand, Conservative
governments, unwilling to have incomes policies, but finding themselves nonetheless the *de facto* employers of a large part of the
labour force, often try to hold back wage rates in the public sector.
In addition, the 1979 election featured a Conservative Party more
than usually determined to cut back public sector employment. On
the other hand, the Labour Party, by standing for an extension of
the state, is generally supportive of staff levels and therefore job

security in the public sector. But the winter before the 1979 election witnessed some pretty vicious disputes between the Callaghan Labour government and the public sector unions opposed to the 'voluntary' incomes policy of the time.

In 1979, with one exception, every occupational category was more supportive of the Conservatives in the private sector than its equivalent in the public sector. The difference, furthermore, is essentially due to a straightforward shift from Conservative to Labour between the two sectors. Liberal voting, though varying vertically inside the sectors, hardly differs horizontally between them. But for one case, the same is true for non-voting. Whatever the explanation, managerial and professional workers in the public sector were 8 per cent more Labour and 10 per cent less Conservative than their equivalents in private enterprise. They were the only exception to the idea that the Liberals had no special attraction to the public sector. The Liberal lead in this occupational category in the public sector *vis à vis* the private was as great as the Labour Party's advantage.

Two groups stand out requiring comment. There is only one category for whom public sector employment does not especially enamour them of the Labour Party. This is working class foremen. In this one case the Conservative lead over Labour is several times better amongst public sector workers than in private enterprise. It is true that the sample sizes are small, but the difference in behaviour is too marked plausibly to be written off in that way. The clue cannot be the previously documented dislike of this group for the Liberal Party (though public sector foremen are even less keen on that party than are those in private enterprise). Nor is the abstention rate unusual. It may well be that the work experience of people at this level differs very little between the sectors, and their seniority left them unworried by the threat of job losses and pay cuts incumbent on an incoming Conservative government. But the fact of this unpredictable Conservative appeal will have to be explained by those who wish to make much of the private/public sector difference.

The other special group here are the semi-skilled and unskilled manual workers. Unlike the foremen, they do not contradict the thesis of public sector radicalism; instead they uphold it in a possibly exaggerated fashion.[2] The Labour vote is an incredible 62 per cent in this group, giving a massive lead for Labour of 48 per cent. This fact alone would be less remarkable were it not that in the private sector this lower working class group demonstrates the not unusual pattern of being *less*, rather than *more* left-wing than the more skilled working class, with a Labour lead of only 7 per cent. Again, we are dealing with a very small sub-sample which prevents detailed analysis. But, again, the pattern is too marked to be dismissed. Here, though, there is less of a problem in offering a tentative explanation. If any group stood potentially to lose from a Conservative attack on public sector staffing levels, it is surely the relatively unskilled workers, who do badly enough, in their own eyes, even when a Labour government is in power. If their high-level managerial colleagues found it less easy to vote Conservative than they would working in private industry, how much more vulnerable must this sector have felt?

Whatever the detailed explanations, and whatever theoretical debate it may be taken as evidence for, the combination of tables 2.3 and 2.4 surely demonstrates the enormous fragmentation of class experience in politically relevant ways in modern Britain.

This chapter, by looking first at non-class but equally deeply fixed personal characteristics, and then by opening up class as a black box, has had one aim. The aim has been to demonstrate the great variety of electoral responses that appear once one admits the huge variety of personal conditions that actually exist. Class may once have been a simple matter, though I suggest in chapter 1 that it never was. Certainly class, along with demography, cannot now be treated as a powerful and simple explanation of voting. It is not simple, and is hardly an explanation. I turn now, in extension of this general position, to look at two further aspects of a voter's economic situation.

3

Economic Status and Family Background

Whether class is a real social phenomenon, or merely an analytic category, class membership by itself does not exhaust the social impact on voting. Economic factors have an effect over and above class location. Family experience does not only mediate social class, it shapes views and expectations directly. In this chapter I concentrate mainly on these direct impacts.

3.1 DIRECT ECONOMIC STATUS AND VOTING

I use the phrase 'direct economic status' to refer to certain matters which can be seen as directly linking self-interest and electoral choice. Class, however measured, sex, age, religion and other variables may define a social role, and this role may carry an economic or other politically relevant self-interest. They are, by definition, 'mediating' variables. Why not look at the hard core of self-interest if one believes it to be linked to voting choice? The two 'hard core' measures I select in this section (and obviously a much more detailed analysis would be desirable) are various measures of economic security. On the one hand, I look at income and living standards; on the other, at the most important institutional arrangement we have, after the welfare state, for providing job and income security — the trade union movement.

Income, living standards and the vote

Although to the layman a voter's affluence would seem so tied up with class as hardly to be worth investigating separately, it is actually the case that we know very little about the matter. Class, if defined objectively in terms of occupation, is only partly correlated with income. Income is only partly correlated with personal affluence. Yet it is distinctly improbable that the standard of living enjoyed by a voter is irrelevant in his voting decision. Indeed, again, to the layman much of the class analysis might now seem irrelevant. Surely the way many see politics in Britain is very simple — the rich vote Tory, the poor vote Labour. In this case the layman's insight may well be worth considering. Much of the theme of part I of the book is that simple class politics have been replaced with complex dis-aggregated economic interest voting. For if economic interest does directly shape the vote, apart from any mediation through family and class traditions, the results will indeed be complex.

The problem of measuring wealth, income, or living standards is partly definitional, partly a matter of how much respondents will disclose. No-one in Britain, by cultural tradition, is very happy about disclosing such matters, and researchers have to use very simple and crude measuring devices. Much of the uncertainty in the analysis and discussion of what follows, then, is inherent as a result of measure-ment. But some light can be thrown on the question. I first take the most obvious measure here — how much does a respondent earn, and does this affect his vote? This simple idea of income is probably closest to the ordinary man's understanding of affluence, if only because wages and salaries are the overwhelmingly greater part of most people's personal disposable wealth. In our case, we are really dealing with the income of economic units. The data is drawn from a question that reports the total pre-tax income of a family, if the respondent is married, or the respondent's own income if he is single. There is no easy way of taking into account the liabilities he may have to face, so the same income bracket could well represent very differ-ent levels of actual affluence. It would say something very strange about the nature of British politics if income, however badly con-ceived as a measure, should have little impact. In fact, what the data show is not quite that income has little impact, but that its effect on voting is not a straightforward matter of the Conservative vote rising steadily with income level. Instead the Conservative vote holds roughly steady, between 40 per cent and 46 per cent for five of seven lower income categories, accounting for about 85 per cent of the sample. It then shoots up to 58 per cent for the next group (9 per cent of the sample) and 82 per cent for the top 4 per cent of incomes.

Roughly what seems to happen is that, over a very large range of incomes, there are random fluctuations of vote around the same level, with the Conservative Party getting about 40 per cent of the vote,

Labour about 45 per cent and the Liberals a fairly steady 15–16 per cent. This range which, in 1979 terms, meant all gross incomes up to about £4,000 per annum, covered then about 60 per cent of the electorate. Because in this wide range there is no systematic pattern, income has no general predictive power. Disconcertingly, at the bottom end, for incomes in a range with a maximum of about £1,200 per annum, there was an actual Conservative lead. Little reliability attaches to the details of this bottom range. Not only are the income figures improbable, but those who actually do have incomes within such a range are in very untypical earning situations. This phenomenon, of the apparently poorest being more favourable to the right-wing party, has cropped up in survey research in other countries, and should probably be disregarded.

The electoral impact of income comes after one gets over the £4,000 per annum point. After this each of the remaining categories shows an increasingly sharp lurch towards Conservative voting as income increases. Those with incomes between £4,000 and roughly £6,000 give the Conservatives a lead over Labour of 9 per cent. Income receivers between that figure and about £8,000 give a very large lead of 32 per cent. Though only 4 per cent of the electorate get into it, the richest category of all behave in a way that leaves no doubt about the economic rationality of at least a part of the electorate. Incomes above roughly the £9,000 mark are associated with an incredible Conservative lead of 69 per cent, partly caused by a total collapse of the Liberal vote to only some 5 per cent. This bears on data examined in the last chapter where Liberal support slumped amongst 'employer' categories. I discuss it more fully later on.

Actual income levels clearly do, therefore, have an impact of considerable theoretical importance, at least at the high levels of income associated with middle class jobs. It is in the middle class, where class consciousness can be shown to be relatively unimportant in determining the vote, that something else has to function. This point about class consciousness is borne out by the discussion in chapter 4.[1] In working class occupations there does not appear to be any great tendency to vote according to income. Certainly 'working class Conservatives' are not those with higher than average working class incomes. This holds true whether or not one takes special note of those who do and do not give themselves a subjective working class identity, as table 3.1 demonstrates. In manual jobs there is, of course, a considerable range of economically and socially relevant factors – such as job security and status – that bear little or no correlation to income (Goldthorpe *et al.*, 1968).

TABLE 3.1 Voting by objective and subjective class by relative income (%)

	Middle class				Working class			
	Identifies with class		Does not identify with class		Identifies with class		Does not identify with class	
Class identification / Income compared to median income for objective class	Above median	Below median	Above median	Below median	Above median	Below median	Above median	Below median
Party vote in 1979								
Conservative	64	64	64	50	23	25	34	41
Liberal	19	17	15	16	13	17	18	13
Labour	17	19	20	34	64	57	49	45
Total	100	100	100	100	100	100	100	100
Number of respondents	120	50	168	179	142	116	181	173

Note: This table records the three party vote percentages for respondents separately by objective social class according to whether or not they spontaneously identify with that class and whether their income is above or below the median *for the relevant class.*

With middle class, non-manual occupations, things are somewhat different. This probably follows from the fact that the typical hierarchical institution in which most non-manual occupations are found tends to give status, security and pay together. Thus, income is a better indicator of overall economic well-being, and correspondingly more closely connected to some aspects of economic voting rationality. Table 3.1 divides both manual and non-manual jobs according to whether respondents do or do not identify with their objective class status. A similar analysis is offered briefly in Butler and Stokes (1974) on 1963 data. In both their case and mine, it is shown that income itself helps to form class consciousness in the middle class. How should it not, given the increase in size of this class over the post-war period with its associated social mobility? Of those non-manual voters who label themselves as middle class, 65 per cent have incomes above the non-manual average. Only 20 per cent of those with incomes below this median point spontaneously see themselves as middle class. More than a third of those who have above average incomes do so. This factor increases still further the importance of sheer economic welfare in determing the middle class vote.

The data in table 3.1 strongly support the contention that, in a context where income is a good measure of overall well-being, and where it is needed as a rationale for vote, it is exactly that. For the voting profiles of three of the four groups are almost identical. If one has a consciousness of being middle class, income level makes no difference. Nor, without such a consciousness, will one vote any differently as long as one is, relatively, well off. In all these cases the Conservatives have a lead of about 44 per cent over Labour. The Labour Party never gets more than a fifth of the vote. However, where there is no subjective middle class identity, income certainly does count. Non-manual workers who earn less than the average non-manual income give the Conservatives only 50 per cent of the vote. This produces a Conservative lead less than half of that in the other three categories. Nor is this a trivial result because it affects only one of four subgroups. It happens to be the biggest of the four, accounting for 40 per cent of the total non-manual category. What one would suggest, in fact, is that there are, for non-manual grades, two different orientations to party voting. For the small section who are consciously middle class, income is largely irrelevant, as their vote is a class vote in a 'sociological' sense of that phrase. This 'middle' class consciousness is investigated in depth in chapter 4. For the current purpose, it can be accepted that as much as three-quarters of the non-manual grades in fact lack any serious subjective sense of being in such a social position.

But this does not imply that their political behaviour in any way fails to be motivated by materialistic or self-interested economic matters. It is precisely in such a group, lacking class identity, that a much more pragmatic and 'instrumental' vote should be expected. The data in our table here are strong grounds for supposing that income does indeed have a very direct impact on their vote in an entirely predictable way. It is an impact, though, which by being instrumental, sets up no special long-term loyalties. The rich 'non class-conscious' middle class voters are not 'safe' Conservative votes. No more are their poorer class brethren beyond the Conservatives' sights (50 per cent of them still vote Conservative anyway). They are very much at risk to the actual likely benefit they see themselves getting from other parties. Thus they are probably the best hunting ground for the Alliance, though the evidence to support this proposition has more to do with opinion polls and by-elections before the 1983 election than the election result itself.

If income is a difficult measure of affluence, there are more direct ways of trapping it. One can ask about the enjoyment of some of the benefits of affluence. This is especially relevant as industrial jobs increasingly make available benefits in kind, rather than cash. Some company directors, for example, have relatively low salaries, more than made up for by company cars, free membership of private health insurance schemes, and so on. Consumption patterns may directly indicate a psychological state tying people to a party in favour of middle class affluence, even when the income that provides the basis for the choice may be spread more widely than the take-up rate on the choices. Many of those without telephones, for example, may be prevented from getting them for reasons having little to do with the capacity to pay the 'phone bills, but they are still thereby cut off from one aspect of affluent modern life.

Those who choose to use some of their funds to pay for the help of a 'daily' in the house may be no richer than neighbours who do not have such help. But by availing themselves of this service they are putting themselves into an economic situation, as employers of domestic service, linked with a tradition of wealth. One could easily go on with such a catalogue. The BES survey did include a few simple questions about consumption choices, from which I have constructed a simple additive index. This is reported in table 3.2, which is broken down into three occupational status groups. I have deliberately separated the intermediate social grades of upper and

TABLE 3.2 Living standards by vote and social grade (%)

Occupational status		Living standards score: 0/2 points					Living standards score: 3/5 points				
		Con.	Lib.	Lab.	Total	Number of respondents	Con.	Lib.	Lab.	Total	Number of respondents
A and B	Higher managerial or professional and lower managerial or administrative	51	21	28	100	181	76	10	14	100	153
C1A and C1B	Skilled or supervisory non-manual and lower non-manual	54	17	30	100	226	78	9	13	100	78
C2 and D	Skilled manual and semi-skilled or unskilled manual	34	13	53	100	675	46	21	34	100	92

Note: A respondent gets one point for each of the following: having a telephone, having private health insurance, paying for domestic help. He gets one point for having use of a car or van for his private driving, and two points if he has use of two or more cars or vans in such a way.

lower white-collar workers from the rest of the non-manual 'middle class'. I have done this, not because their voting patterns under various degrees of affluence are different from the higher and lower managerial groups (grades A and B), but precisely because they are not. What is most intriguing about table 3.2 is that the whole of the non-manual sector reacts politically to affluence in exactly the same way. This suggests, much more powerfully than the previous table on income, that economic rationality does indeed directly affect voting, rather than being a surrogate measure of a social status.

The index is very simple. The survey asked whether respondents had: (1) a telephone, (2) one or more cars or vans for their private use (which does not mean privately owned — thus it includes the ubiquitous 'company car'); (3) whether they were members of a private health insurance scheme; (4) whether they hired domestic help with cleaning, and so on. Each respondent gets one point for every 'yes' answer, and two points if they have two or more cars or vans. The maximum score is, therefore, five. Table 3.2 divides each 'objective social class' into two groups — those scoring 0–2, those scoring 3–5. The voting differences are stark.

Those who enjoy less affluence amongst non-manual grades give only slightly over half of their votes to the Conservative Party. They give somewhere between 17 per cent and 21 per cent to the Liberals, and approaching 30 per cent to Labour. This pattern is the same across both the higher and lower categories amongst the non-manual grades. For all of these grades, possession or enjoyment of more of the goods I use as indicators boosts the Conservative poll to over three-quarters of all the sub-sample. Again this applies as much, indeed more, to the lower white-collar jobs inside the 'objective' middle class. We note something else here too. As was the case with income, the Tory dominance comes about by an equal drop in the attraction the affluent feel to both the other parties. In both non-manual sectors, the Liberal vote is cut in half once one crosses the affluence border. It seriously appears that being well off produces an automatic support for one particular party, the Conservatives, rather than an opposition to the Labour Party. This effect is very strong indeed. The lead enjoyed by Conservatives over Labour jumps from around 23 per cent amongst the less affluent to over 60 per cent amongst the well off, a multiple of around three.

Amongst the manual 'working class' voters, affluence still has an equally dramatic impact, though from a lower base. The less affluent give Labour a clear majority, 53 per cent against 34 per cent for the Conservatives. For that (naturally small) part of the working class who also score highly on the living standards index, the Conservative vote does not jump as high, or by the same relative amount, as it did amongst the affluent middle class. Nonetheless the change in absolute Conservative lead is of much the same order. Here, amongst working class affluent voters, the Labour vote drops as low as the Conservative vote amongst the non-affluent manual workers. Instead, the Liberal vote jumps up; the Conservatives have a lead over Labour of 12 per cent, when Labour leads them by 19 per cent amongst the less affluent. Why Liberals should gain by relative affluence amongst the working class, and lose by it amongst the middle class, is perhaps unclear.

What is beyond doubt is that owning the good things of an affluent society makes voters very keen to protect that affluence by voting for the party they most see as protecting property and wealth. There are innumerable other signs of the same pattern. For example, one can explain the preference of council house tenants for Labour, and of owner occupiers for the Conservatives, without necessarily opting for a theory of rational economic interest voting. But can one avoid such a theory to explain that, amongst owner occupiers, those who have a mortgage are less Conservative than those who do not? Or that inhabitants of privately owned detached houses give a much bigger share of their vote to the Conservatives than do the owner occupiers of semi-detached houses? Yet that is what the data showed at the end of chapter 1.

So far most, if not all, the material covered in this book has been to the detriment of the Labour Party. More which is to come, especially on the role of parental socialization in section 3.2, and class consciousness in chapter 4, continues this theme. Yet the real reason that Labour seems to be doing badly is that much of its vote has been, in the past, from reasons other than rational self-interest choice. In turning to examine the role of trade union membership I am turning to the one remaining real strength of the Labour movement, as well as to its birthplace. This is because unionization is like income in having a direct economic link to vote choice.

In some countries, Italy being the best case, trade union membership is almost the most important determinant of the vote. In Britain, though less vital, affiliation to organized Labour is still extremely important, and will rank above most other 'background' variables in any multivariate analysis.

Unionism and the vote

Union membership is very important in shaping voting, not only where it might be expected, amongst manual workers, but also amongst non-manual, 'middle class' voters. Unionism as a political force can be approached in a variety of ways. What to do with unions, whether or not they have too much power, and similar problems are in themselves political issues. As such they have been dealt with elsewhere in this book. At the other end of a spectrum from 'issue in itself' to 'political institution', one might ask about the substantive content of being in a union: How do people see the efficacy of their own union? What direct political education or experience do they offer? and so on. Here, however, we are concerned only with a fairly formal membership or proximate membership in a union. We ask no more than this, Does membership of a union in itself, regardless of the content of that experience, have an effect on voting behaviour? If so, does it do this across class lines, and does it have an impact on what I turn to in a later chapter to discuss, class consciousness? (Butler and Stokes, 1974, ch. 9.)

The first slightly surprising thing about union membership, at least going by stereotypes, is how little class related it actually is. Membership of a trade union is not, perhaps, quite so much of a personal characteristic, a 'background' variable, as others discussed in this book. But inasmuch as it is an often involuntary aspect of a voter's working life, it would surely qualify for inclusion in any election study. In the 1979 election, argument about trade unions played so large a part that union membership is likely to have been even more a significant aspect to a voter.

Somewhere around 40 per cent of non-manual workers are members of trade unions of some sort or other, and perhaps 10-15 per cent more amongst manual workers. Hence the comment that membership at least is not so much a class-related variable as one might think.[2] The sorts of unions people join in different classes, the nature of that membership, and its ability to shape political beliefs naturally varies a good deal, both within and across classes. A full analysis of union membership would have to take account of which unions are being discussed, and how actively involved in their affairs the voters were. I can only sketch an answer to the obvious questions that arise about such membership and voting.

To start with, we can derive a scale of closeness to unions by arguing that not only one's own membership, but that of members of one's family, can be relevant. This follows because the political implications of unions, especially in the 1979 election, are not only personal to the voter. It is not just an ideological or pragmatic influence on members *qua* union members. Because industrial relations were so important as an issue, and because images of what unions and unionists are like can so easily have been distorted, especially after the events of the winter preceding the election, any proximity to a union could have affected a voter just by giving him more information on the issue. So I have constructed a four-point scale of union involvement (table 3.3). The most intense point on the scale is where the respondent is a member of a union, and at least one other member of his immediate family is a union member also. Next comes the point where only the respondent is a member in his family, followed by the state where the respondent is not himself a member, but at least one person from his family is. Finally, we have those with no union connection at all, directly or through family.

Unions being so closely tied up, in practice and in myth, with the development of an industrial working class in Britain, the question of class consciousness cannot be left out here. So table 3.3 reports

TABLE 3.3 Labour voting in manual occupation by subjective class and degree of trade union connection (%)

| Degree of trade union connection: membership of trade union | Subjective class identity | | | Percentage of each row category with spontaneous working class identity |
	Middle class or no class	Working class	Total	
Self and other in family	66	63	65	50
Self only	63	48	54	40
Someone else in family only	70	51	59	38
No connection; nobody in family a union member	53	30	39	37

Note: Respondents in occupational status categories C2 and D are divided according to subjective class as well as degree of trade union connection into nine sub-categories. Entry in each of these sub-category cells is the percentage voting Labour. The total entry is the Labour percentage of each row category. The right-hand column in the table gives the percentage of each row category who spontaneously identified with the working class.

four figures for each of the four points on the union involvement scale. The table covers only those in manual grades. It gives the Labour vote for each scale point in the manual working class, and it also gives this separately for those who do and do not spontaneously offer a working class subjective identity. Finally, it reports on this last phenomenon directly by giving the percentage of each unionism scale category who do not have such a spontaneous working class identity. What stands out most strikingly from the table is that any connection, however slim, with a trade union enormously boosts the chance of a Labour vote. Those manual workers who do not even have a member of their family in the union movement give only 30 per cent of their vote to Labour. Those without a subjective working class identity, over 60 per cent of this group, give Labour less than a third of their vote. But even only having a family membership connection, without oneself being in a union, pushes this up by 20 per cent to a 50 per cent Labour vote across the manual workers as a whole. Amongst the class identifiers Labour gets 70 per cent of the vote. There is a slight anomaly here in that being oneself a member without family support is, according to the data here, actually less conducive to Labour Party support than having a close family member in a union, but not oneself being a unionist. Whether or not this is an accident of the data collection, as it may well be, the crucial point is that any connection with a union markedly increases Labour sympathy. At the top of the scale, those who are members in their own right and come from a union family are still more Labour oriented. Fully 65 per cent of those with such intense ties vote Labour. This is a figure as high as nearly any middle class vote for the Conservatives so far documented, when I have systematically reported Labour never really doing well in any category, and the Conservatives so often pulling in a huge vote. The most striking point is that amongst the majority of manual workers who do not spontaneously identify with the working class, those very closely connected to unions are more than twice as likely to vote Labour than those with no connection.

Perhaps this offers an explanation of the importance of unionism, one in some ways parallel to the impact of income in the non class-conscious middle class described earlier. For while union membership may be a functional substitute for class consciousness, it is not the same, nor does class consciousness seem to follow from membership of a union. As the final column of table 3.3 demonstrates, being a member of a union, or having a family member in one, does not itself give rise to spontaneous class identity at any significantly greater rate than is found amongst those totally unconnected with the union movement. Only in the intensely union-connected category, respondents who are themselves members and have a relation in the union, does the incidence of working class identity rise. Even here only half do have a spontaneous working class identity. Here one is presumably dealing with the most solidly entrenched traditional Labour voting working class families, and even then half do not have the relevant subjective class image. There are other reasons for seeing union membership as most probably having an instrumental impact rather than being a substitute source of working class solidarity and consciousness. The impact of unionism is actually much greater amongst those who are not self-consciously working class. The class-conscious are indeed more likely to vote Labour if they are connected with unions, but the maximum difference between the non-unionists and those with union connections amongst this group is only 17 per cent (only 13 per cent if one treats the 'family member only' score of 70 per cent as suspicious and uses instead the 'self and family member' group). Where class consciousness is absent, the comparison gives a Labour increase nearly twice as big as this at 33 per cent.

Comparing these data from manual working union members with the non-manual middle class unionists is instructive and helps support the argument above that union membership has a pro-Labour effect in its own right, and not by strengthening some basic working class party loyalty. It also disposes of another superficially attractive explanation, that the only reason union membership appears to boost Labour voting is that it is a surrogate measure for the more 'truly' working class manual jobs. This argument would claim that unionism picks out a 'lower' working class, or just indicates that such voters come from particularly troubled industrial sectors. As non-manual union membership is such a different phenomenon, the general tendency for union connection markedly to boost Labour voting would not then subsist also in the non-manual middle class. Yet table 3.4 continues to give evidence of a Labour Party advantage amongst union members, even where it exists outside its natural habitat.

Although the actual level of Labour voting, even amongst unionists, is much lower in the non-manual social class, the pattern is most decidedly still there. There are not enough unionists in the middle class, especially in the interesting sectors like the self-consciously middle class, to allow of the full four-point scale used before. So we operate on a straightforward dichotomy union member/non-member, which still gives enough leverage to make the point. The points are

TABLE 3.4 Labour voting in non-manual occupation categories by subjective class and union membership (%)

	Subjective class identity	
Union membership	Middle class	Working class or no class
Union member	35	39
Non-union member	12	21

Note: Respondents in categories A–C1B are divided according to subjective class as well as union membership into four subcategories. Entries are the percentage who voted Labour within each of the four categories.

twofold. First, that union membership makes non-manual workers much more likely to vote Labour, with around 38 per cent of those in unions doing so when not more than 20 per cent of non-members vote Labour. This is a ratio of much the same order of magnitude as existed amongst the manual workers. The second point is that, far from being tied to any relationship with class consciousness, the union membership factor appears to be able to transcend it. For the Labour vote amongst union members in the non-manual category is much the same, between 35 per cent and 38 per cent, whether or not they spontaneously see themselves as middle class. But subjectively middle class non-manual workers who are not union members give only 12 per cent of their vote to Labour. Where there is no class identity, non-unionized middle class voters give 21 per cent to Labour. Union membership nearly triples the Labour vote amongst self-labelled middle class non-manual workers.

TABLE 3.5 Subjective class identity by union membership in non-manual occupational categories (%)

Subjective class identity	Union membership	
	Union member	Non-member
Middle class	22	29
Working class or no class	78	71
Total	100	100

Final evidence that union membership in the 'objective' middle class does not particularly depend on diminishing a voter's sense of what class he comes from is given in table 3.5. This reports how subjective class identity in the non-manual middle class is affected by union membership. Although those who are union members are slightly less likely to see themselves spontaneously as middle class, the impact is only slight, in a class that is not in any case very prone to carry a subjective class identity. Only about 7 per cent less of trade unionists amongst non-manual workers think of themselves as middle class than do so amongst non-members, and even then more than one in five do so.

We would suggest then that union membership, like income, and — in a slightly different way — like educational level, is a variable which has a secular, essentially 'classless', and certainly more pragmatic than ideological, effect of notable importance on the vote. It is impossible to be sure to what extent the particular salience of unionism in the data is a long-term phenomenon, or partly affected by the politics of the 1979 election. Even if the latter account is partially true, there is no doubt that union membership, perhaps next after class itself, is of tremendous importance. This is why I have been so careful to try to throw light on the nature of its impact. It is precisely because it does seem to have an effect quite independent of class consciousness that I regard unionism as best treated in this chapter. I argue that increasingly a disaggregated 'economic interests' model, rather than a dichotomous class interest model seems to fit. This is shown earlier in terms of detailed location in the industrial structure and here, in terms of union membership, itself part of the industrial experience. The same argument is backed by, for example, the impact of income and wealth. The decline in inheritance of parental voting habits, and the impact of social mobility to be considered next in part explain why this disaggregation might take place. Part II of this book, which suggests that the electorate consists of nine class–party sub-cultures, makes further sense of this phenomenon.

3.2 FAMILY BACKGROUND AND THE VOTE

So far in this book I have treated voters as though they appeared, fully fledged, with political opinions and class interests at the minimum voting age of 18. There is a long tradition of studying instead the development of such attitudes and preferences. The most obvious single thing a new reader picks up from Butler and Stokes, for example, is an argument about whether voting preferences are inherited. This may well be overdone, and the tradition of electoral sociology has probably erred in the other direction from me, by attaching too much importance to the learned and inherited instinct and too little to adult calculation.

Still, there may well have been real changes in the importance of childhood political learning in recent decades. In any case no study of class and voting can afford to ignore the considerable impact of social mobility.

I turn then first to a consideration of how much voters inherit a party loyalty from their parents. The earlier studies of voting behaviour made much of the way electors cast the same vote as their parents did, especially casting the same vote as their fathers (Butler and Stokes, 1974, chs 3 and 5; Campbell *et al.*, 1960). Table 3.6 reports the 1979 data on this inheritability of the vote, and in so doing supports a suggestion in chapter 2 that recent trends in voting changes have hurt the Labour Party much more than the Conservatives.

TABLE 3.6 Voting in the 1979 election by
parents' party preference (%)

| | Parents' partisanship | | |
Own vote	Both parents Conservative	Parents divided	Both parents Labour
Conservative	72	47	28
Liberal	13	18	13
Labour	15	35	60
Total	100	100	100
Number of respondents	376	69	530

Note: The table includes only respondents who voted Conservative, Liberal or Labour in 1979, and who remember their mother and father as either Labour or Conservative voters.

In order to mean much, table 3.6 needs to be read in conjunction with table 3.7, which reports similar and comparable data from a 1963 survey.[3] There seems little change in 16 years in the inheritance of votes from Conservative parents. This is not so for Labour, whose ability to rely on inherited vote has been drastically reduced. In 1963 three-quarters of voters who remembered both their parents being Conservative voted in the same way. Labour did even better, for 81 per cent of those with united Labour voting parents followed their lead. By 1979 this had dropped to only 60 per cent of people with a solid Labour parental background voting for the Labour Party. The inheritance of Conservative votes had been reduced by only a few per cent, mainly because of the rise of the Liberals.

TABLE 3.7 Party preference in 1963
by whether parents' preference was Conservative or Labour (%)

Respondent's own present preference in 1963	*Parents' partisanship*		
	Both parents Conservative	*Parents divided*	*Both parents Labour*
Conservative	75	37	10
Liberal	8	10	6
Labour	14	49	81
None	3	4	3
Total	100	100	100

Source: D. E. Butler and D. Stokes (1974) *Political Change in Britain* (2nd edn), London: Macmillan, ch. 3, p. 52.

TABLE 3.8 Vote in 1979 by parental vote and sex (%)

Own vote	*Parents' vote*		
	Both Conservative	*Divided*	*Both Labour*
Male respondents			
Conservative	68	38	29
Liberal	15	24	13
Labour	18	38	57
Total	100	100	100
Female respondents			
Conservative	76	54	27
Liberal	11	13	11
Labour	12	33	62
Total	100	100	100

In the context of our earlier discussion of sex differences in voting, table 3.8 is interesting. It reports the 1979 inheritance rates for the vote separately for men and women voters. Not only is the decline in importance of parental vote different across the parties, it is different across the sexes too, in a way that goes some way towards explaining the sex differences amongst the middle class voters we have noted. Amongst men, the table shows a decline in tendency to vote as did their parents for both parties, though the decline is very much greater for the Labour Party. Labour gained the votes of only 57 per cent of the sons of united Labour families. Amongst the women the actual drop in inheritance of the Labour loyalty is not quite as great, with 62 per cent of daughters of firm Labour families voting that way. But, and it is a vital point, daughters of Conservative families have not changed at all in their probability of voting as their parents did — 76 per cent still vote Conservative.

It is not surprising that women should follow parental patterns more than men who have still been culturally more important in politics, but it is interesting that it should be a pattern that benefits one party so much more than the others. It does explain one of the potential problems in chapter 2, which was that women in the young and old middle class categories were considerably more Conservative than men, when this did not apply to their sisters in the middle age group. What seems likely is that younger women are more likely to retain a parental influence than older ones, being still closer to their parents, and that women in the 55+ age group are in any case, because of the socialization of their cohort, more likely to be Conservative (see Crewe, 1972; Peele and Francis, 1978). Those in the middle group are far enough away from childhood for parental influence to have been eroded, but young enough to have been originally socialized and re-socialized through life experience into a Labour-supporting attitude.

Clearly one of the most obvious explanations for the recently noticed volatility of the electorate and the breakdown of traditional voting loyalties would be something to do with early socialization patterns, and table 3.6 might suggest this. If people are less likely to inherit political attitudes, they are by definition going to be less predictable by background factors, because in the past there was so strong a 'background to vote' causation. Alternatively, one could invert the argument and suggest that if social background ceases to be much of a determinant of the vote, parental influence will also appear to decline. Whichever pathway may actually be true, we must suspect that experience of political influence and of social background in one's early years has diminished in importance. This can be tested in several ways. One useful thing to look at is the connection between social mobility and voting. Butler and Stokes (1974, pp. 100ff.) found a decade ago that those who changed their class position from that of their parents were less likely to vote along class lines than those whose social location was static. Table 3.9 replicates, as nearly as possible, their analysis.

TABLE 3.9 Conservative and Labour support by class among socially stable and socially mobile voters in 1979 and 1970 (%)

| | Socially stable | | | | Socially mobile | | | |
| | Middle class | | Working class | | Middle class | | Working class | |
Vote	1979	1970	1979	1970	1979	1970	1979	1970
Conservative	87	87	28	29	65	56	62	50
Labour	13	13	72	71	35	44	38	50
Total	100	100	100	100	100	100	100	100

Note: Data for the 1970 election are from D. E. Butler and D. Stokes (1974) *Political Change in Britain* (2nd edn) London: Macmillan, p. 101.
My data and Butler and Stokes' relate to those who voted either Conservative or Labour in the respective years.

The table gives the figures for the Labour and Conservative vote amongst the socially stable and mobile according to their current class position. The 1970 entries for each cell are the comparable figures from Butler and Stokes (1974, p. 101). They used a measure, roughly equivalent to my use of the Alford index, discussed previously, to determine how much class-based voting existed amongst the two sectors of the electorate. They showed that while the index stood at the very high level (58 per cent) for the socially stable, it was almost negligible (6 per cent) amongst those with class positions different from their parents. The BES data give virtually the same result for the socially mobile, the index figure being this time round only 4 per cent. This is predictable, because the socially mobile are very likely to have, as Butler and Stokes (1974, p. 99) put it, 'blurred' class images. If long-term background influences are decreasing at all, they should certainly not increase amongst those with conflicting experiences. Support for the idea that socially learned voting behaviour is less and less important comes from the decrease in the index amongst those with stable social class positions. In 1970, this stood at 58, because 71 per cent of those who were, and had always been, working class voted Labour, but only 14 per cent of the long-term middle class did so. By 1979 this had dropped to 47 percentage points, mainly because of a change in the stable working class Labour vote from the previous 71 per cent level to only 61 per cent.

The intensity of class voting decreases, but only because of a drop in stable working class party loyalty. The stable middle class voting figures are almost exactly the same in the two data sets collected nine years apart. The actual figures for voting amongst the socially mobile are different, because the Conservatives did better than they had in 1970. In fact, the swing recorded amongst both socially mobile current class identifications, between 8 per cent and 10 per cent, is more or less the overall average amongst our sample. Nothing seems then to have happened unusually to those whose votes were already cut loose from structural influences. They just reacted as the population as a whole did. Those in the stable middle class continued an apparently unshakeable loyalty to the Conservatives. But those who ought to have been equally solid for Labour were not. When there is a situation where one and only one social group shows an unexpected shift and where that group is especially defined around a criterion directly relevant to early socialization, it is quite likely that a breakdown in the inheritability of social attitudes favouring the party in question is happening. It might also be pointed out that the reliability of these data is high. Both time points we are comparing are years of Conservative victory. This being so, a jump of stable working class voting to the right, with no change in stable middle class support, is even more striking.

Although the sheer fact of the inheritability of the vote is important in its own right, there are sociological problems involved in interpreting it, as has already been shown by the connection with social mobility. We need to consider together the two factors that appear to affect such a tendency to vote as did one's parents. These are the sex factor, women appearing to inherit more than men, and the social mobility factor. It is first worth getting a clearer idea of the details of vote inheritance across mobile and stable class groups. Table 3.10 sets out the 1979 vote for two categories of voters, those who remember both parents as having a united loyalty to either the Conservative or Labour Party. These two categories are broken down according to current and family social class, except that two of these sub-categories have too few respondents in them to be worth reporting. These are the sub-categories for respondents who remember their parents as having been Labour voters, but who also remember their family as being middle class. It is hardly surprising that few should remember an earlier generation as having been middle class but supporting the working class party, though in practice there must have been quite a few such families. Most of the interesting comparisons I wish to make are still available.

TABLE 3.10 1979 vote by parental vote,
according to past and current class status (%)

		Both parents Conservative			Both parents Labour	
Current class	*Middle*	*Middle*	*Working*	*Working*	*Middle*	*Working*
Family class	*Middle*	*Working*	*Middle*	*Working*	*Working*	*Working*
1979 vote						
Conservative	79	71	62	63	46	24
Liberal	12	21	17	13	8	11
Labour	9	8	21	24	46	65
Total	100	100	100	100	100	100

The results of this analysis again support the idea that Labour has lost out in terms of inheritance rates even when one takes social mobility into account, though it is clearly true that social mobility does affect inheritance of partisanship. The Conservatives retain at least a clear majority of support amongst children of Conservative parents in all the four categories into which they are divided. The worst loss to Labour that they sustain is about a quarter of children of Conservative parents voting Labour amongst the stable working class. If the class-socializing forces on those who themselves have manual jobs and who remember their parents that way can only reduce inheritance of a Conservative vote by this amount, parental influence must still be very strong indeed for conservatism. Butler and Stokes tended to comment more strongly on a 'drift' back to the 'natural class' amongst those with a deviant class vote amongst the working class. Any such drift is now clearly attenuated (Butler and Stokes, 1974, p. 102).

Labour voters, as noted above, can only usefully be divided twice by class, into those whose Labour voting parents were working class and are themselves either working class or middle class. One of these groups, the stable working class, I have just discussed when they had Conservative parents. Such two generation working class voters have a tendency to inherit a Labour loyalty as high as most tendencies to inherit conservatism. But children of working class Labour families who themselves become middle class are only marginally more likely to vote Labour than they are to support the party of their new class (Thorburn, 1977). In contrast, voters who have themselves fallen to a working class status from the middle class, had they Conservative parents, are still three times more likely to vote as their families did than to change to their dominant 'class' party.[4] Two-fifths of those who are upwardly mobile desert Labour for the Conservatives, only one-fifth of the downwardly mobile desert in a similar manner to Labour. This pattern is neither new nor restricted to the British electorate, but it is as clear and strong, perhaps more so, as ever.

A second and quite striking pattern in the table refers to the Liberal vote. We are not concerned with the inheritability of Liberal voting, mainly because it was never high enough in the past as covered by the respondents' memories for them to have much chance of inheriting it. But the Liberals are important as an avenue of desertion from united family loyalty to the two major parties. Of the six columns in table 3.10, three involve socially stable voters, whether from Conservative or Labour families. The 1979 Liberal vote in these three categories is more or less the same, regardless of parental politics, somewhere between 10 and 12 per cent. This is close to the usual figure in the tables, most of which show no class connection to the Liberal vote.

The other three columns refer to those whose class experience is mixed, being upwardly or downwardly socially mobile. In each case the Liberal vote is very much higher. Those who are downwardly mobile from a Conservative background give nearly one in four of their votes to the Liberal Party. The upwardly mobile with Conservative parents give over a fifth to this party. Even the current middle class who come from a working class family with a Labour background give 17 per cent of their votes to the Liberals.

There are two obvious explanations, between which one cannot choose. On the one hand, the Liberals might be a halfway house for adjusting a family vote to class location. If this were true, one might expect the children of the respondents, if they stay in the same class the respondent himself has arrived at, will switch to the dominant party of that class. Thus, where the respondents had middle class Conservative parents, and, having become working class themselves, give nearly a quarter of their votes to the Liberals, we would expect much of that Liberal advantage to go to Labour amongst their own children if they stay working class.

The alternative thesis would be that it is the socially mobile who are shaken loose from class ties, and who therefore are especially attracted to an apparently classless party. If this version is true, we would expect the Liberals not only not to lose the support they gain here, but in fact to increase as an increasingly mobile population shifts away from the politics of class loyalty. Certainly this would fit into the picture I frequently describe of the Liberals benefiting from a breakdown of class loyalty. The more complex class model in part II, and chapter 4, where I turn to the question of subjective class consciousness, supports this contention.

So far I have not picked up the earlier suggestion that inheritance rates might be higher amongst women than men, partly at least because of stronger socialization links between girls and parents. If these links are stronger it is partly because women are less likely to be socially mobile, and I turn now to an analysis that includes sex as well as social mobility. In so doing I can represent the data in table 3.10 in another way which helps answer an obvious question. The question is the extent to which social mobility has been the principal cause of decline in voting inheritance. The best way to answer this question is to consider the loss from an early generation vote as consisting of a series of components. Thus the stable middle class inheritance loss amongst male descendants is one component of the total Conservative loss. If we look at the loss rates in each 'social mobility by sex' group we can draw conclusions both about sex differences and about the relative importance of loss due to mobility as opposed to the loss of inheritance amongst the socially stable.

The most direct evidence comes from table 3.11, from the first column headed 'Loss rate'. This is the percentage by which the vote of the later generation for the relevant party falls below 100 per cent inheritance. In the part of the table referring to the Conservative Party, one can see that in two of the three generational groups women have stayed much closer to their parental vote than men. Only 3 per cent of women who are now, and were as children, middle class and who had Conservative parents, have changed their vote, while 16 per cent of men in that situation have deserted their parents' political allegiance. Similarly, a quarter of women who are and always have been working class have lost their Conservative background, while less than a third of such men have. It does seem, then, that where nothing has happened to shake general patterns of socialization, socialization is stronger amongst women than men and, indeed, that amongst stable middle class women from Conservative backgrounds it is well nigh perfect. One reason for regarding the general decline in vote inheritance as representing a weakening of such socializing pressures comes from the figures in the rest of the 'Conservative' part

TABLE 3.11 Components of loss of vote inheritance
for the Conservative and Labour Parties in 1979 (%)

	Loss rate	Size of group	Effect	Effect in each group as percentage of total effect
(A) Both parents Conservative Component				
male, stable middle class	16	29	5	29
female, stable middle class	3	25	1	6
male, upwardly mobile	11	8	1	6
female, upwardly mobile	11	8	1	6
male, stable working class	30	16	5	29
female, stable working class	25	15	4	24
Total		100	17	100
(B) Both parents Labour Component				
male, stable working class	26	38	10	32
female, stable working class	27	42	11	35
male, upwardly mobile	58	9	5	16
female, upwardly mobile	42	11	5	16
Total		100	31	100

Notes:
Section (A) of the table comprises respondents who remember both parents as Conservative.
Section (B) comprises respondents remembering both parents as Labour.
Loss rate = percentage of respondents in the appropriate row group who did not vote for their parents' party.
Size of group = the size of the group as a percentage of all respondents remembering both parents as Conservative (A) and Labour (B), respectively.
Effect = percentage points of total loss of parents' party vote inheritance due to decline in the party's vote in the group. The extreme right column in the table gives the effect in each group as a percentage of the total effect.

of the table. One cannot simply argue that the sex difference above is actually based on any direct tendency for women *qua* women to be either more Conservative, or simply more loyal to their parents. Were this simple explanation true, then the sex difference should also show up amongst the socially mobile. However, amongst women who have been upwardly mobile from Conservative working class backgrounds, the loss of parental vote is higher than it is amongst men. Seventeen per cent of women in this category shift away from conservatism, when only one in ten men do. Class mobility of this sort does not itself involve necessarily any shift of political perception. Indeed, for a Conservative to move into the class which the Conservative Party naturally represents ought, *a priori*, to harden that political allegiance. That there is a tendency to home onto the natural class party is well documented, and shown in this table itself with the very high rates of Labour desertion amongst the upwardly mobile. Despite this, upwardly mobile Conservative women are four times more likely to desert conservatism than stable middle class women, and not that much less likely so to do than stable working class women. Shifting class does, through a wide variety of mechanisms, cut one off from not only parental, but many other early socializing forces, and the pattern in this table can be argued to be indirect evidence for this general thesis.

Though less marked, the tendency of women in general to retain their parents' political allegiance shows also in the Labour Party section of the table. It is unfortunate that the sample does not allow us to look at as many component groups for those from loyal Labour families, but the two important categories — the stable working class and the upwardly mobile — again show women tending to desert Labour less than men. In this case also, women who undergo class mobility are more likely to change from their parents' vote than those who are socially stable. Here they are not more prone to do so than men, but with a massive 58 per cent loss rate for ex-working class men with Labour parents it would be hard for that to be the case.

The question of the extent to which it is social mobility in general that has reduced the inheritability of voting loyalty is largely a question about the Labour vote. The Conservatives have, in any case, lost much less of the older generations' vote — less than 20 per cent — while Labour has lost at least a third. The Conservatives are less at risk to this form of loss. Formerly middle class voters who sink in the class system account for only 10 per cent of respondents remembering having had Conservative parents. Of these the Conservatives lose the support of only a quarter of them anyway, suffering therefore a loss of only about 2.5 per cent in support. This is the way one has to consider the question; the rate of loss in a group by itself cannot tell us about the impact on the party. One must also consider the size of the group as a proportion of the relevant body of electors. This is what the second and third columns of table 3.11 give us. The column marked 'Effect' is arrived at by treating the figures in columns 1 and 2 as proportions and multiplying them together. Thus, inheritance loss amongst upwardly mobile men from Labour families is 58 per cent, and that group accounts for 16 per cent of all respondents remembering united Labour parents. Thus, calculating 58 per cent of 9 per cent gives us the 'effect' figure of 5 per cent. This means that the Labour Party lost 5 per cent of its total inherited vote through whatever it was that happened to upwardly mobile men. The last column simply re-expresses this result in overall percentage terms to make the comparison between the groups easier. Overall, Labour lost 31 per cent of its older generation's votes. If 5 per cent was lost by the group we are using as an example, then one can say that 5 per cent of the whole loss of 31 per cent is equivalent to that group accounting for 16 per cent of the whole loss.

Whichever way we look at it, we get a slightly counter-intuitive result. The two upwardly mobile groups do indeed exhibit much greater desertion from parental vote than the two stable groups, a contrast of about 48 per cent to 25 per cent. The stable working class are only half as likely to desert. But the ultimate impact on Labour's vote is roughly equal, because of the much greater size of the stable population. In the end, over half of Labour's vote loss came from those who did not change social class. Similar comparisons can be made between any of the components in either part of the table. The results tend to re-affirm the first part of our discussion. There has been a tendency for women to retain a Conservative vote in such a way as to diminish the impact on Conservatives of a weakening in general of parental vote inheritance. Thus, the three female groups discussed amongst the Conservative parental vote group account for only a third of the inheritance loss, though they are nearly half of the group. This is mainly because one subgroup, stable middle class women, who amount to over a fifth of those with Conservative parents, have lost the Conservatives only 6 per cent of their total vote loss.

Labour has not, however, benefited from any tendency like this. Although women with Labour parents are more likely to keep the parental vote than men, the relative sizes of the subgroups mean that in the end women account for exactly half of the vote loss. One must conclude that, for a variety of reasons, there has been an attenuation of family political socialization, partly connected, but not restricted, to social mobility, and that this has hurt the Labour Party notably more than it has the Conservatives. On the assumption that this trend continues in the face of greater equality of opportunity between the sexes, and that social mobility itself continues, perhaps at an increasing rate, the long-term prospects for Labour, in this sense, look grim.

This may, of course, not help the Conservatives directly, because of the tendency shown in table 3.10 for Liberals to gain amongst the socially mobile. Assuming the Alliance of 1983 holds together, most of this chapter should read optimistically for them.

In the final chapter of part I of this book I turn to my first serious discussion of class consciousness. This, at least in the guise of sub-jective class identity, has perforce cropped up from time to time already. In many ways chapter 4 can be seen as a bridge between the orthodoxy of part I, and my more heterodox treatment of social class and political attitudes in part II.

4

Social Class as a
Subjective Phenomenon

Throughout the history of sociological analysis, theorists have recognized that social class involves not only external descriptions of the wealth, income, or job status of citizens. Before a class position can have much impact on a voter, he must be aware of his class, and indeed must think that class has some bearing on his life. One can, of course, have an entirely objective scheme within which people who just happen, without knowing it, to share economic interests, act in the same way. Few theorists, however, have taken this claim, what Marx would call a class 'in itself' as opposed to a class 'for itself', as of central importance.

The aim of this chapter is to tease out some of the points that follow once one admits that what people think about social class is at least as important as what analysts think about their class location. Two obvious sorts of question suggest themselves. Along one dimension is the question of whether or not people do admit to class membership, how willingly, and to what class they adhere. Cross cutting this identification question is one of salience. Regardless of what class a voter identifies with, and how willingly he does this, does he actually think about social class at all? Does he think his own path through life is made easier or rougher because of his (self-assessed) social class?

These dimensions cannot, in fact, be treated as completely independent of each other, because there are natural asymmetries involved. For example, given most people's idea of class, it makes no sense to ask a (self-avowed) member of the middle class if he thinks being middle class has made life harder for him than it would have been had he been working class. It does make sense to ask the question the other way round, because those in the working class (by

80

their own judgement) who see themselves as disadvantaged, relative to the middle class, are sensibly taken as a different political animal from those who do not. Even where this sort of non-symmetry does not obtain, one cannot expect the internal effect of class perceptions to be the same across the great divide of the middle and working class. Take, for example, the question of whether class is so important to a voter that he usually notices the social class of someone he meets for the first time. We would expect the answer to this question to vary across self-ascribed class boundaries. We might also expect the division so created to have a differential impact on voting for the traditional 'class' party inside the two subjective classes.

But even though the logic of class is bound to be complex, it is unavoidable that we pursue these two dimensions in some detail if we are to begin to understand social status and voting in what may well be the Western world's most class-ridden society.

I have already described the techniques of tracking subjective social class feelings in an earlier chapter in part I. At that stage there was no need to discuss fully two of the results of any such exercise that must now concern us. Investigations of subjective class identity nowadays regularly show two things that lead to problems in treating British politics as class based. First, relatively few people do, in fact, easily and spontaneously offer a class label unless the interviewer 'prompts' them to do so. Second, there is no very strong connection between what class label respondents do offer and their objective social location in terms of the manual/non-manual breakdown. Though this latter breakdown still proves to be useful in political analysis, and though it is still acceptable to refer to it as a 'middle class' versus 'working class' distinction, voters' private classifications, spontaneous or forced, frequently contradict the 'objective' labelling.

Table 4.1 presents detailed information on this preliminary matter. It gives, for each of the six occupational grades, the percentage who spontaneously, and unspontaneously, accord themselves middle or working class status. In no occupational status group do more than half of the voters offer a class label for themselves without being prompted by a second question, as described in chapter 1. Nor do the spontaneous labellings coincide very well with the standard equation that to be a non-manual worker is to be middle class, and that working class voters are those who do manual jobs. Indeed, only in one group do as much as 40 per cent of the sample give spontaneously a label which would coincide with the analysts. This is C2, the skilled manual workers. It is not just that groups which are indeed marginal in their class position fit badly. It may not be surprising that the

TABLE 4.1   Subjective social class by occupational status

Occupational status	Spontaneous class label			Prompted class label		
	Middle class	Working class	(None)*	Middle class	Working class	Total
A Higher managerial or professional	20	8	(72)	48	24	100
B Lower managerial or administrative	35	15	(50)	28	22	100
C1A Non-manual skilled of supervisory	22	15	(63)	30	33	100
C1B Lower non-manual	18	33	(49)	16	33	100
C2 Skilled manual	9	41	(51)	10	41	100
D Semi-skilled manual or unskilled manual	8	39	(55)	9	46	100

Notes:
   *The third column (for those with no spontaneous class) is the sum of the fourth and fifth columns.
   The percentage distributions show (for each occupational status category) the percentages who spontaneously and after prompting, described themselves as middle class or working class. Respondents who, even after prompting, failed to describe themselves with either of these class labels are excluded from this table.

group (C1B) which consists of the lower status white-collar workers, a group usually but uneasily credited with middle class status, should agree with analysts so little that only 18 per cent of them do give a spontaneous middle class label. It is considerably more odd that group A, the higher managerial and professional non-manual workers, should be prepared only in one case out of five to admit easily to being middle class. If one combined spontaneous and forced class labelling for this, the highest status group of all, one finds indeed that 32 per cent actually regard themselves as working class. Table 4.2 summarizes these results in terms of the most useful dichotomy, which is to contrast 'spontaneous and correct' with 'all other' responses. The use of the phrase 'correct class labelling' is naturally not meant to imply any arrogant claim to superiority in the analyst's perception. It is just a quick, convenient way to indicate congruence between private labels and external categorization.

   The summary backs the suggestion above, that is that a spontaneous sense of social class that accords with well-established external categorizations is rare in Britain. Much less than half of the manual working voters spontaneously offer a working class identity, and only one-quarter of the non-manual workers see themselves as middle class. But this difference cannot just be accounted for by the problem of the socially marginal non-manual workers in occupational grades C1A and C1B. Even if we adopted a much more restrictive definition of middle class status, putting only the higher and 'other' managerial and professional workers into this class, only 30 per cent would spontaneously give a middle class self-label.

TABLE 4.2
Objective class by subjective class under conditions of spontaneity (%)

	Spontaneously and 'correctly' giving class identity	Having no spontaneous class identity, or having an 'incorrect' identity	Total	Number of respondents
Objectively middle class	25	75	100	684
Objectively working class	40	60	100	907

Does it then follow that subjective class is irrelevant for voting behaviour, both because it is a relatively rare phenomenon and also because it so often fails to coincide with external classifications? It would be rather surprising were this so. How could social position have a voting relevance except through personal perceptions? It turns out that subjective social class is, under certain conditions, of considerable use in explaining voting, but that these conditions are rather specific and complex. It is also true, however, that external class, even when not backed up by a private class identity, can be equally important. Furthermore, the decline in class voting, already discussed at length, is itself connected to a decline in subjective class identity. I show later that the *average* levels of spontaneous class identity have not declined monotonically during the last 15 years, but that *working* class identity has declined.

4.2 SUBJECTIVE CLASS IDENTITY AND VOTING BEHAVIOUR

As we now know that objective and subjective class combine to mark out a set of complicated subgroups, we need immediately to study the way these groups cast their vote. Most previous studies have used only one or other of the ways of classifying and thus have obscured

much of the class/vote connection. Table 4.3 reports the 1979 vote
for each of the six groups obtained by using objective class with
subjective class, splitting this latter in a special way. I have argued
that forced responses to subjective class identity questions are best
left out here. So for each objective class we have three groups, those
spontaneously saying they are middle or working class, and those
refusing any *spontaneous* label at all.

TABLE 4.3   Party division of the vote in the 1979 election
by objective and subjective class (%)

Class group	Party vote in 1979			
	Con.	Lib.	Lab.	Total
Non-manual with spontaneous 'middle class' self-label	67	16	17	100
Non-manual with spontaneous 'working class' self-label	26	15	59	100
Non-manual with no spontaneous self-label	66	16	19	100
Manual with spontaneous 'middle class' self-label	42	15	43	100
Manual with spontaneous 'working class' self-label	25	14	61	100
Manual with no spontaneous self-label	43	14	44	100

It is obvious that class self-perceptions do affect voting – there is
a steep decline in class–party voting links under certain conditions of
objective/subjective class. The difference between the percentage of
manual workers who vote Labour amongst those who spontaneously
see themselves as working class (61 per cent) and either of the other
categories is around 17 per cent. Far fewer of the working class who
have this identity, only a quarter, vote Conservative, while over
40 per cent of those who think they are middle class, or have no
spontaneous image, do so. Amongst manual workers the important
question is clearly whether or not they have a 'correct' self-image.
If they do, they are strongly Labour and strongly anti-Conservative.
But, failing that, it appears to make no difference whether someone
objectively in the working class is merely unconscious of this or if
he actually thinks himself to be in the opposite class.

While the impact of class consciousness is no less amongst the non-manual 'middle class', the nature of the impact is reversed. Those who spontaneously offer a middle class self-image, and those who refuse any spontaneous image at all have identical voting profiles. They give 66 per cent or so to the Conservatives, and less than a fifth of their vote to Labour. But where a non-manual worker believes himself to be a member of the working class (and nearly 20 per cent do so spontaneously) they support the Labour Party nearly as intensively as the most class conscious of manual workers. Indeed, the voting profiles of those who have an unprompted working class identity are virtually identical, whatever objective class they come from. This, noticeably, is not true of those who have a spontaneous middle class identity. Although manual workers who believe themselves to be middle class split their vote roughly equally between the two major parties, those who share their subjective class identity, but from an objectively middle class background, are only half as likely to vote Labour and 50 per cent more likely to vote Conservative. It may be remarked in passing that Liberal voting strength has virtually nothing to do with class consciousness. Just as all tables of objective class show each category giving virtually the same proportion of their vote to the Liberal Party, so do the subjective/objective groups in table 4.3 This table invites us to see the electorate in terms of three basic groups. There is that group who believe themselves to be working class, regardless of their actual occupational status. These are the most intensely loyal to the Labour Party, which has a lead of about 35 per cent over the Conservative Party amongst them. Then there is the group consisting of non-manual workers who do not deny their middle class status, whether or not they spontaneously offer it. These are the strongest supporters of the Conservatives, whose lead over Labour amongst them is huge, somewhere between 45 and 50 per cent. Finally, there is an intermediate group. They are the manual workers who lack a spontaneous working class identity. After giving the usual handful of 14 per cent or so of the vote to the Liberals, these split the rest more or less equally, 43 per cent or so going to each major party.

The picture is fascinating and may tell us a great deal about the mechanism of class voting in Britain, especially after we look, in part II, somewhat deeper into the nature of class identification. At this stage it seems fair to suggest the following hypothesis: middle class support for the Conservative Party is relatively automatic, based on perhaps more pragmatic and 'real' connections between middle class life-styles, incomes, and so on, and a perception of likely policy from a Conservative government. In contrast, working class support for Labour, to reach any great intensity, must be based on an ideological, or at least conscious, direct perception that one *is* working class and that therefore the Labour Party is naturally one's party. Where this consciousness is present, it would seem to override any actual class–life-style considerations. The suggestion is that, unlike middle class life, there is nothing about the conditions of life in the objective working class that particularly predisposes someone just because of what his objective class is, to vote for a particular party. Accordingly, the vote of this group goes more or less at random depending on individual considerations, producing a roughly 50:50 split between Labour and Conservative. The point worth stressing is the nature of the contrast. In the objective middle class all that hurts the Conservatives is when someone 'wrongly' thinks he is actually working class; otherwise objective class is enough to give them a high vote. In the objective working class, the only thing that helps Labour is the positive spontaneous identification with the working class. Labour, to repeat, requires class consciousness, the Conservatives do not.

If something like this is true, and the data are very suggestive, the Labour Party would be very much more at risk to a class secularization of society than the Conservatives. It is one thing to *be* a class party, and there is nothing in table 4.3 to say the Conservatives are not (though perhaps earlier discussion does lead that way a little). It is quite another thing to have to be *seen* as one, which is what the Labour Party seems to require. Some caution is needed, however, because even if we have located a theoretically important part of the Labour Party's vote, it is not very large as an actual proportion of all those who voted Labour in 1979. The objective middle class who think themselves working class account only for 8 per cent of the total sample. The 'correctly' spontaneously working class account for another 22 per cent, and the two groups together make up only around 45 per cent of the 1979 Labour Party vote. Still, the Conservatives got only 22 per cent of their vote from those who spontaneously think of themselves as middle class.

4.3 THE PARTIAL DECLINE IN SUBJECTIVE CLASS IDENTITY

There is some evidence that the prevalence of subjective class identity may be declining in the electorate. If it is, it is doing so in a way especially harmful to the Labour Party.

TABLE 4.4
Objective and subjective class and voting over four elections (%)

		1964	*1970*	*October 1974*	*1979*
				Election	
(A)	Sample giving a spontaneous class label	48	42	42	47
(B)	Non-manual workers giving a 'middle class' label spontaneously	26	23	24	28
(C)	Manual workers giving a 'working class' label spontaneously	46	35	36	39
(D)	Non-manual workers giving a 'working class' label spontaneously	20	12	15	15
(E)	Manual workers giving a 'middle class' label spontaneously	6	10	10	8
(F)	Non-manual workers with 'middle class' image voting Conservative*	78 (59)	80 (65)	58 (51)	67 (57)
(G)	Manual workers with 'working class' image voting Labour*	74 (57)	70 (57)	70 (52)	61 (43)

Note: *Figures in parentheses refer to the percentage in that objective group *without* the 'correct' self image voting for the relevant 'class party'.

Table 4.4 gives comparative figures for four elections since 1964. The data for 1964 and 1970 are taken from precursor surveys carried out by David Butler and Donald Stokes. Such comparisons must be taken with some care, as I discussed in chapter 1, because of lack of comparability between questions. In the two Butler and Stokes surveys chosen there were several versions of the class consciousness questions used on different split samples. The ones used here are fairly well comparable as they adopted the same 'open followed by forced' choice system as the BES did in 1974 and 1979. Unfortunately, the split sampling means the relevant samples are very small, particularly in 1964. The data can, nonetheless, be useful as we are interested only in broad trends.

Both stability and change show in the table. After the 1974 elections some people claimed to detect as a trend a general decrease in willingness to give spontaneous class labels (Crewe, 1977). Our data shows this was only a temporary decline, in 1970 and 1974. The 1979 proportion willing to give a self-label without being forced is 47 per cent, effectively the same as at the beginning of the period. Similarly, the willingness of those categorized as middle class (because of non-manual occupation) to see themselves as such, experienced a temporary decline in the middle of the period, but now stands higher than ever before. No trend at all is visible in row (E), for objective working class voters who give themselves a 'middle class' label.

Where there is a trend is just where the Labour Party can least afford it, supporting the general conclusions we have begun to come to about the eroding of its most loyal base. Although the proportion of manual workers who were prepared spontaneously to label themselves working class has increased a little from its 1970–4 dip — a dip shared, as we note, by the non-manual equivalent in row (B) — the general decrease over the period is confirmed. In 1964, 46 per cent of the manual workers were prepared to say they were working class, this figure dropped in the middle two elections by around 10 or 11 per cent, and is still only 39 per cent, which is 7 per cent less than at the beginning of the period. This is a crucial sector for the Labour Party, and it is not the only change that adversely affects them. The subjective working class has another vital component. As described earlier, part of the objective middle class think of themselves as working class. The support for Labour amongst this group is higher than any other sector of the population apart from manual workers with a spontaneous working class identity. But these non-manual 'middle class' voters who are subjectively working class are also in decline as a proportion of the electorate. In 1964 a full fifth of the non-manual workers saw themselves as working class, but the proportion has been steady for the last two elections at only 15 per cent.

There is another comparison in the table which suggests that the decline in the conscious working class must damage Labour more than any trend in the table can damage the Conservatives. Consider how important it is for the two parties to have the members of their 'natural support' class being class conscious. Row (F) of the table shows that the Conservative share of the vote in the 'conscious' middle class has declined over time from the very high 1964–70 figures of about 80 per cent to less than 70 per cent, even in a very successful election like 1979. But its share of the vote in the (much bigger) part of the non-manual group which does not spontaneously recognize itself as middle class has not declined. What has happened is that the extra advantage the Conservatives used to have amongst the conscious, rather than the non-conscious, middle class, has been eroded. But it can, as we noted earlier, rely on a very strong support from any member of the middle class who does not actually think of himself as working class.

With the Labour Party the opposite has happened. Until 1979, the Labour Party's share of the vote amongst the 'consciously' working class did not really decline. But also its need of them has stayed constant. In none of the four elections did Labour fail to do very much better with 'consciously' working class voters than with voters who just happen, objectively, to be working class without seeing themselves that way. The difference in the Labour vote between these two sections of the working class has always been at least 14 percentage points.

Though the Conservatives used to enjoy a similar advantage, when one compared the 'consciously middle class' with those merely object-ively so, this has been much reduced. The Conservative equivalent advantage has declined from a similar level in the earlier elections to only 7-10 per cent in the last two elections. In summary, then, there is evidence, if not dramatic, of two things happening. First, the importance of class consciousness for producing high levels of class voting for the Conservatives has declined, and is now low. But it has not declined, and is still very high for Labour. At the same time, it is the prevalence of working class consciousness, both amongst manual workers and the non-manual social strata, that has declined over the years since systematic surveys were started, while middle class con-sciousness on the whole has kept its (always lower) level.

A final documentation of what these changes in the prevalence of class consciousness and class conscious voting mean is given in table 4.5, where the index I used in chapter 1 to measure the degree of class voting in general is now applied to subjective class voting. I measure the intensity of class voting over the period according to whether middle and working class labels are present or absent amongst manual and non-manual groups. The first row of the table measures the intensity of class voting where it should be at its highest, reporting the index as calculated between spontaneous middle class identifiers in non-manual jobs, and spontaneous working class identifiers in manual jobs.

This simple index, which I have used before and will use again, is an intuitive measure of great flexibility. So here the 1970 figures show, for example, that the 'conscious working class' percentage voting Labour is 61 per cent higher than the 'conscious middle class' Labour percentage, whilst there is a gap of only 40 per cent between the manual and non-manual Labour vote, taking account only of those who refused to give any class label when asked.

TABLE 4.5 Comparison of the party difference index of class voting by degrees of class awareness

		Index of class voting in the elections in			
Groups		1964	1970	1974	1979
(A)	Index for non-manual with spontaneous 'middle class' self-label and manual with spontaneous 'working class' self-labels	67	61	51	44
(B)	Index for respondents with no spontaneous class labels in non-manual and manual occupational status categories	40	35	35	24
(C)	Difference between (A) and (B)	27	26	16	20

Source: For 1974 and 1979 elections: BES election surveys. For 1964 and 1970: Butler and Stokes' surveys. Details of these are given in Butler and Stokes *Political Change in Britain* (2nd edn).

Overall, the table confirms the argument so far developed. The intensity of class voting has declined amongst both class conscious and unconscious groups, and about at the same rate. Earlier in the period it was enormously high amongst the conscious groups, with indexes of above 60 in the first two elections, declining by 1979 to only 44. Though this figure is still higher than the index level at the beginning of the period for the groups without class consciousness. In fact, the table probably shows that as class voting has declined in both sectors of the population, it has become relatively less important now than it was. For when in 1964 the index stood at 67 per cent for the conscious groups, the difference in degree of class voting between them and the unconscious groups was 27 per cent. By 1979, the difference between the two indexes had dropped to 20 per cent, suggesting not only that there is less class voting, as we know from earlier tables, but that there is relatively less amongst the highly class conscious. The cause of this is almost certainly the increasing broadness of the Conservative Party catchment which allows it to do better than the Labour Party while actually getting less of the class conscious middle class vote, the rest going most probably to the Liberals.

4.4 HOW MUCH DOES CLASS MEAN TO PEOPLE?

I have used the concept of 'class consciousness' in this chapter, although political scientists are more prone, perhaps, to use less theoretically loaded words. Class consciousness might more usually be found in purely sociological works, and those of a more theoretical nature. It is part of my contention, however, that voting can only be properly understood if external characteristics are involved with investigation of how actors see themselves. In the following sections I investigate in more depth than is often found a set of questions about how people do in fact see class, how they think it affects their lives. The only comparable investigation on the British electorate in large-scale survey work is part of Butler and Stokes' (1974, pp. 81ff) *Political Change in Britain*. Here they study the extent to which voters do see classes as in conflict, and whether that conflict is seen as reconcilable or not. Probably that section tells us more about British politics in the mid-sixties than much else, however admirable, in the book. It was open to the BES to try to replicate those results, and study change over time in this part of class politics. While this would have been worthwhile, so little has been done in understanding just how British voters do actually think about class that I opted for a different tack. Instead of seeking information about class conflict, I have taken deliberately, a tangential route. Questions have been asked, instead, about personal experiences of class, about its immediacy in everyday life. From such questions — necessarily few because of the size of the questionnaire — are created class consciousness profiles and indexes to check against voting behaviour. This is why I do feel entitled to use the more sociological phrase 'class consciousness' rather than some anodyne like 'class feeling'. What I have to say in the rest of this chapter should very much be read against the context of Butler and Stokes, and against the other admirable and pioneering work *The Affluent Voter* by Goldthorpe and Lockwood (1968).

It is so common still for commentators to see British politics as class based that it is slightly counter-intuitive to claim, as I have earlier, that increasingly people do not have class self-images, and even when they do, their votes are often not affected by them. Very little academic research (though a massive amount of theorizing) has gone into the question of what social and economic consequences people believe attach to class, or indeed, to what extent class as a phenomenon is an everyday presence in their minds. In a general election survey such as this one, there is limited scope to remedy this, nor is a book on one election a particularly suitable vehicle for exploring such general sociological problems. The survey did manage, though, to include a short battery of rather crude questions with which to sketch the meaning, and consequent electoral implications, of class to the general populace. The first question is aimed at finding out just how aware most people are of class in everyday life:

> When you first meet someone, how aware are you of their social class? Would you say you usually notice their social class, some-times notice, or never notice?

The second question attempts to find out how much people admit to allowing class to influence them in everyday life, and also, hope-fully, to what extent class is seen as a natural community, a focus of loyalty, as opposed to being a rational economic factor alone. It follows directly the question about noticing class and reads:

> What about friends? How easy do you think it is to have friends in other social classes? Which of the answers on this card comes closest to what you feel?

The answers the respondent can pick are:

(1) It would be hard to have friends who belong to other classes.
(2) It might be a little difficult to have friends who belong to other social classes.
(3) There is no difficulty about having friends who belong to other social classes.

Those two deal with the extent to which people are generally aware of class and feel constrained in their own initiatives by it. But there remains a vital question — do people think the class system has a major systematic effect, harmful or otherwise, on their life chances? It would after all be a little silly to expect class to affect voting, even if the two previous questions had elicited a great deal of class consciousness, were it to transpire that most people still did not believe the class system affected their life much. So immediately after the respondents had given a subjective class identity (spontaneous or forced), they were asked the following question:

Some people think that a person's social class affects his life a good deal. Others think that class does not matter much. How do you feel about this?

They are then offered five sentences to pick from:

Being middle class rather than working class (or *vice versa*, depending on class identity):

(1) . . . makes life a good deal easier.
(2) . . . makes life a bit easier.
(3) . . . makes no difference.
(4) . . . makes life a bit harder.
(5) . . . makes life a good deal harder.

The question may not exactly tap a social theorist's views about what is wrong with the class system, but it should provide some pretty robust evidence for us. The logic of having class-based parties if the electorate does not think class affects their life much is, to say the least, a refined one. Taken singly, the questions throw light on important aspects of the class/vote nexus. Put together they make a scale of class consciousness that not only allows us to categorize groups of the electorate with some refinement, but to do so with some degree of theoretical meaning.

Let us immediately look at the, quite surprising, basic data, the marginal distribution of answers to the questions. Table 4.6 gives these, for the whole sample and, where relevant, separately for non-manual and manual workers. Answers to the first question certainly show that the British do notice class in everyday life. Only a quarter of the non-manual and just over a third of the manual sector claim never to notice the social class of someone they meet, though the answers at the top end of the scale are less than one might have expected. The objective middle class is slightly more aware of the phenomenon than the manual sector, with nearly a third admitting 'usually' to noticing social class. Class being a sensitive question, these are probably underestimates, but the rough proportions will be reliable, and, by itself, the question does not do too much to disturb assumptions about class politics. It does not remove the necessary class awareness from the population.

TABLE 4.6   Attitudes to social class and its impact —
attitude by occupational status (%)

Question	Non-manual	Manual	Total
Do respondents notice class?			
usually	31	25	27
sometimes	43	38	40
never notice	26	37	32
Total	100	100	100
Is it harder to make friends from other social classes?			
hard	4	8	6
a little difficult	21	26	24
no difficulty	75	66	70
Total	100	100	100

When we turn to the second question, the results do begin to surprise. The idea of social class as anything like a natural community
to which loyalty might be paid, especially in any context of class
conflict, does not fit the data. Three-quarters of the middle class
respondents claim that they would expect no difficulty in making
friends across class lines. Even the objective working class, less
sanguine in all these tables than the non-manual workers, can only
amount to 8 per cent to say that such friendships would be hard to
make. At most, less than one-third of the population feel there is any
difficulty at all about transcending in their social life the barriers that
English novelists and sociologists have portrayed as creating two separate and often opposed communities. These data are actually quite in
keeping with what little previous data we have as, for example, Butler
and Stokes' discovery that very few people felt class antagonisms to
be irreconcilable in the early sixties.

It is table 4.7 that really makes one doubt that British society any
longer has the material for class-based party loyalty. It is just possible
that voters might only sometimes be aware enough of class to notice
the class of those they meet and still be class voters. Even if, in addition, they believed there were no class barriers to social intercourse,
they might yet see their social class standing as affecting their lives so
strongly that a party–class link would be primary when they went to
the polls. Yet, as the data abundantly demonstrate, this is not so.

TABLE 4.7 Attitude to social class and its impact —
attitude by occupational status and subjective class (%)

Subjective class	Middle		Working	
Occupational status	Non-manual	Manual	Non-manual	Manual
Does being in (whichever class is self ascribed) make life harder or easier?				
a good deal easier	7	4	2	3
a bit easier	32	24	6	8
no difference	53	68	68	61
a bit harder	7	4	18	23
a good deal harder	1	1	5	5
Total	100	100	100	100

A majority of voters, at least in every group, believe that their class position makes no difference to their life. Across the whole sample, 61 per cent believe this. Nor do those who believe that class has an impact consist principally of people thinking they suffer. About 30 per cent of the subjective middle class feel they have easier lives. Those who probably do have a social advantage are the objective middle class. Such voters, when they see themselves as subjectively middle class as well, produce a 39 per cent confession to benefiting from their class position. We return to them shortly. In contrast, the most 'suffering' group is, again, the one that can most plausibly make that claim, the manual workers who are consciously working class. Here, though, only 28 per cent feel that their lives are at all disadvantaged compared with the middle classes. Hardly anyone in any group feels that class has much effect. Never more than 5 per cent of the subjective working class feel their life to be 'a good deal harder' and no more than 7 per cent at most of the self-ascribed middle class feel it 'a good deal easier'.

What then for any thesis that class rests heavily on the shoulders of the British populace? Clearly the proportion of the electorate that can score highly on any index of class consciousness will not be great. But the psychology of class is bound to be complex, if only because of the natural inversions of response in the third question. It is, after all, perhaps psychologically more comfortable to deny that middle class status is helpful if one is solidly Tory. Something like this may well explain the way in which the middle class are more likely to notice class but incredibly unlikely to let it affect their friendships, much more so than the subjectively working class. It certainly looks as though the raw material for intense class-conscious voting does not exist. If Britain is to be seen as a political society within which two opposed social classes are represented by competing powers, the answers to these questions should be different. If class is important in politics, it should be recognizable, and perhaps is. But it should also represent community and members of the 'working class' community should feel disadvantaged. Neither of these assertions can be backed up by the data. If anything, a rather Tory view of a society where class exists, but where there are no attendant conflicts, might be indicated. We can get little further just by these data. The next section asks about the connection between degrees of class consciousness and voting.

4.5 CLASS CONSCIOUSNESS AND THE VOTE

The preliminary questions about class consciousness profiles and voting are answered by table 4.8. This reports the 1979 voting behaviour according not only to answers to particular questions, but to combinations of them. Because so few respondents chose some categories, the table reports voting for collapsed answer categories which sustain the basic dichotomies involved. For example, on the question of whether middle class life is harder than for the workers and *vice versa*, the quixotic handful of the self-ascribed middle class who thought they had it rough, and the working class who thought their life was actually better, have been collapsed into the 'no difference' category. This retains the distinction we are after. Amongst the middle classes what mattered is feeling privileged or not. For the working class the question is, do they feel disadvantaged or not. The whole table is divided on subjective class lines because, as table 4.7 shows, the subjective groups are much nearer each other in what is, after all, an entirely subjective arena than they are near the other half of their objective class category.

To start with the middle class group, both the question of noticing others' class, and the question of finding friendship across class lines difficult, does indeed clearly differentiate voting tendencies. To admit to noticing class makes one 11 per cent more likely to vote Conservative than denying this. So does denying that friendship is constrained by class. The curious point here is that these two indicators operate

TABLE 4.8   Vote by subjective class identity and attitudes to class (%)

Subjective class/ attitudes to class	1979 Vote					Conservative percentage minus *Labour* percentage
	Con.	Lib.	Lab.	Did not vote	Total	
SUBJECTIVE MIDDLE CLASS						
Notice class						
usually or sometimes	60	13	16	11	100	+44
never	49	15	19	17	100	+30
Believe friendship across class lines						
hard or a little difficult	49	17	14	20	100	+35
not difficult	60	13	17	10	100	+43
Think being middle class makes life						
a good deal or a bit easier	50	18	17	16	100	+33
makes no difference	62	11	16	11	100	+46
friendship hard and class not noticed	45	16	16	23	100	+29
no difficulty for friendship and usually notice class	61	14	17	8	100	+44
SUBJECTIVE WORKING CLASS						
Notice class						
usually or sometimes	30	12	41	16	100	– 11
never	31	11	42	17	100	– 11
Believe friendship across class lines						
hard or a little difficult	22	16	45	17	100	– 23
not difficult	35	10	40	16	100	– 5
Think being working class makes life						
a good deal or a bit harder	24	16	45	16	100	– 21
makes no difference	33	10	40	16	100	– 7
life harder and friendship hard	19	19	47	14	100	– 28
life no different and friendship no difficulty	36	9	39	15	100	– 3

Source: BES, May 1979 Election Survey.

in different ways. *A priori* one would have thought them both to be logically similar as measures of intensity of class awareness. In fact, the most Conservative are those who, while being closely aware of class in relationships, deny that it affects them. The differences between these categories, in terms of Conservative voting, would be even greater were the table based only on those who voted. The least Conservative group, who claim not to notice class personally, but fear its impact on human relationships, do not vote very much more strongly for the Labour Party, but do abstain a good deal more. Those who believe class does not affect friendship not only give 11 per cent more of their vote to the Conservatives, but abstain from voting only half as frequently as their opposites. They also, of course, vote Liberal somewhat less frequently. Generally then, attitudes to class amongst the self-ascribed middle class seem to affect class voting loyalty to the Conservative Party. One brand of middle class voter turns out to be rather keen on the 'natural' class party, and more prepared to support the Liberals or to abstain. These, who deny their own awareness of class but think the class system damages human interaction, are not, though, apparently forced into supporting Labour, which is, after all, yet another class party. Indeed, this all rather neatly defines a quite predictable middle class ideology of class. There are those to whom a middle class status, and the existence of a class system, is entirely natural. They do, of course, notice a person's social class, are aware of their own, but refuse to see this system as having unfortunate consequences. They have, in fact, a proper middle class 'class consciousness', and they accordingly vote for the proper middle class party.

On the other hand, there appear to be those who, though (often, of course, under pressure) admitting that they are middle class, do not find it natural. They themselves do not notice social class (or would like to think that they do not?). But they certainly see it as an unfortunate phenomenon. Perhaps, lacking any strong tie to a middle class culture, these are not very strongly tied to the paradigm middle class party. It is not at all surprising that they should not vote for Labour – the other class party – however, which would be even worse, given that they are after all middle class. Instead they tend to support the classless Liberal Party in slightly greater numbers, or to announce a plague on all the political houses and not vote at all. This analysis is, admittedly, in part speculation. I could document it further by a closer inspection of the other attitudes and background data on the groups, but I have no space here for a sustained investigation of British social attitudes.

Other data in the table support the argument. When one asks the self-ascribed middle class whether being middle class has made life easier, 37 per cent admit it has done so. They are again different in voting habits to the majority who do not believe their class position has helped them. And, again, by not accepting their class position, they are less Tory. Only 50 per cent of them voted Conservative, compared with the 62 per cent Conservative vote of those who believe class makes no difference to their lives. Once again, the feeling of privilege they have does not turn into a Labour vote. Only 1 per cent more of this group vote Labour than for the majority of their class on this question. Instead, they give the Liberals a 7 per cent lead, and 'not voting' a 5 per cent lead. In summing up, one can surely say that the class ideology of the middle class is to deny the importance, while accepting and noting the fact, of class. This is precisely the old *Tory* rather than *Conservative* Party ideology on the subject. The 'deviant' class ideology is, personally not to notice class, but to admit it has its advantages, and to regret this. This ideology is not, however, strong enough to transcend class lines. It does not lead to support for Labour, a party even more clearly class based. Note also that the Conservatives have the advantage that the mainline class ideology is very much the majority view amongst the subjective middle class. Those who hold both deviant beliefs — that friendship is hard across class lines and that they do not notice social class — represent probably under 10 per cent of the subjective middle class.

Turning to the section of the table dealing with the self-described working class, we can see that attitudes to class again make quite sharp differentiations in voting pattern, but that the pattern is very different. To start with, the question of whether or not one notices class in people one meets has no impact at all. The voting profiles of the two groups defined by their answer to the question are virtually identical. Despite this, the questions do sort out different voting groups, and indeed do so more effectively than amongst the middle class. The differences I commented on there made relatively little impact on the really crucial measure, the Conservative lead over Labour. The gap between the biggest and smallest lead, those who think being middle class makes no difference to their lives, where the Conservatives had a lead of 46 per cent, and the least important position, those who claim never to notice class, at 30 per cent, is only 16 per cent. The gap between the biggest and smallest Labour lead amongst the working class is 25 per cent. This refers to the two sides on a combined measure. The contrast is between those who think their life is made harder by being working class *and* who feel class restricts friendship, with those who deny both suggestions.

The important thing amongst the working class is the impact of the class system, or, rather, whether or not the respondent notices an impact. At least some evidence that class can constitute a natural

community with political implications is given by the answers to
the question about friendship being affected by class membership.
Amongst those who feel it is difficult to make cross-class friendships,
only a little more than one voter in five votes Conservative, while
45 per cent vote Labour. Where this constraint is not felt, where class
does not take on a direct impact in everyday life and thus can hardly
be a community, more than a third of the voters supported the
Conservatives and 5 per cent less voted Labour. Inside the potential
'communal' class the Labour Party had a lead of 23 per cent; amongst
the rest, Labour's lead at only 5 per cent was derisory, considering
that we are dealing with the subjective working class. A similar
impact is shown when we ask whether being working class makes life
harder. Here the leads contrast 21 per cent to 7 per cent, with a very
similar voting profile.

Putting together these two questions gives us an even more powerful discriminator. If we separate the subjective working class into
those who both think that their lives are harder than in the middle
class, and also that class constrains friendship, one gets a lead for the
Labour Party over the Conservatives of 28 per cent, with only 19 per
cent voting Conservative. In contrast, those who feel neither of those
things give the Labour Party a lead of only 3 per cent, so small as to
be indistinguishable from zero with our sampling error. This group,
for whom admitting to being working class appears to carry no
connotation at all of disadvantage or resentment of the class system,
give 36 per cent of their vote to the Conservatives against only 39 per
cent to Labour. They are like the earlier example of the unconscious
working class when talking about the willingness to give oneself a
label, who seemed to give their votes on an individual basis ending
up with an almost even distribution. These voters, the subjective
working class with no class ideology of constraint and disadvantage,
might just as well be randomly distributed between the parties.

What is crucial is that they are the majority! The group with the
full class consciousness, aware of constraints and harm from class,
amount to less than 20 per cent of the subjective working class. They
are probably less than 15 per cent of the electorate. Here is a crucial
difference between the class consciousness base of the two parties.
The vote polarizing class ideology in the working class, from which
Labour can hope for great loyalty, is only a tiny minority. The
dominant class ideology supporting the Conservatives in the middle
class is a very strong majority. But that is not the only difference in
the operation of class ideology between the parties. One obvious
point is how little Labour does benefit from even the strongest sup-

porting ideology amongst the subjective working class. The highest share of the vote Labour got in 1979, from that sector of the self-identified working class whose ideology was most favourable to Labour, was only 47 per cent. This is lower than the *worst* the Conservatives did amongst the subjective middle class who held the deviant, anti-class loyalty views on the impact of class!

There are other differences too which hardly helped Labour in 1979 and which, if repeated, seem to make class consciousness of even less avail to it as the most deliberately class-based party. Amongst the middle class, having a deviant class ideology was likely to do two things when it reduced the Conservative vote — to increase the Liberal vote, and to increase the abstention rate. This at least avoids directly strengthening the major opposition party. But in the subjective working class, those who have no strong identity with that class favour the Conservatives, not the Liberals, and they do so at a direct cost to their own 'class' party. The differences in Conservative voting between the most and least class-conscious working class voters is 17 per cent. The difference in Labour voting amongst the most and least 'typical' middle class voters was only 5 per cent. The Labour vote amongst the subjective working class actually varies very little. Even the highly class conscious never gave it that much of their vote, and those indifferent to class gave it only a little less, but they do vote Conservative much more. Abstention amongst the working class is unaffected by class consciousness, being more or less constant over all the categories.

What is perhaps even more remarkable, and something of an omen for the future, is the Liberal vote as it is distributed over class consciousness categories. We saw that in the subjective middle class those who saw class having an impact tended to vote Liberal more than those who were indifferent to class. So it is amongst the subjective working class. The respondents who felt friendship to be affected by class, and those who felt their life had been made harder by class, were markedly more likely to give their vote to the Liberals than those who were indifferent. The proportions were 16 per cent compared to 10 per cent. When the questions were combined, to mark out the most class-conscious group, the Liberals had a lead of 10 per cent (19 per cent to 9 per cent) over their vote in the least class-conscious group. The implication is quite clear. Britain does indeed have class consciousness, but its political implication is not what it is often seen to be. Basically there are those indifferent to class who are the great majority. These, if they see themselves as middle class, will most probably support the Conservative Party. Then there is a much smaller group who exist in both the social classes and who feel that class impacts on private lives and on their life chances. This may be an impact favourable (amongst the subjectively middle class) or harmful (amongst the subjective working class). In deserting their class party, those in the middle class will certainly not go to the opposite class party, but do to some extent go to the apparently classless Liberal Party. Inside the working class, being sharply conscious of class does indeed reduce the chance of voting for the party of the middle class. Instead of strengthening their own traditional class party, though, a large part of this group's vote also goes to the Liberals. In short, there is only one party in Britain which openly bases its appeal on class loyalty, the Labour Party. Those who have the relevant class ideology are not only a very small percentage of the relevant class, but do not particularly support that party anyway. Nor does Labour stand much chance of a sympathetic vote from those in the middle class who are worried by the class phenomenon. For all such voters, there is a classless party to support in the Liberals, and perhaps now in the SDP.

Summarizing this chapter, I would argue that the data seriously call into question any orthodox class model of electoral politics in Britain. Consider the questions I have asked and answered. Do British voters actually offer class labels of themselves? The answer seems to be that, on the whole, they do not. When they do offer such labels, either spontaneously or after an interviewer prompts them, does the self-labelling accord with a common distinction between the manual and non-manual workers on which is erected the usual class division between the middle and working class? Again, on the whole, no. Nor is the mismatch between external class description and private self-labelling confined to those who are, by any standards, ambiguous in terms of class location. Nearly a third of the highest two social grades in Britain claimed to be actually working class.

Of course class is so sensitive and so complex a subject that I cannot possibly claim any last word on the matter. But if class is hard to grasp, for the respondent, and embarrassing of confession, why should it be more so than one's party affiliation? Yet the proportion of those able, with no prompting, to give a party-label to themselves is far higher than the proportion confessing to class identity. And when I go below the surface of class identity, to its meaning, I consistently find that it has very little. Few people think class could be a barrier to friendship, hardly any voters think their class has harmed or helped them unduly in life, although, in keeping with a society where class (as status at least) manifestly exists, most admit the phenomenon to be near enough to their ordinary life to recognize social class in new acquaintances.

These results might be treated more sceptically were it not the case that, where one can find class ideologies, voting patterns do indeed fit them. We are forced to the conclusion that class in anything resembling the overall communitarian and ideological sense is vanishing from British politics. But we know from preceding chapters that class as an external, occupational status matter continues to have a dampened, circuitous, but real, impact on voting. Parties do still clearly get their votes in a way related to the class of their followers and the class-related policies they espouse.

Is this in any way contradictory? No, not in the least. Nothing in any part of this book suggests that voters are not rational, perhaps self-seeking, and certainly 'canny' people. Nor is it suggested that economic and financial matters are anything but supreme in the voter's choice. What appears to have happened, and the whole theme of this book supports the argument, is that rational self-interest has become partially divorced from standard class patterns, whether they be objective or subjective. Economic groups continue to be vital, but the parties have not yet orientated themselves to the new patterns that may be replacing traditional class groupings. Unless the marked victory of the Conservatives in 1979, with an enormous vote amongst the self-consciously, and very conscious, working class, argues that one party, at least, has done so. If there is a new Conservative electorate, it is one in which orthodox beliefs about class and its impact have been seriously changed.

PART II

An Alternative Model of Class and Partisanship

5

Classes and Parties

5.1 HOW MANY CLASSES?

As I argued in chapter 1, there are a variety of ways in which one can operationalize class, and however one does it, one is dealing with an analytic construct. It is still preferable that the construct should match as much as possible the 'social fact' of class. Through most of part I of this book I have restricted myself to the orthodox definition of class, as used in most voting studies. With this definition there are only two social classes in Britain, the non-manual 'middle' class, and the manual 'working' class. There were two principal reasons for using this standard dichotomy up to now. First, so far I have been examining class and voting, especially in 1979. In order for patterns of voting behaviour in 1979 to make much sense, it has been necessary continually to make comparisons with previous studies, especially those of Butler and Stokes. These comparisons are possible only if one uses the same class definition. A second related reason is that a simple dichotomous operationalization of class is very attractive when dealing with voting. Even with the upsurge of Liberal support in the seventies, the voting choice in Britain is itself largely dichotomous. In terms of actually voting for a party, the traditional class connections to the two major parties fit better theoretically with a two-class model than with a plurality of classes. Indeed it is precisely the fact that data on voting fits that class model decreasingly well, despite the theoretical fit, that is one reason for investigating just how the complexities of the British class system should be modelled.

In part II it is not the act of voting but how people hold opinions and beliefs that takes first place in relation to social class. When one moves from the voting act to the area of political attitudes, one is moving from the domain of the near dichotomy to a much richer and pluralistic set of dependent variables, and there remains no longer any good reason to use the traditional non-manual versus manual class dichotomy. It remains to be seen, of course, whether there are theoretical and empirical reasons to adopt another scheme for operationalizing social class.

By far the most useful discussions of this as an empirical problem come from the group of sociologists who constitute the Oxford Social Mobility Research Group. They have been coping with massive data analysis in the area since 1972. Particularly useful are the works by John Goldthorpe (1980) *Social Mobility and Class Structure in Modern Britain*, and A. H. Halsey, A. F. Heath and J. M. Ridge (1980) *Origins and Destinations*. Anthony Heath (1981) has also analysed the relationship between social mobility and voting in his book *Social Mobility*. Though a variety of different class structures are posited and analysed in these works, the basic operationalization is the one adopted by Goldthorpe. The quotation below is from Halsey, Heath and Ridge, giving the arguments for their own way of using the occupational groups derived from their sample to make up a pluralist class model.

> Schemes of social division derive from many different conceptions of society in both social science and common language. We were anxious to avoid implicating ourselves in a conception of stratification in Britain as a monolithic hierarchy or a 'layer-cake' of strata. Similarly, we would emphasise that the schema we have adopted is not to be identified with a scale of prestige or socio-economic status. . . . This classification . . . follows the scheme used by Goldthorpe in his *Social Mobility and Class Structure*, but also differs from it. The degree of differentiation provided by the Hope–Goldthorpe categories in terms of both occupation function and employment status enables us to bring together, within the eight occupational groups and the three broader social classes we distinguish, occupations whose incumbents will typically share in broadly similar *market* and *work* situations – which, following Lockwood, we take as the two major components of class position. It should be noted, however, that we have modified the sevenfold schema of occupational groups used by Goldthorpe in that we have separated agricultural labourers and small-holders into an eighth category. We use this eightfold scheme throughout the book and also a further combination of it into three social classes. The labelling of these three social classes has caused us difficulty and

hesitation but, while conscious of the linguistic inelegance and logical impurity of terms in common use, we have, with John Goldthorpe, adopted the labels 'service class', 'intermediate class', and 'working class' (Halsey *et al.*, 1980, p. 17).

They summarize the 'contents' of their classes thus:

Class I: all higher-grade professionals, whether self-employed or salaried; higher-grade administrators and officials in central and local government and in public and private corporations (including company directors); managers in large industrial establishments; and large proprietors. Class I might thus be taken as largely corresponding to the higher and intermediate echelons of what Dahrendorf, following Karl Renner, has termed the 'service class' of a modern capitalist society — the class of those exercising power and expertise on behalf of corporate 'authorities': plus such elements of the classic bourgeoisie, independent businessmen, and 'free' professionals, as are not yet assimilated into this new formation.

Class II: lower-grade professional and higher-grade technicians; lower-grade administrators and officials; managers in small business and industrial establishments, and in services; and supervisors of nonmanual employees. Class II could then be seen as complementing Class I in comprising the subaltern or *cadet* positions of the service class. Putting Classes I and II together, we have formed a social class, amounting to 13.4 per cent of our respondents by origin (i.e. classified by their father's occupation when they were aged 14) which we refer to as the *service* class.

Class III: routine nonmanual — largely clerical — employees in administration and commerce; sales personnel and other rank-and-file service workers. In contrast to the service class, Class III covers essentially subordinate positions whose incumbents could perhaps be taken as forming a nonmanual labour force.

Class IV: small proprietors, self-employed artisans; and all other 'own-account' workers apart from professionals. Class IV may thus be equated with that of the petty bourgeoisie.

Class V: lower-grade technicians whose work is to some extent of a manual character; and supervisors over manual workers.

This class might be seen as constituting a latter-day 'aristocracy of labour' or 'blue-collar élite'. Putting Classes III, IV, and V together we have formed an *intermediate* class constituting 30.8 per cent of our respondents by origin.

Class VI: skilled manual-wage workers in all branches of industry, including all who have served apprenticeships and all those who have acquired a relatively high level of skill through other forms of training.

Class VII: all manual workers in industry in semi-skilled and unskilled grades.

Class VIII: agricultural workers, including small-holders. Taken together, we have termed these groups the *working class*. Constituting 55.7 per cent of our respondents by origin, they are mainly composed of the industrial working class, but also include the agricultural workers (Halsey *et al.*, 1980, p. 19).

There are three crucial differences between this model and the one used both earlier in this book and throughout Butler and Stokes. First, and most obvious, they have taken eight basic occupational categories and turned them into three social classes, compared with the political science norm of taking six, broader, categories and creating two much broader social classes. Second, and perhaps most important, the manual/non-manual split does not coincide with either of their class boundaries — there are manual workers in their 'intermediate' class, the rest of which covers our 'middle' class. Third, and related to the last point, the distinction between being employed and self-employed is used to move some manual workers from the 'working' class into the 'intermediate' class. This, coupled with the removal of manual working foremen and supervisors from the working class into the service class, means that it is not so much the actual nature of the job as the conditions of autonomy and authority attached to it that are crucial in defining social class.

The basis of Goldthorpe's argument is one I touched on earlier when examining the voting behaviour of certain detailed socio-economic groups, especially that of the manual working foremen on which he also concentrates. It is that there is a crucial distinction between a work life in which one is paid purely to exercise skills and effort directly under orders, and a work life where one is either free to organize one's own life, as with the self-employed, or actually involved in the planning and controlling of the activities of others, as with supervisors and foremen. Goldthorpe (1980, p. 297) himself alludes to the problems for any class analysis of electoral behaviour which treats all manual workers as occupying the same class position. Commenting on the 'partisan dealignment' thesis presented by Ivor Crewe from data up to 1974, he notes '. . . the solidarity of working class partisanship might have appeared great in the data presented by Crewe *et al.* had they not included in their "working class" self-employed manual workers and manual supervisory grades'. If one considers my earlier analysis of voting along with these arguments, there seems to be a good case for taking such people out of the C2 (skilled manual worker) occupational category, although this has been their position up until now in my 'working class as manual worker' definition.

This apparently restricted change, however, opens up an interesting avenue. Can we just put these grades (I shall refer to them for convenience from now on as the 'intermediate grade') into our existing middle class? If one does so, the class becomes almost meaningless, because it has lost the coherence bestowed on it by the exclusively 'non-manual' character of the previous definition. If that goes, we have a putative single social class which ranges all the way from a Permanent Secretary to the Treasury, or the Managing Director of ICI, to a self-employed plumber and a night-shift supervisor on the factory floor. One possibility would be to leave the intermediate grade by itself, as an intermediate class, but further investigation seems called for.

If the place of those in my intermediate grade has only recently been called into question, there is another occupational category that has long been in doubt in political science class models. Again this is one I have commented on earlier, the white-collar worker. When Butler and Stokes took over the market research social grading scale for their surveys in the sixties, they made one alteration to it. The market research scheme has one category, C1, for all clerical and similar white-collar workers below the lower managerial and professional ranks. Butler and Stokes divided this into C1A, the more senior of this group, often again with supervisory roles or extra responsibility, and the lower or junior white-collar jobs, C1B. They also undertook considerable and important research into just how these grades should be allotted to classes. Their answer then was that, in terms of self perception and some other matters, both halves of the C1 category belonged more easily with the A and B grade professionals, who are obviously middle class, than with the manual workers who formed the working class (Butler and Stokes, 1974, pp. 71-3). Subsequent research has tended to support this division

(Rawlings, 1979). There are grounds for unease, however. My analysis of voting in the first part of this book consistently shows them as being clearly in between the rest of the middle class and the working class in voting profile. I also showed that, when one took account of social mobility, especially amongst the C1A group, there was good reason to think that members of the white-collar worker group who did not have middle class antecedents were much nearer to the working class than the rest of the middle class.

The only way one can allot such marginal groups is by comparison with clearly identifiable classes, A and B to represent the clear middle class, and C2 and D to represent the working class. But if it makes sense to take away some part of what has previously been seen as the working class, two prospects emerge. One is that the newly re-defined working class may no longer be anything like the white-collar workers, the other prospect is that the real similarity may be between the new 'intermediate' grade who do not fit the working class, and these white-collar workers, whose similarity with the professional and managerial classes is, after all, somewhat slight. One might then end up with a three-class model contrasting the managerial and professional on the one hand with those who are marginal to them, the lower white-collar workers, and those who are marginal to the working class.

This is effectively what Goldthorpe's scheme does. Our occupational coding is not identical to the Oxford Social Mobility Project gradings, and we do not use the very precise 'Hope–Goldthorpe' scale, (Hope, 1972) but it is still very close, and the schemes are safely comparable. His 'service class', containing his classes I and II, is basically our grades A, B and C1A, his working class (VI and VII) is our skilled and unskilled manual workers (C2 and D). If we extract manual supervisors and the self-employed manual workers from C2, and put them with our grade C1B, we have very roughly his 'intermediate class' (classes III, IV and V). There would still be some difference, especially in the way the intermediate class is defined, but essentially we would have a three-class model based on the same logic.

Rather than take this definition immediately, it seemed worthwhile collecting further information about the actual similarities of putative elements of a class before loading them in together. My reasoning is as follows. Theoretical arguments, and evidence from, for example, social mobility studies, can help us arrange a set of occupational categories on a hierarchy. We can thus say that it makes good sense, in terms of the data I have to analyse, to propose the following full hierarchy of occupational categories. A simple political science test of this is to show the decreasing proportion of Conservative voters as one goes down the seven steps. This is given in table 5.1.

TABLE 5.1 Voting in 1979 by seven social grades (%)

Grade	Con.	Lab.	Lib.	Did not vote
A	58	16	17	7
B	56	22	13	8
C1A	54	15	15	13
C1B	46	26	11	15
I	43	32	7	17
C2	24	44	13	17
D	29	43	12	17

Note: The C2 group here is *not* the same as in previous similar tables, because it now *excludes* the manual working foremen and supervisors, thus making it more 'purely working class', and resulting in a higher Labour vote.

But the question of how one concatenates inside this hierarchy requires one to think not just about the social structure of the political system, but also about the relative similarities of political feeling between various pairs of these seven categories. Class is, at least in part, a matter of similarity in beliefs, and political beliefs are amongst the most important that can help define class. So for the next stage of my analysis I constructed a similarity model. Each coefficient in this model represents how different the social categories are in terms of the category average over a series of political attitude measures. The higher the coefficient, the more dissimilar are the two occupational categories making up the pair. The attitude measures used are factor scores from factor analyses of a series of sets of attitude questions, and it is the occupational category mean on each factor score which is compared. I leave discussion of these factor analyses for later in this book, when they are important in their own right. For the moment they can be treated in the abstract as measures used for calculating the overall similarities and differences between occupational categories.

The question is this, Can such similarity coefficients tell us anything about a natural grouping of occupational categories into a smaller number of relatively homogenous social classes? And if so, does the standard Butler and Stokes model, the Goldthorpe model, or some other, appear to fit best?

Smaller 'distances' all correspond with pairs of occupational categories we would expect to see fairly proximate in any class scale. In particular the distance between skilled and less skilled manual workers is the smallest of all, and represents surely a natural class. If that is so it turns out to be sensible to extract my suggested 'intermediate' category, manual foremen and manual self-employed. The distance between this category and the definitely working class is three or four times greater than the distance inside the manual group. At the same time the intermediate category is very near the lower non-manual group, who have traditionally been put into the middle class in the dichotomous model based on the manual/non-manual distinction. At the same time distance between this lower non-manual category and the other half of the C1 grade, C1A, the supervisory white-collar jobs, is rather large. This is, in fact, bigger than the overall average gap between occupational categories across all the categories. What C1A really seems to fit with is the indubitably 'middle class' category B, the lower managerial and professional workers. The distance between these two is only slightly greater than that between the two categories of manual workers. Indeed C1A is only slightly less far away from the manual working class than are the junior managers of the B category.

Two points at least would seem to be supported from a cursory inspection of such similarities. If political views are to have any place in helping to define a class model, manual self-employed and supervisory workers do not belong in the same class as the ordinary manually employed who wield no authority and exercise little autonomy. The other point is that the lower half of the routine white-collar workers do not belong with their seniors, those whose white-collar work involves managerial and supervisory functions. At this stage it would be premature to go further.

Something a good deal more rigorous than eyeball inspection of the data is called for. I have used a multi-dimensional scaling programme (Minissa) to 'unpack' the similarity data into a spatial map of these proximities. This technique works by using the original distance between entities (in this case the occupational categories) and searching for a spatial mapping of them. Given as many dimensions to the space as there are entities, any such similarity matrix can be reproduced perfectly. The point of the technique is to see how few dimensions are needed to reproduce the patterns in the table without unduly distorting the exact distances. Take a simple example. Cities in Britain could be put into a distance matrix by measuring the distances between them on three dimensions, longitude, latitude and height above sea level. A perfect fit to this distance matrix would require three dimensions, that is a map with height contours. But the altitude difference is so trivial compared with distance on the plane of the Earth that we would be perfectly happy, and are happy, with a two-dimensional map. What we are doing with the multi-dimensional analysis is directly analogous. The original distances were measured over six 'dimensions', yet to see more easily how the categories group together it would be much better if we could represent the relationship between the categories in a 'map' of far fewer dimensions, provided this can be done without unduly warping the exact distances in the table (Macdonald and Ridge, 1974).

As figure 5.1 demonstrates, this is in fact possible, because the multi-dimensional scaling routine is able to unpack the data into only two dimensions, with, as it happens, virtually a zero stress coefficient. (The stress coefficient measures how much violence has been done to the original exact distances. In the example here effectively none has, so we have a perfect representation of the six pairs of distances in the shape of a traditional two-dimensional map.)

The dimensions in a multi-dimensional analysis have no meaning in themselves, and, unlike the factor analyses I discuss later, no attempt is made to 'interpret' the meaning of the scales. It is enough to see that the categories do form three very neat and clear clusters, with most of the distance between being along the first, horizontal, dimension. Our class model is obvious. There is a cluster consisting just of the two manual working classes, close together, and at the far end of a dimension that more or less ranks the categories as they have been presented in the past, and as similar rankings of roughly equivalent categories appear in other sociological analyses. There is a clear 'upper class' at the other end, consisting of the higher and lower categories of the professional and managerial grades and the supervisory grades amongst white-collar workers. Finally there is an in-between class, the lower white-collar and the 'intermediates' from the manual category, sitting roughly halfway between the centres of gravity of the other two classes. This, noticeably, is separated from the other two classes on both dimensions of the map, rather than just on the one that mirrors the orthodox hierarchical ordering.

No analysis like this can give a definite answer to classification. In the end the analyst has to make a private decision about how to group the components of his class model. There are problems for the interpretation I have given above. One might argue, as Heath (1981,

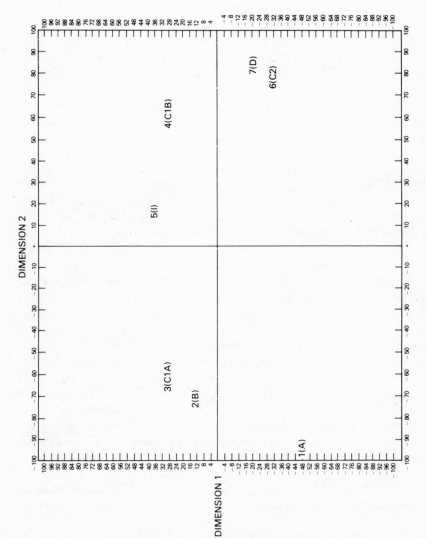

Figure 5.1 Seven social classes in a two-dimensional similarity space

p. 53) has done in his *Social Mobility*, that the very top category is best understood as an 'elite' rather than part of a broader social class which also comprises the lower managerial and even the supervisory white-collar categories. Certainly the figure would give comfort to this claim, because my category A is much further from the other elements in the class to which I assign it than is any other class member. My assignment is based more on there being no possibility of mistake about which other categories it could be associated with than a claim that it is particularly near them.

Further support, both for the grouping I propose, and for the idea of occupational category A being a rather distant elite, only included for convenience in a social class along with categories B and C1A, comes from trying to force the similarity data into just one dimension, a purely hierarchical class model. The stress coefficients are still vanishingly small, and most analysts would regard the results as near enough to a perfect fit. In this case the differences between my proposed classes are so much more important than distances between class constituent categories that the latter are treated as having zero distance between them. The figures in the table refer to the co-ordinates on the one dimension, and we clearly have the three social classes of the previous analysis along with the elite. Going downwards through the seven categories from A to D, the positions are: 1.7, 0.7, 0.7, -0.3, -0.3, 1.3, 1.3!

It may be thought that overdue reliance is being placed on a data analysis technique seldom used in political science, and on rather mysterious similarity measures. Support for this class model can be produced more simply. Questions in the 1979 survey allow the creation of very simple scales of partisanship which allow for negative as well as positive identification. Respondents are coded on the familiar party identification scale, which runs from very strong identification via fairly strong and weak identification to no identification at all with a party. Those who do not identify with a party are also asked if they feel very strongly or not very strongly 'against' the party in question. Taking the two together one can construct a six-point scale of degree of positive or negative identification with each party. If we take such a scale for the Conservative and Labour Parties, we can use them, with no further statistical creativity, as the axes of a two-dimensional graph. Figure 5.2 plots the average position of each of our seven occupational grades in such a space. A position in the lower right-hand quadrant implies approval of the Conservatives and disapproval of the Labour Party. The opposite position, identifying with Labour and feeling 'against' the Conservative Party, is found in the upper left-hand quadrant. Once again the basic three-class model presents itself.

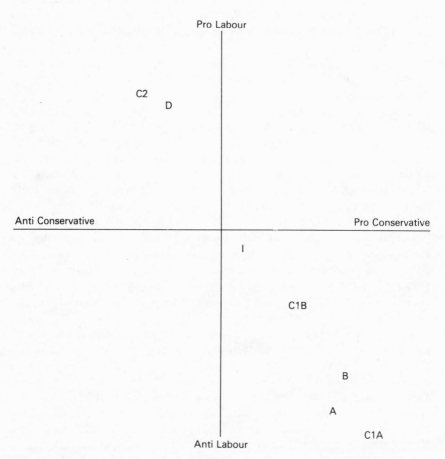

Figure 5.2 Seven social grades in a party identification space

The exact relationships are not quite the same — our elite class looks slightly nearer the rest of what we choose to regard as the upper social class, for example, and the order in which the inter-mediate category and lower white-collar workers come is reversed. But all in all, the positions of the categories in this 'political space' firmly support a three-class model rather than a dichotomy, and confirm fully that manual/non-manual is an irrelevant distinction.

It remains to be seen whether a three-class model like this actually

works — are the classes (a) distinct from each other, and (b) homogenous amongst themselves? To a large extent the rest of this book
is a test of this. In using the three-class model to investigate the
relationship between class and political belief, both (a) and (b) need
to be true for the enterprise to be successful. One simple and rather
revealing test can be given at this stage, and concludes this section.
Two points require brief discussion first. One problem is the exact
nature of the classes defined, the other the provision of suitable
labels. My three classes correspond closely to the Oxford Social
Mobility Research Group's class division. Their nomenclature is
rather difficult to introduce, however. The 'top' class they call
the 'service class', a notion derived from sociological theory of the
sort that sees managers and professionals as 'serving' a capitalist
economy. I do not share the ideological perspective of this theory,
and in any case I fear the label of 'service class' is likely to be opaque,
mysterious, and even misleading to most political scientists. One
could opt for 'middle class', inasmuch as the top class accounts for
much of what has been treated as middle class on the old manual/
non-manual division. But I feel this is actually dodging the issue.
I propose, therefore, to call the class that comes at the top of the
status/market/hierarchy, and which is politically at the 'right-wing'
extreme, quite simply, the 'upper class'. I shall label the next class,
of those insecure between the upper class and the manual work
force, the 'intermediate class' (as do the social mobility researchers,
but for different reasons). To keep consistency, and for honesty,
I shall describe the manual working class as the 'lower class'.

The 'intermediate class' raises a second problem, for which its
proposed title is apt. Basically our sociological justification for this
class model rests on two propositions. These are that there is a
crucial difference in the economic well-being of those who command
and control the work places, and those who obey them, and secondly
that the distinction of authority and autonomy between the com-
manders and the obeyers is itself vital in forming social entities and
political values. This double distinction serves well to establish the
'upper' and the 'lower' classes. But the others are ambiguous as a
class. The intermediate strata consists of two groups who may well
not have that much in common, the manual workers (therefore of
lowish social status) who nonetheless either exercise authority or, as
self-employed, enjoy autonomy, and the low white-collar workers,
whose status takes them out of the 'lower class', but whose conditions of work and economic rewards are no better. In other and
traditional words, we are dealing with two 'cross pressured' groups.

They form a class not because of what they have in common, which is very little, but because they share an ambivalence. They are, both, intermediate between the 'real' classes. This theoretical distinction is useful in my later data analysis, and, putting it the other way round, their behaviour as displayed by the data justifies treating them as, indeed, intermediate between, or cut off from, the basic class distinction of British society. In this sense it could fairly be argued that I am not in fact offering a three-class model, but a two-class model which is not treated as embracing the whole of society. For my purposes that distinction is unimportant, but I admit the possibly serious theoretical consequences it may have.

An immediate example of what I mean also serves to demonstrate that the three-class model does indeed make sense of British political attitudes.

Table 5.2 is, on one sense, very familiar. It reports vote by class in the 1979 election. But it does this on the three-class model, and the focus of interest lies not in the actual figures, but in the extent to which they depart from the statistical predictions of a very simple model.

TABLE 5.2a
Vote by class (1979 election) using three-class model (%)

	Con.	Lib.	Lab.	Total
Upper class	63	16	20	100
Intermediate class	54	11	36	100
Lower class	31	15	53	100

TABLE 5.2b Deviation from expected values
and chi square percentage contribution

Upper class	Con.	Lib.	Lab.
Upper class	+72	+9	-81
	17%	1%	27%
Intermediate class	+22	-12	-9
	1%	2%	1%
Lower class	-95	+4	+90
	23%	1%	26%

Table 5.2a gives the percentage from each of the three classes voting for each of the three major political parties in 1979. There is an immediate surface plausibility to the three-class model. The intermediate class lies between the upper and lower classes in the percentage voting Conservative and Labour. It also has rather fewer Liberal voters than either of the other two classes. This may well be because the higher Liberal vote in the opposed classes comes about as a result of their unwillingness, when unhappy with what might be seen as their natural party, to vote for the opposition. It is really the second part of the table (5.2b), though, which gives the best theoretical support both for the class division I propose, and for the argument of the next section. Table 5.2b is based on the simplest theoretical model which can be fitted to a contingency table. This is the model which says that columns and rows of a table should be unrelated. In this case we would assume that class and voting are quite independent of each other, that the upper class were no more and no less likely to vote Conservative than any other class. This model (false, empirically, of course) can be used to generate the 'expected' entry for each cell of a table — the raw number of cases that would occur were class really not to condition voting. The purpose is to examine deviations from this expected value, to find which cells, and which class–party connections are strongest. There are two entries in each cell of table 5.2b. The upper entry gives the difference between the actual and expected number, so that a positive entry of 72, in the cell for upper class Conservatives, shows that there are more than there 'should' be. Either the upper class are more likely to vote Conservative than the simple model would predict, or Conservatives are more likely to come from the upper class, or both. The lower entry refers to the percentage of the total chi square, the statistical measure based on these deviations and used to test for significant departure from the simple model, accounted for by that cell.

For our purposes here the striking fact is that virtually all of the chi square is accounted for by only four of the nine cells in the table. These are for upper and lower class Conservative and Labour voters. What this means can be stated in two complementary ways. One is that Liberals draw their strength proportionately from each class — a fact well attested in part I of this book. Of more immediate interest is the fact that the intermediate class gives its support more or less proportionately to each party. Our class model works, therefore, because we have identified not only a strongly Conservative upper class and a strongly Labour lower class, but also an impartial intermediate class. The intermediate class gives each party almost exactly the vote that would happen were there really no class connection in British politics.

I have gone into this simple table in some detail both because I build on this notion of the 'non-partisan' elements in the British electorate quite heavily later, and because the very simple methodology of fitting a model to a table, rare in political science, is one I use continually hereafter.[1] At this stage I need only stress that table 5.2 both justifies the use of a three-class model, and shows something of potentially considerable importance, which is that at least part of the British electorate can be given a class position not previously recognized, and which runs against any assumption of class voting. Three classes, then, are to be used henceforth—three classes identified for both general theoretical reasons, and on account of their similarity of political views. We turn now to the question of who they are, what sort of backgrounds and current social experiences they have.

With all we know about the permanence of class, over generations as much as over political barriers, the best way of showing the real political relevance of my three-class model is by demonstrating that voting choice follows from not only the current but also the childhood class position of voters in 1979. If a three-class model of the previous generation fits with a three-class model of the respondents to give a social mobility pattern which clearly shows a political consequence, then we have a further reason to take my class model seriously. Table 5.3 therefore gives a social mobility table of voting in 1979 using, for both generations, the upper, intermediate, and lower class divisions. One point needing immediate comment is the small size of the intermediate class for the parental generation. Though our actual figures for class distributions may well be artifacts of the particular sample, it seems clear that the intermediate social class has grown proportionately with industrial development and the expansion of white-collar jobs. (On this point it is worth consulting Goldthorpe (1980, chs 5 and 9). While the classes split 24:10:66 for the parents of our 1979 respondents, the respondents themselves split 33:26:42. The reduction in the lower class is inevitable, and though the way it has grown into the intermediate class certainly makes sense, it has not been documented in political science literature. The obvious conclusion is that our modern intermediate class consists largely (70 per cent) of those risen from the basic manual grades. Yet they do now occupy positions in the social structure which makes them genuinely intermediate, and they show a corresponding ambivalence in voting behaviour. Had this class not grown so enormously, by a factor of more than 2.5, much of our political uncertainty might not exist. Table 5.3 shows, really, two things. One is the linear decline of Conservative voting inside each current class group as the class of the respondents' fathers declines towards the lower end of the spectrum. This grows into a general decrease of conservatism as both earlier and current class decline. Thus the overall idea that the three-class model fits class–voting assumptions at least as well, if not better than, the older non-manual/manual distinction is shown. The other basic point is that, in the election of 1979 at least, only one of the nine groups actually preferred Labour (though by a huge margin): those who were themselves, and whose fathers had been, in the lowest social class. Were this group bigger than it now is, the Labour Party might be happier. As it is, only two other social mobility categories come anywhere near supporting the Labour Party, those who are lower class but came from the upper class, and the current intermediate class whose parents had lower class jobs. Both of these give the Conservatives a lead of around 6 per cent.

TABLE 5.3 Respondent's class by father's class by vote in 1979 (%)

Respondent's class	Father's class	Con.	Lab.	Lib.	Con–Lab	N
Upper	Upper	70	14	16	+56	155
Upper	Intermediate	71	13	16	+58	45
Upper	Lower	54	29	17	+25	168
Intermediate	Upper	75	19	7	+56	59
Intermediate	Intermediate	70	11	19	+59	27
Intermediate	Lower	48	42	10	+6	198
Lower	Upper	41	35	24	+6	58
Lower	Intermediate	50	34	16	+16	38
Lower	Lower	26	59	15	-33	368

Note: N = Number of respondents.

This is roughly what the overall national lead ended up as, and it seems a fair guess that in this, and perhaps most elections, these cross-pressured groups are so balanced as simply to mirror the national swing pattern. In any case the Labour Party would be ill-advised to ignore the fact that their only loyal voting block has declined, according to this data, from 66 per cent to only about 40 per cent of the electorate, and the next two most favourable groups amount only to a further 23 per cent. This gives us a suggestion that social mobility, if measured on a three-class model, produces a Labour support only in a decreasing long-term lower class group, and no more than an average chance of doing well in the next biggest group. All others are very solidly for the Conservatives, though in a way which continues to show the impact of earlier chaos. Anthony Heath (1981, p. 240) working on 1972 data with a more powerful set of class membership categories, shows a very similar result.

Another way of showing that the three classes I propose are not only currently in existence but carry a politically important message from the past is to consider the electorate's self-image of class against the same sort of three-class mobility table just used to analyse current vote. Table 5.4 reports an 'average' self-location on a class spectrum according to social mobility types. I use the dichotomous class identity measure reported in earlier chapters, because the respondents were never given a stimulus that might have evoked anything but the standard middle/working class split. In this case I have constructed a scale using both the 'spontaneous' acceptance of a class identity and the 'forced' responses of those who initially denied having a subjective class identity. The scale is constructed by giving one point to those who spontaneously admit to being middle class, and four points to spontaneous working class identifiers. Those in between, who have to be prompted, are given two points if they finally confess to middle class status, and three if, under pressure, they admit to being working class. An average calculated over each group then gives one a quick impression of both the direction and immediacy of the typical subgroup class image. At the same time, by looking at this measure broken down by class of origin as well as current tri-class location, we can check that the tri-class notion has enough reality to impact on current self-image even when tested by a breaking down of the respondents' parental class according to a scheme they do not even use themselves.

The group scores show a nearly perfect monotonic increase (i.e. a move towards spontaneous working class identity), as one moves down from being stable upper class, via various types of social mobility, to being solidly lower class for at least two generations. The three parental class groups have average scores of, respectively, 2.1, 2.9, 3.2, for upper, intermediate and lower parental class (all three possible pair comparisons being statistically significant at the 5 per cent level). At the same time, the current class positions can also be seen to produce notably different average senses of subjective class looked at inside 'class of origin' groupings. The thesis that we do

TABLE 5.4 Subjective class index scores by
social mobility in a three-class model

Father's class	Respondent's class	Score
Upper	Upper	1.8
Upper	Intermediate	2.3
Upper	Lower	2.5
Intermediate	Upper	2.4
Intermediate	Intermediate	2.8
Intermediate	Lower	3.0
Lower	Upper	3.0
Lower	Intermediate	3.1
Lower	Lower	3.2

Note: The score is derived by giving each respondent 1 point if he spontaneously offers a 'middle class' self-ascription, 2 points for a forced 'middle class' response, 3 points for a forced 'working class' response, and 4 points for those who spontaneously offer a 'working class' identity. The scores are averaged for each group.

have an intermediate social class, distinct over two or more generations in political loyalty (the vote) and politically relevant social perceptions like subjective class, seems well established. With the additional figures mentioned about the growth of the intermediate class, and with the data of the 'middle' positions taken up by such a group, any class model of British politics clearly has to be more subtle and complex than it has been hitherto.

What we must now consider is the additional problem of linking class to political party loyalty, for parties are, if anything, perhaps more obviously rooted in the British political scene, even at a time of partisan dealignment. After all, it remained true even in 1979, as it had been in the great dealigning elections of 1974, that far more people confessed readily to a psychological identification with a party than admitted spontaneously to a class label.

5.2 THE PARTY–CLASS INTERACTION

Table 5.2 earlier does not only show that members of the intermediate class give their votes proportionately to all parties. It equally shows that Liberal Party voters come proportionately from all classes, whilst the two major parties of the state draw their support in a very disproportionate way from the two basic model classes. This leads us to a further problem in analysing class and political attitude. To what extent must we take 'party' as being an equally deep cleavage in Britain, one that must be taken into account along with class in portraying the basic building blocks of our political society? Sometimes it can seem dangerously tautologous to use partisanship as though it were causally prior to actual voting, or to the holding of opinions which are, after all, arrayed on a party-political spectrum. The impetus to treat 'party' as though it were logically independent of political action or belief, as though it had much the same deep-seated and structurally relevant role as class, comes from the whole tradition of 'party identification' theory in voting studies. To the champions of the Michigan school, and to their followers in later studies, it makes perfect sense to study the actual votes cast, or the opinions held, by those of a known party identification. This is because identifying with a party is seen as a matter of inheritance from parental allegiance, or otherwise holding for non-rational reasons an important psychologically simplifying construct about the political world. It does not go too far to say that 'party', to such analysts, is a political family. You are born, willy nilly, into that family, and live with it, more or less at ease, being guided and constrained by it all your life, unless something almost as traumatic as divorce occurs.

Those who hold to this approach may have done themselves some disservice in portraying the relationship with undue emphasis on its intellectually empty, un-ratiocinative nature, as commentators have suggested (Robertson, 1976b). But it cannot be denied that there is good empirical evidence to support them. The rate of inheritance of family political loyalty, even when class position varies, is one of the sharper pieces of evidence. I concentrated in chapter 3, for good reason, on the decline of this voting inheritance. But it remains true that an enormously large part of the population does vote in the way its parents did, even when its own social situation varies a good deal (Goldberg, 1969). Historically also we are, in fact, used to the idea of 'party' as a family tradition, with all the trappings of associated social life and peer group expectation. The danger of tautology, in using party just as much as class to analyse either voting or political belief, arises only if the evidence used to allocate people to a party is logically or empirically dependent on the data to be examined. Thus studies of actual voting which use the standard 'party identification' question to explain that people who 'usually thought of themselves as' party X voted for party X are indeed engaged in an odd activity.

But if one is actually analysing a different matter, in my case political opinions rather than voting, and if care is taken to use data somewhat separated, logically, temporally and empirically, from the holding of any specific belief, it does make sense to claim that a deep and rather unfocused and general membership of a party family is a serious independent explanatory variable. The real proof of this comes, indeed, from investigating the empirical relationship between 'party' and 'class' as dual predictive variables in analyses of attitude variation.

It would be possible to write the rest of this book basing the analyses of political attitudes only on classes. If one did so, however, much would be missed. Classes do average positions on the various dimensions I discuss later. These are, usually, significantly different. But it remains true that the variation around the class mean is very large. How could it be otherwise when a small, but vital, part of the upper class is dedicated to the Labour Party, and a large minority of the lower class always votes for the Conservatives? Were this a very tight fit, tautology might again creep in. But ignoring class and taking only party as an independent variable produces equally large deviations. To repeat myself, as it were, how could this be different? The answer is that class does exist, is socially vital, and large numbers of the Labour and Conservative loyal voters come from the 'wrong' class. One must recognize that political beliefs, and political actions like voting, are products of community affiliation, and that both class and party, in this very general sense of party, act as communities. So broad are British political parties that there is no automatic connection between membership of one and the holding of any specific belief. Nor, most importantly, is membership of a party community general to the political system. There are two basic political families in post-war British political history, the Conservative and Labour Parties. Membership of these in any deep sense is restricted to not much more than a bare majority of the population.[2] During the rest of this book I treat the requirement for membership of either of these political families as having voted for the same party in both 1974 and 1979. All others, those who failed to vote at all in 1974, those who voted only once for the major parties, or consistently voted for a minor party, are treated as politically 'neutral'. They are the political counterpart of the 'intermediate' social class.[3]

As these two elections present roughly similar victories for each of the two major parties, with a large swing between them, consistent voting over both is a good, if tough, test of family membership. Much of the ensuing analysis can be described in terms of table 5.2, treating

'Liberal' voters as those without membership in the basic political families, those who are politically intermediate. If one takes these two dimensions, in a manner reminiscent of Weber's writing on party and class, the population is divided into the nine cells of table 5.2. Of these nine, only four can be expected to show the evidence of ideological subgroups. These are the upper and lower class Labour and Conservative family members. They account for about two-thirds of the electorate, leaving one-third which is intermediate in either class or party membership, or both. The intermediates are those whose cells in table 5.2 do not deviate from the 'expected' entries, and who show on most of the following figures and tables a position typically halfway between the extremes of any dimension.

To take class and party as more or less equal, deeply-rooted constraints on voting and belief is capable of two rather different analytic descriptions. One version is to say that both exist, that they are independent, and that each has a separate and unconnected impact on, say, economic radicalism./In the language of statistical analysis this would mean the following. If we take a measurable dimension of belief, called radicalism, for example, the population has an average position, the 'grand mean'. The position of any specific individual is then a matter of adding and subtracting effects from his class and party position. To be part of the Conservative family might give an average of $-X$ points on radicalism, while to be a member of the lower class might give an average increment of $+Y$ points on that dimension. With this purely additive model we would be seeing the two communities, class and party, as unconnected. There would be an upper class and a Conservative family, a Labour and lower class family, but there would be no interaction. Membership of any cross combination would be, as the model suggests, purely a matter of taking the two effects and adding them together. This would be, sociologically, an unlikely eventuality. Surely there must be something special about being both upper class and Labour? Will not the patterns of association, kinship, the sources of support and validation and the positive and negative life-style consequences of being an upper class Labour supporter produce a difference in both the nature of the class perceptions and the political ideology? Is the experience and evaluation of upper class life to be the same for those from both political families, and the politically neutral? Are these experiences the same for the Conservative who directs the Board and the one who attends the machine in the factory? Can we expect the foreman and pay clerks in that same factory who are intermediate between these two not to have yet another, different, experience of life?

The model which can be put against this additive, disaggregated picture of class and party membership is an 'interaction' model. Here we not only expect Conservatives to be different from Labour supporters in their attitudes, and the politically intermediate to be different again. We also expect the upper, intermediate and lower class members of each political family to be different from their opposite numbers by more than the simple difference arising from the class or party contrast. In this model we are thinking of several crucially different sub-cultures in the population which cannot be treated additively. The actual model I wish to argue for has in fact only four real sub-cultures, plus the general intermediary floating population. I suggest that we can expect there to be four clear sub-cultures – an upper class Conservative culture and a lower class Labour culture are the prime ones, predictable from all the history and theory of this century's voting. We know also to expect the counter, or deviant, cultures, those of lower class Conservatives and upper class Labour family members. In calling these sub-cultures I mean, amongst other things, that their views will not be the same as would be predicted if one took party and class and added them together. Let me have a more or less concrete example. If we take a dimension of economic radicalism, anyone would correctly predict that the upper class would be less radical than the lower class, and that Conservatives would be less radical than Labour supporters. Additively, ignoring the special nature of subgroups, one would therefore expect the deviant sub-culture of upper class Labour family members to be somewhat average – more radical than non-Labour upper class, less radical than lower class Labour. My model does not yield certain predictions, simply that no such cross-pressuring, no averaging over socio-political cleavages, necessarily happens. The views of the sub-cultures are formed by an interaction between these two basic aspects of class and party.

This basic assumption of my model, that we really have four crucial sub-cultures in the electorate, plus a large minority of those intermediate between at least one, if not both, polar dimensions, can easily be tested by looking for such statistical 'interaction' effects.

In order to investigate this I derive, in chapter 6, a simple ideological model of the electorate, using the sorts of variables that earlier provided the 'similarity matrix' I employed for assessing the correct class location of the several socio-economic grades. As this model also has considerable interest in its own right as a map of basic ideology in Britain, the flesh on the bones of party–class interaction, it requires the whole of a chapter. Before dealing in such detail, however, it seems worthwhile to give a demonstration that my three class–party schema does work in a general sense. What I need to show is that the overall measures of political belief do separate the population into the families I have argued for. Basically there are two hypotheses that have to be tested and confirmed at this stage. First, that on at least some measures of ideology or political belief there are differences between members of different 'parties' *inside* the same social class. This is hardly to be doubted, and is the easier test to pass. (I should remind readers that from now on, when I talk of 'parties' I am referring to three political groups: those who voted for the Conservatives in both the last two elections, two time voters for Labour, and then all the rest as a 'neutral' party.) The second hypothesis is that, within any party family, there are differences on at least some measures according to class. The use of the phrase 'on at least some measures' in the formulation of the hypothesis arises because we have no warrant to assume that the separate and interactive effects of class and party must always operate in the same way on all areas of political belief. If I am right in thinking of the party–class groups as real 'sub-cultures', then considerable complexity should arise in the constraining of political attitudes. Table 5.5 gives a simple test of these two hypotheses.

The table reports the mean score on four general attitude indicators derived from factor analysis of a large number of questions. The most important of these, the first two columns in the table, which form the basis for the ideological model discussed in the next chapter, are described in detail there. In practice the actual meaning

TABLE 5.5 Average scores party–class families on four political attitudes

Class		Socio-economic radicalism	Social liberalism	Peaceful protest or participation	More radical protest
Upper	Neutral	0.25	0.37	0.04	−0.15
Upper	Con.	0.79	0.03	0.37	−0.06
Upper	Lab.	−0.54	0.66	−0.19	−0.40
Intermediate	Neutral	−0.01	−0.15	−0.08	0.08
Intermediate	Con.	0.53	−0.21	0.31	−0.03
Intermediate	Lab.	−0.58	−0.12	−0.05	−0.05
Lower	Neutral	−0.22	−0.13	−0.24	0.10
Lower	Con.	0.16	−0.35	0.17	0.13
Lower	Lab.	−0.45	0.01	−0.11	−0.06

Note: Technical details and interpretation of the first two measures are given in chapter 6. These scores are from factor analyses. As such they are constrained to give an overall mean of zero, and a standard deviation of unity. Hence apparently small differences can be significant statistically.

of all four scales is largely irrelevant — they can serve just as lines of political longitude and latitude by which we can hope to see class and party differences.

The first two columns represent: a dimension of (i) economic radicalism and (ii) social liberalism. The other pair are measures of preparedness to engage in protest activity of various types. The first measures a willingness to take legal and orthodox protest activity, such as the signing of petitions and attending public meetings. The second measures willingness to go on proscribed demonstrations, block traffic, occupy a building, and so forth. Thus we are able to ask whether party and class severally affect what might be called matters of participation and protest.

These latter two variables are chosen for demonstration because party–class sub-cultures, to be politically important, ought to vary in attitudes to political engagement, as well as in views about what is politically desirable. The graph in figure 5.3 plots into a map the positions of the four major party–class families, according to the basic idea that those intermediate in class or faith are essentially floating between the four major ideological entities, on whom attention should be concentrated. On all four variables including the second pair which could be used to draw a similar map, the twofold test suggested passes easily. There are clear differences between party groups inside classes, and usually, though not always, between class groups inside faiths. As the next chapters are largely taken up with investigating the complexities of these 'interactions', I need make no detailed comment here. It is enough to point out that, of the significance tests carried out on pairs of positions, nearly all show statistically significant differences between party-class families. On each variable there are four crucial tests: one needs to test the difference in score between Conservatives and Labour in both classes, and between upper and lower class voters inside each political faith. Of the ensuing 16 tests, 14 show differences in position that are statistically significant. The two tests which show an absence of an expected difference are highly important.

The most important refers to the fact that, on matters of socioeconomic egalitarianism (dimension 1 on figure 5.3), there is no difference between upper and lower class Conservatives. This is a matter to be taken up at length, and discussed theoretically in the rest of the book.

The second is a similar closeness of position on the question of the more peaceful protest, or, which comes to the same thing, an equal preparedness to indulge in active though law-abiding participation.

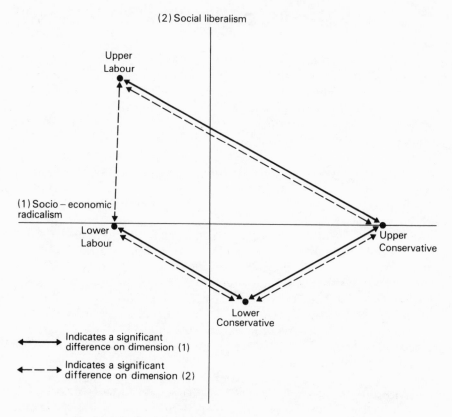

Figure 5.3　Socio-economic radicalism and social liberalism

Otherwise the two different sorts of test show clearly that, both in terms of political preference, and engagement in political action, both class and party work together to present a set of four central ideological homes. The rest of the book is dedicated to exploring these homelands. One major theoretical concern is to demonstrate and explain a feature that shows already in these simple graphs. This is the extreme radicalism, in attitudes to protest as much as in political aims, of the upper class Left. Indeed much of what follows concerns not only just four of nine class-party families, but more specifically two. For, in the data as always in theory, two political animals stand out as curiosities in British politics — upper class Socialists and lower class Conservatives. My redefinition of class in no way reduces, but rather enhances, the analytic visibility of these groups.

6

The Four Quadrants of British Politics

6.1 PARTY AND CLASS INTERACTION IN IDEOLOGICAL SPACE

The opinions voters have about political questions can be seen in two lights. They can be seen as specific answers to particular questions, Should the House of Lords have its powers reduced? Has the granting of equality to women gone too far? Or the answers to questions like these can be seen as indicators of more general underlying political attitudes. The same item in a questionnaire can be used in both ways, depending on the analytic needs of the writer. In the next two chapters I take such questions as separate and not necessarily interconnected issues on which class and party may have an impact, and the examination of which may tell us a lot about the political culture of the four basic subgroups of British voters. At this stage it is more useful to have a small number of rather general attitudinal dimensions, preferably describing an ideological space in which we can chart the position of class–party groups and investigate the interactions or separate effects of class and party. With an eye to this latter need, the directors of the 1974 and 1979 British Election Studies derived two batteries of questions, one set of which has already been used in a rough and ready manner earlier in this book. The idea was that these sets of questions, internally homogenous in format, could be scaled. By scaling a set of question responses I mean that I take not individual answers, but the patterns of answers to similarly-oriented questions as cumulatively giving a general picture of where a respondent is on an underlying dimension that each question partially measures. The two sets of questions each render two or more sets of logically related underlying dimensions. These dimensions were used to measure the similarity of occupational categories in section 5.1. The first set refers to actions that the government might be felt obliged to carry out or refrain from. They measure individually the

desirability or otherwise of a series of possible policies, and collectively 'tap' one or more general orientations to what might be considered desirable government directions of policy. Each question in the
'battery' is of the form, 'How important is it that the government
should do X', where X can be, for example, 'establish comprehensive
schools', or 'repatriate immigrants'. To each question respondents
were allowed to answer on a five point scale: 'very important that
the government should do X', 'fairly important that the government
should do X', 'does not matter either way', 'fairly important that the
government should not do X', and 'very important that the government should not do X'. The actual topics questioned are discussed in
some detail in chapter 7, and tested in the Appendix.

The familiar technique of factor analysis was used to produce
underlying general policy attitude dimensions from the responses
to this battery of questions. (Those not sure of the nature of factor
analysis are referred to the Appendix, where the two useful dimensions which were extracted from the factor analysis are described.)
I interpret these two dimensions as according with much that has
been written from the factor analytic approach to political ideology
from the early work of Eysenck (1951) onwards. The first factor after
rotation is very clearly a straightforward socio-economic egalitarianism version of a left–right radicalism dimension. Four variables load
in an important way on the first dimension–demands for the creation
of comprehensive schools, governmental control of land for building,
the redistribution of wealth, and reduction of power of the House of
Lords. Other variables with non-zero loadings support the contention
that high scores on these variables go together to produce a syndrome
of support for a more egalitarian distribution of power, wealth and
opportunities in the country. It is a very basic dimension of all that
is contained in the notion of a left–right dimension to politics. The
second dimension is, by the formula for factor analysis, constrained
to be statistically independent of the first. Thus, if it picks up a
left–right meaning, it must be one that is statistically, and hopefully
logically, a meaning such that a voter can plausibly have any position on it regardless of where he may be on the first dimension. The
second dimension is one fully familiar from journalistic coverage of
British politics, one intuitively easy to comprehend, but difficult to
label. It puts together a different sort of right-wing syndrome, represented by a desire to see the repatriation of coloured immigrants, the
re-introduction of the death penalty, the giving of stiffer sentences
by criminal law courts, and, at a lesser level, an opposition to taking
our troops out of Northern Ireland and an opposition to increasing

our Foreign Aid budget. No label matters very much anyway, and one could choose several for this. It combines a clear chauvinism with another meaning of left–right, the holding of authoritarian and retributive attitudes. In fact both dimensions coincide with Eysenck's (1951) well-known two-dimensional map of ideology in *The Psychology of Politics*.[1] There he chose the titles for his dimensions as, for the first, radicalism/conservatism, and, for the second, tough minded versus soft. In this case, wishing to be less emotive, I choose to label them thus: the first dimension contrasts the Left with the Right, understanding this to be principally concerned with socio-economic radicalism. The second contrasts the authoritarian with the 'liberal', whilst accepting that this easily recognizable dimension might well be described in other terms. I choose to call it 'social liberalism'.

The two dimensions describe very well most ordinary perceptions of the structure of modern political debate. They are statistically, and ought to be logically, distinct, though in the minds of much of the intellectual elite there is an assumption that left and liberal go together. I would argue that this assumption is not only unwarranted, but has led much of the left-wing of Britain's intelligentsia into serious mistakes about the constituency of the Labour Party.[2] At this stage in the argument we are concerned only to show that the position in the two-dimensional space described by this data analysis does indeed show the party–class interaction posited above. The first step, intended as a largely intuitive demonstration which may well be enough for most readers, is shown as figure 6.1. Further statistical evidence of party and class interaction follows.

Figure 6.1 plots the position of each of the three basic classes described in the previous chapter, taking account also of their 1979 vote. Thus there are nine positions marked.

In many ways the four quadrants of this figure summarize the areas of British political rhetoric. The top right-hand quadrant belongs to those who take an unsympathetic line to demands for increasing egalitarianism in economic and allied matters, in other words a Conservative approach, but a conservatism that does not spill over onto other issues, for this quadrant is on the 'liberal' side of the 'authoritarian versus liberal' dimension. Of the nine groups formed by combining the three-class model with 1979 voting, only two have average positions in this quadrant. Upper class Conservatives just get into it, though being close to the frontier of authoritarianism. They are joined by those from the upper class who voted Liberal, who are less 'right-wing' on the egalitarianism axis, but, quite properly, definitely 'liberal' (see Alt, 1975). The next quadrant belongs to

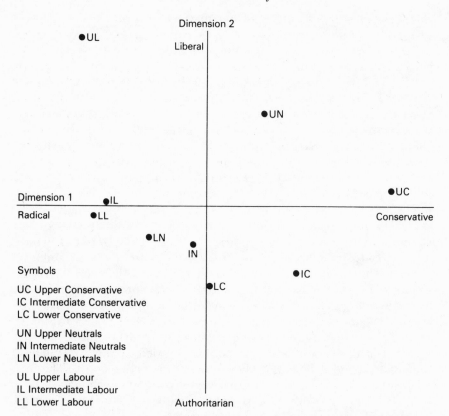

Figure 6.1 Positions of nine class–party groups in two ideological dimensions

those who are conservative on the socio-economic radicalism or egalitarianism dimension, but right-wing, pro-authority, on the second dimension. Two groups appear here: one, of intermediate class position but clear Conservative preferences, fits easily into the most 'Tory' of positions, authoritarian anti-egalitarianism. The other is almost on the border as far as the left–right axis of egalitarianism goes, but even more clearly authoritarian; this is the lower class Conservative segment.

So far the best indication of the interaction that creates real political communities out of the party–class division is this very large gap between upper and lower class Conservatives. Lower class Conservatives are much more egalitarian than Conservatives of any other class (though much less so than the lower class voters from the opposite political family), but they are also much less 'liberal' than what one might call 'non-deviant' Conservatives, those from an upper class background. Following clockwise we come to the most populated quadrant of British politics, the area of those who, while being 'illiberal' on the 'authority versus liberalism' dimension are also 'left-wing' on the basic 'egalitarianism' dimension. At least four political-class groups belong here, five if one has doubts about the lower class Conservatives. A suggestion that those who are cut off from the major political debate by being Liberal in vote may be less than liberal in policy outlook comes from the clearly authoritarian position of the intermediate and lower class voters who are either Liberal or, at least, not affiliated to the major parties. This very fact shows the class relevance to political attitudes. None of the three political groups from the upper class fall below the borderline of the liberal/authoritarian cut-off, and no political group from either of the other classes gets above it. Otherwise this quadrant is not surprising. The Labour Party family and the Liberals find both their intermediate and lower class segments on the 'left-wing' side of the basic egalitarianism dimension. This being said, the face validity of the analysis is surely increased by the near identity in position of lower class Conservatives and those from the intermediate class who do not have a major party affiliation. Perhaps it is when we turn to the final quadrant that we actually see the evidence of real party-class interaction communities in political attitudes. This quadrant, judging from the pages of *The Guardian* and *The Observer*, and the beliefs of university teachers throughout the land, should be highly populated. It represents the apparently logical connection of egalitarianism and liberalism. In fact only one small segment of the population, though clearly a very vociferous one, lives here, the upper class Labour supporters. This group, though it amounts to only about 7 per cent of the whole population, is the best single example of the class–party interaction communities I am concerned with. Here we most clearly have a sub-culture whose views cannot be explained on the lines that to be upper class reduces egalitarianism by X points, and to be of the Labour persuasion decreases 'authoritarianism' by some such amount. In fact there is no class difference amongst Labour supporters on the egalitarianism dimension (though there is a significant difference for those who are either Conservative supporters or belong to neither party family). But there is a very large distance between the liberalism/authoritarianism positions of the upper and other class Labour supporters, and between the Labour and other political supporters from the same class, on both dimensions.

This sort of visual inspection may well satisfy most readers that the class–party interaction I suggest exists. I still need, however, to produce reliable statistical evidence for this pattern. An analysis of variance test was conducted on the scores on the first and second dimension, partitioned by both class and party. The analysis shows clearly that the sort of interaction I have suggested exists. An analysis of variance works by fitting a set of statistical models to the data. In this case three models are fitted. First, both possible explanatory variables, party and class, are tested to see if they separately account for the variance in the average position of the nine party–class groups on the ideological dimensions. As would be expected from the previous figure, both explanatory factors are relevant, so there is a statistically significant difference on both the egalitarianism and the authoritarianism dimension according to both the class and party characteristics of the voter. Much more important, though, is the significance of the 'interaction' term. As surmised, a special effect sets in where certain combinations of class and party coexist. This effect makes the upper class Labour supporters very radical on the egalitarianism dimension, and very liberal on the cross-cutting authoritarianism dimension, even though other upper class voters are disproportionately anti-egalitarian and other Labour supporters are much more authoritarian. It is precisely the impact one expects from a political culture in which both class and party have not only their own separate impacts on ideology, but coincide to create whole sub-cultures.

Statistically, at least, the interaction effect is very highly significant in both cases. The 'F' ratios produce, at the worst (which is the class–party interaction on the social liberalism dimension), only a 1 per cent chance of getting such a result by accident. We can accept both the four quadrants, and the class and party influence on their populations, as real social facts. (The interaction term yields an 'F' value of 17.3 with 4 degrees of freedom, statistically highly significant.)

I will review quickly the suggested model. I have argued that a primary dimension of political attitudes, one which correlated most closely with a layman's understanding of the problem in terms of the traditional 'left–right' dichotomy, is a dimension dealing with egalitarianism. Questions of the proper distribution of values — whether they be very pragmatic issues of wealth redistribution, or mediating considerations like those of the comprehensive school system, or rather remote matters of equality in political power as displayed by differences of opinion about reforming the House of Lords — are primary to our political and social system. Such matters are clearly influenced by the overall partisanship of members of the electorate. But they can also be seen as powerfully influenced by social class. The higher one's class, the more one is unlikely to worry overmuch about unequal distributions. Details of the somewhat unsurprising thesis must wait for later chapters, but the relative positions of the nine party–class averages have been shown. Tories are less worried, on average, by inequality than Labour Party supporters; people from our 'upper' social class are less worried than those from our 'lower' class.

This most familiar of ideological distinctions is cross cut by another. The second dimension we discern in British politics is something that any reader is likely to grasp intuitively, and is indeed the stuff of much social comment and even official BBC humour. It represents a concatenation of attitudes on less pragmatic, perhaps less structural, matters. Should we hang murderers? Are the courts too soft on other criminals? Has the rush to ensure equality of opportunity for women and racial minorities gone too far, or too fast? Are standards of morality or social discipline being eroded by easier abortion, a lack of respect for traditional authority, by 'modern methods of education'? Should coloured immigrants be repatriated, and should we really be spending more of our GNP on aid to underdeveloped countries? These and endless other questions raise in our minds a syndrome of political opinion which is instantly recognizable but exceptionally hard to name. One might do well to use the (in)famous television characters of Alf Garnett in Britain (or Archie Bunker in the American version), the best public descriptions of the illiberal populist 'small man' ideological syndrome ever given.[3] Yet there is one crucial reason why these public portraits will not do. The authors of these television serials made life too simple for themselves by assuming a correlation that does not exist, at least in my data, between positions on the liberalism/illiberalism dimension, and appropriate positions on the equality/inequality or simply 'left-right' dimension of political attitudes. Alf Garnett and his American confrère were Conservative in every way — not only were they illiberal, they voted Tory or for Nixon and believed that social service expenditure and nationalization were just as stupid as equal opportunities and modern maths. This fits well, of course, into the media assumptions of how ideas fit together, perhaps because they really do fit for the cultural elite of journalists and dons who give us our impression of the politically important *Weltanschauung*. In fact there is no such correlation.

Those who wish to redistribute wealth and abolish grammar schools are by no means automatically in favour of sexual and racial equality. Those with 'enlightened' approaches to abortion and pornography do not necessarily think that socialist economic policies are a good thing. This is why there are four quadrants to our political life. One can be right- or left-wing on the fundamental question of increasing overall equality in society. One can be more or less liberal on the cross-cutting dimension which Eysenck called the 'tough–tender minded' contrast. And while one can hold any combination of such positions, social class will tell a lot about which of the cross-cutting positions one is likely to take up.

So much I have already shown. If social class really does have a determining force on the political quadrant one ends up in, it ought to be fairly deep-rooted. To further the evidence already adduced, we can look deeper than the immediate social class of a voter. We can look at the class he or she has come from. If a two-generation class effect successfully predicts the political quadrant, we can have a good deal of faith in the model. We can also, perhaps, hope to understand the apparent inheritability of voting choice.

Using the four quadrants, and using essentially a 'nominal' or at best 'ordinal' level measurement like class, would usually lead to a standard cross-tabulation approach. The analysis of contingency tables, once one gets further than a single explanatory variable is exceptionally difficult. Throughout the rest of this book I shall principally be presenting three-way tables, where a specific social attitude is seen to depend on both a voter's social class and his political loyalty. As there are, in my schema, three classes and three party loyalties (Conservative, Labour, and none), we have immediately nine categories in the analysis, before we even consider the variable of political attitude which is to be explained. If the attitude variable is measured even at two levels only, 'yes' and 'no' say, eighteen cells appear in the table. Were the two explanatory factors always to be independent of each other, so that, for example, to be lower class made one left-wing and to be Tory made one right-wing, and one could simply add these two causal elements together, the analysis, while still awkward of exposition, might be feasible. But we have already seen that this is unlikely to be so. In figure 6.1 the average position of upper class Labour supporters was much further to the left and much more liberal than could be explained on the (essentially correct) notion that to be upper class was to be liberal but also to be right-wing, while being a Labour supporter was to be left-wing but not terribly liberal. Where such special effects set in, where the impact of two or more social characteristics is that they do not simply add together to produce an overall result for a category, we have 'inter-action effects'. Such interactions, which I have already shown using analysis of variance on the dimensional scores, though theoretically interesting and rich for our understanding of the development of political ideology, are extremely difficult to disentangle and demon-strate given the usual approach to contingency tables. In order to deal effectively with the possibility of such interaction effects and, more simply, to test separately for the impact of two or more causal elements on the distribution of attitude opinion data, I make use often from now on of a technique that has gained much popularity in the last decade of social science data analysis, usually called log-linear modelling (see Upton, 1978). Though the details of this technique are not particularly difficult to grasp, they can be a little confusing, and only the simplest explanation will be given here. Those who wish a fuller exposition should look at any of the several good general texts that have become available in recent years. The essential point of log-linear modelling is that it allows one to treat the sort of data we have, typically un-ordered nominal data, with the same sort of precision and theoretical complexity that is usually found only with fully measured real variables in regression analysis or the analysis of variance.

I shall apply a log-linear analysis to the data in table 6.1, partly to demonstrate the technique, partly because the data are important for our general investigation. Table 6.1 gives the distribution of the sample over the four ideological quadrants according to the current social class of each respondent, and the respondent's father's class. It is typical in design of the tables analysed later; with three classes for each generation, and four political quadrants, one gets 36 cells, demonstrating a very complex pattern of class influence on political attitudes.

TABLE 6.1 Respondent's position in the two-dimensional space by current class and father's class (%)

| Current class | Upper | | | Intermediate | | | Lower | | |
Father's class	*U.*	*I.*	*L.*	*U.*	*I.*	*L.*	*U.*	*I.*	*L.*
Ideological quadrant									
right/liberal	50	43	31	24	23	13	25	10	13
right/illiberal	30	26	33	31	43	27	14	25	17
left/illiberal	6	8	18	28	11	39	30	34	44
left/liberal	14	22	19	17	23	21	31	31	26
Total	100	100	100	100	100	100	100	100	100

The table shows fairly clearly that the probability of being both right-wing rather than left-wing, and liberal rather than illiberal, depends on one's current social class and also one's class of origin. For example, amongst those now upper class, only 20 per cent of those with upper class fathers are on the 'left' side of the left–right dimension. However 35 per cent of those with lower class fathers but who are themselves upper class are on the left. Equally revealing is the fact that of those on the left who are upper class in their own right as well as by descent, the bulk are in the 'liberal' left-wing quadrant, while only half of the other left-wing group we have noted fall into the liberal aspect of the left. Throughout the table these patterns emerge. But have we no way of systematizing the analysis, of asking about the relative strengths of class as measured on one or other generation? Indeed, are the apparent patterns in the data real? Do they diverge enough from what one might get by accident?

The traditional analysis of contingency tables would either stop at this point, or it would separately test to see if the two purported class influences were statistically significant. The usual technique would be to apply a chi square test (Upton, 1978). With that old and familiar technique one sets up a null hypothesis, the thesis that the data reported in a table are no different in pattern and distribution from those which would emerge were all the variables involved quite independent of each other. Effectively one predicts how many people should fall in each cell of the table from simple probabilities. If there were an X per cent probability of being upper class, a Y per cent probability of having an upper class father, and a Z per cent probability of being in the right-liberal quadrant, then there is an X*Y*Z per cent probability of being all three of those things.

Similar probabilities can be used to calculate all the other cells. Having predicted, therefore, what the results ought to be, given no impact of class on attitude, one can contrast the actual distribution against this predicted one. If the difference between the actual or 'observed' data and the predicted data is large enough, as measured by the chi square test, one rejects the null hypothesis and accepts a thesis that class and opinion are interrelated. However, with the simple chi square test, nothing can be said about the relative impact of each class measure, nor about the possibility that interaction, as discussed above, exists between the two class measures and the 'dependent' variable which is to be explained. Indeed the very language of causal or explanatory sequence, familiar to those who are used to applying regression techniques to harder data, is missing. A log-linear analysis allows us effectively to do to this sort of data what regression can do to interval level data.

We start in much the same way as with ordinary chi square, with the assumption of no connection at all between predicting and dependent variables. In this case we fit a very simple model to the data, which says effectively that the data are the result only of a series of uninteresting patterns in the table. These are: (1) the fact that one's own and one's father's class are not themselves unrelated. This is, of course, something that in a different context one might actually want to test. Here, though, relationships between the predicting variables are unimportant to us; (2) we add also the uninteresting fact that the total numbers in the different quadrants vary. The model can be given the following symbolism, which will make further use of the technique easier to explain. We assert that the entry in each cell is effectively the overall average entry for all the cells, or general mean (GM), plus the effect of the two class measures being interrelated, FC (for father's class) and RC (for respondent's class), plus the sheer fact of varying total numbers in each cell of the quadrant variable (Q). This simplest model then is: GM + FC*RC + Q. The symbol (*) between two variables indicates that all the interrelationships between those two or more variables are being fitted to the model in order to predict what the cell entries should be were the model true. By leaving out a term like (RC*Q), for example, we are denying that there is any relationship between respondent's social class and his ideological quadrant.

The reason we test out this uninteresting model first is twofold. Firstly we do need to see if such a model accurately predicts the actual data. Were it to do so, we would have to admit that there was no evidence for a connection between class and attitude in any way we could model it with our two-class variables. Naturally we hope this is not so. The second reason is that by using this null hypothesis we can get a measure of error in predicting attitude to take as a base line against which to measure the success of our preferred models. This measure, called 'deviance', is directly analogous to chi square, and can be tested against the chi square distribution. For the base line model here, GM + RC*FC + Q, the deviance score is 309.9, with 24 degrees of freedom. (For a discussion of degrees of freedom and other technical points see the Appendix; for our purposes they matter only as a technical part of significance testing.) A deviance score of 309.9 with 24 degrees of freedom is huge. It means that our prediction of the data is very bad indeed, in other words that we do indeed need to take account of social class and its relationship to attitudes. Of course this is only to be expected. We can use the deviance score from this model to measure the improvement in prediction when other terms are added. Let us immediately add the term RC*Q. That is, we will test the model GM + RC*FC + Q + RC*Q. In this model, respondent's class is allowed to predict attitude, but father's class is not. This model produces a deviance of 70.9, with 18 degrees of freedom. This is a vast improvement on the base line. The original error in predicting the distribution of political opinion has been reduced by 239 units, to 70.9 from 309.9, a reduction in error of the predictions of 77 per cent. The statistical significance of this is given by comparing the change in the deviance measure and the change in degrees of freedom in the original and fuller models on a chi square table. It reaches such a level of significance that the probability of being wrong in asserting that respondent's class affects attitude is vanishingly small.

We need not stop at this point, however, because the model can be tested in another sense. Admitted that adding respondent's class vastly improves the fit to the real data, has it gone far enough? Is there still enough error left to require further explanation? Or in terms of the actual table, does our impression that attitude also varies according to parent's class over and above respondent's class test out? There are really two tests involved at this stage: Is the existing model good enough? That is, is the remaining error small enough to be due purely to random chance or measurement error, meaning that GM + RC*FC + Q + RC*Q is a complete explanation for the data? We test this just as we tested the base line model to see if any explanation was needed at all, by testing the remaining deviance of 70.93 with 18 degrees of freedom. Is this deviance high? The answer is yes. We do need further explanation before we can say the errors in prediction are meaningless. This then requires us to test the fuller model in which father's class is also allowed to predict someone's political quadrant. This model takes the form GM + RC*FC + Q + RC*Q + FC*Q. This returns a deviance score of 16.3 with 12 degrees of freedom. Exactly the same process applies. Is the difference between the previous error of 70.9 and the new one of 16.3 significantly large? Again the answer is yes, and the reduction in error shows that both measures of class are important in explaining the vote. In this case, though, we can compare the relative predictive capacities by pointing out that, while the first class variable reduced the error by 239/309 points, over 70 per cent, the second one makes a much smaller reduction of 70.9 − 16.3 or 54.6 units, a reduction of the original 309 of only 18 per cent. This again is what one would expect: the class of origin should not have so serious an explanatory power as current class, though it cannot be disregarded.

Two points remain to be made about this technique. First, we have not just established that two measures of social class both affect political attitude, but that they do independently, when the other is controlled for. Here we have an important general point — because one's own and one's father's class are themselves correlated, it might be thought the demonstration of the impact of the earlier class was dubious, inasmuch as it might be said simply to be repeating to a large extent the class measure. The relationship, in other words, might be thought to be spurious. Log-linear modelling ensures one does not make such a mistake, however, as in regression the impact of the later variables is measured after controlling for the effect of any spurious correlation arising from the inter-correlation of the two predicting variables.

The second point is that the model we have just tested is an additive one. That is, the two class impacts add together, and no account has been taken as yet of an interaction between the two predicting measures and the dependent variable. However, interaction is something we have already commented on and which we can plausibly expect to find from time to time in the later analyses to be performed. The .og-linear technique makes it very easy to test for such interactions. In fact, with the simple three variable model demonstrated above, the test is automatic. The final model we have fitted is GM + RC*FC + Q + RC*Q + FC*Q. There remains only one possible extra term we could add, before completely constraining the data and ensuring a perfect fit. This term, FC*RC*Q, is in fact the representation of the three-way interaction between father's class, respondent's class and quadrant. Were it significant, then the model lacking it would still leave a deviance measure which showed too much error left in the predictions to be accounted for by random disturbance. So if we test the remaining error after adding the parental class variable, to see if it remains in need of further explanation, our only choice would be to accept an effect of class of origin and current class that transcended the purely additive. The deviance measure after the last model was fitted was 16.3, and there remained 12 degrees of freedom. Testing this against the chi square distribution, we find the probability of getting such a difference between predicted and actual data by accident is 17 per cent. Thus we must accept that there is no good reason to think there is a significant interaction. In this case the effect of parental and current class do just add together. How they do so we can see from the original table — the higher the social class, the more right-wing and the more liberal a person is in general. Furthermore, the class one came from has an impact over and above the class one is in now.

The two class effects are of very different magnitude, and doubtless there are other factors which this simple model does not take into account. But we have in this chapter and the previous one shown that the four quadrants of British politics suggested here economically, neatly and reliably summarize the confusion of our political ideologies. That such a summary measure should show so firm an impact of social class over two generations demonstrates how vital class still is in shaping our political life. There is a good deal more to say about these quadrants, and I shall continually return to them. In continuing this chapter I choose to go to a very different sort of data. I try to put an intuitively comprehensible flesh on what might seem too abstract a skeleton to be fully accepted as a picture of class and political attitudes.

6.2 UNSTRUCTURED POLITICAL VIEWS AND SOCIAL CLASS

One trouble with survey data on political attitudes is that our results are inevitably constrained by the researchers' assumptions about what issues are important. Detailed interview questions of the sort I have been using to construct the four-quadrant model of political attitude can give us much, but there is always the problem that both the issues and the answers are predefined by the researcher. There is an alternative that can be used to give some extra support for the sort of description I have given. The 1979 Election Study started with a section of 'open-ended' questions. Respondents were simply asked what they liked and disliked about each party. Their answers were taken down verbatim by the interviewers. These responses allow voters' own concerns and reactions to characterize their attitudes, rather than reporting simply how they responded to the researcher's assumptions about what was politically important.[4]

The data are not easy to analyse because a huge range of 'likes' and 'dislikes' emerge. Also, unsurprisingly, many people are unhappy with the free format and find it difficult to think of any answer, especially when asked what they 'like' about a party they would never dream of voting for. We cannot use even this data in the full richness of the original responses. Instead the responses are 'coded'[5] into a large range of general categories, doing as little violence as possible to the original intent of the respondent. Respondents are encouraged to give as many likes and dislikes as they can think of.

Most manage one, a few two, hardly any more than that. They are allowed to give highly specific or very broad answers. In the tables that follow I have taken the first and second answers given and combined them to get a rough idea of the half dozen or so topics that came up most frequently for the different categories of respondents when asked what they liked about the two major parties. The data can only be used impressionistically, because the sub-sample sizes giving any particular response are often very small. Nonetheless, tables 6.2 and 6.3 do give a readily understandable portrait of political attitudes, and one that backs up my characterization of the four political quadrants. Again I use the ninefold classification by class and party as defined in the previous chapter, which we shall follow through most of the rest of the book.

The three parts of table 6.2 give the most common reasons adduced for liking the Conservative Party, according to whether the respondent is a Conservative loyalist, a Labour loyalist, or has no party loyalty. In fact the section for Labour loyalists is of restricted use. The tables are all broken down into the three classes, and as the sample contains very few upper class Labour loyalists, of whom only about one half could think of any reason for liking the Tories, the results are highly speculative. The other 'slices' of the table are, however, revealing. Consider first the reasons given for liking the

TABLE 6.2a Reasons for liking the Conservative Party:
political neutrals

Upper class	*Intermediate class*	*Lower class*
General support for capitalism and *laissez-faire*	General support for capitalism and *laissez-faire*	Tax policy
Tax policy	Law and order policy	General support for capitalism and *laissez-faire*
Educational policy	Tax policy	General policy competence
Support for freedom and individualism	Trade union policy	Housing policy
Other social values	Other social values	Leadership
Trade union policy	General policy competence	Race relations and immigration policy
	Leadership	Law and order policy
		Social service policy

Note:
In tables 6.2a–c and 6.3a–c the lists of reasons are given in order of relative importance.

Conservative Party amongst those with no party loyalty. Here we can see a sharp contrast between the classes. To be sure a general sense of liking the Tories because they are seen as adhering to some element of a general capitalist or *laissez-faire* policy ranks high with all three classes. (For that matter it comes top amongst upper class Labour loyalists!) But apart from Conservative policies on taxation and public expenditure, which in many ways are logically connected, the lists diverge a good deal. The upper class attach considerable importance to the Conservatives as a party which stands for individualism, freedom and liberty. This is not an aspect noticed by the politically neutral amongst intermediate and lower class respondents. The other two specific policies which lead these respondents to like the Conservatives are trade union policy, shared by the other two classes, but the least important to the upper class, and educational policy, which does not enter the lists for the other classes at all.

As far as the intermediate class goes, the seven types of reason given contain only three which directly relate to policy preference, and the most important of all these is their attraction to the Conservatives' supposed tough line on 'law and order'. Otherwise the Tories attract either through an identification with one of a series of general normative stands, or simply because they and their leadership project an image of competence and authority. The contrast between the upper class attraction to the idea of liberty and individualism and the intermediate class attraction to the law and order policy is crucial. This, arising as it does from the spontaneous rather than prestructured responses of the electorate, helps well to explain the varying liberal/illiberal position of voters who have much the same position on the left–right dimension. A glance at the lower class reasons furthers this. Six policies appear amongst nine dominating reasons (against three out of six for the upper class). This general tendency to go for specific policy preferences rather than generalized ideological or value positions further down the class scale stands up throughout this data. While it may not be surprising, it is an interesting reflection on the different intellectual approaches to political choice across class lines. Law and order, and trade union policy appear again here, but in connection with a liking for Conservative race relations policies. (In this context this can only mean a perception that immigration was likely to be rather more restricted by the Conservatives than other parties.) In addition, we see the appearance of policy stands with a direct pragmatic link to lower class needs, the liking for policies on housing and social services.

One gets from this part of the table a vivid image of differing class orientations, partly in terms of the way in which a party can be liked for conflicting reasons, in the preference for its individualism and liberty for some, compared with its reputation for highly illiberal policies in areas of crime and race relations — and, perhaps, trade union reform and social service provision. The latter is opaque in our data, but may well refer to the notion of being tough on 'welfare scroungers' just as much as to ensuring welfare payments at an adequate level. It would be hard otherwise to explain the constant mentioning of the Labour Party record on social services which we note later, were the Tories not liked for something rather different about their welfare policies. The other difference, one that shows up again later, is, as I have pointed out, the varying tendency to go for abstract rather than concrete reasons for approving of the Conservatives.

TABLE 6.2b Reasons for liking the Conservative Party:
Conservative supporters

Upper class	Intermediate class	Lower class
General support for capitalism and *laissez-faire*	General support for capitalism and *laissez-faire*	General support for capitalism and *laissez-faire*
Support for freedom and individualism	Other social values	Tax policy
General policy competence	General policy competence	Trade union policy
Tax policy	Tax policy	Law and order policy
Other social values	Stands for people like us	General policy competence
Educational policy	Support for freedom and individualism	Housing policy
Law and order policy		Leadership
Trade union policy		

It is unnecessary to go into such detail commenting on the following tables. Amongst those who are treated as Conservative loyalists because they have voted for that party in both 1979 and 1974 there is much the same picture (table 6.2b). True, and to be expected from their relative positions on the quadrant model, upper class Conservatives are less 'liberal' than upper class neutrals, but the relative difference between the classes is clear. 'Capitalism' comes first in importance as a reason for their adherence in all three classes. But support for the liberalism and individualism of the Conservatives is second in importance for the upper class, last for the intermediate class, and not present at all amongst lower class Conservatives! In fact the intermediate class in this case are quite hard to characterize. They demonstrate less concern for specific policies than the upper class (tax policy being the only policy reason to stand out in their top few mentioned), and the reasons tend to be very vague. This class seems moved by a set of general social values or an approval of the Conservatives' general competence on all policy issues. Perhaps most important in a way, there is a general feeling that the Tories 'stand for the interests of the people like the respondent'. Analysis of data like this from the surveys in the sixties often threw up this sort of generalized identity with a party, most often for the working class support of the Labour Party. This case, intermediary social class support for the Conservatives, is the only one to appear in our analysis. It may well reflect the uncertainties of such voters, nearly all of whom are socially mobile, in an ambiguous class context.

Lower class Conservatives give a list almost entirely of policies as reasons for supporting the party, with law and order fairly high on that list, along with housing policy and trade unions. For only the second time in this analysis, mere approval of the leadership appears as a reason for liking the party. Noticeably again, education policy is present only for the upper class and housing policy only for the lower. Bluntly, only the upper class is to gain by a policy of strengthening public schools and selective education, only the lower class stand to gain by a policy of selling council houses to tenants. But why should trade union reform be more important to the class most likely to be unionists and so much less important to the upper class? After all, one of the primary social values attached to such reform, the support for individualism and liberty, is only important to the upper class. The whole pattern is again one of a contrast in authoritarianism, a contrast between different ways of being right-wing, and a class-based concentration on pragmatic interest politics as opposed to intellectual generalizations between the classes.

The reasons given by Labour Party supporters (table 6.2c) for liking the Conservative Party are unreliable, as already explained. They do, however, point out quite sharply how little any social class or political category is immune to some of the concerns of the opposition supporters. It may well be that only the most obvious, even crass, appeals of the opposition can elicit support from another party's loyalists. These are likely to be important especially when they occur in areas where one's own party cannot effectively compete. Certainly it is intriguing to find 'law and order' and tax policy

TABLE 6.2c Reasons for liking the Conservative Party:
Labour supporters

Upper class	Intermediate class	Lower class
Support for some aspect of capitalism or *laissez-faire* Law and order policy Other social values Tax policy	Law and order policy General policy competence Tax policy Social service policy	Law and order policy Tax policy Support for some aspect of capitalism or *laissez-faire* Race relations or immigration policy Trade union policy Housing policy

of vital interest to Labour loyalists in all classes, and even to find 'capitalism' of varying but high importance in two of the three classes. There is no absurdity here, in fact. The most loyal of upper class Socialists can be forgiven for being irritated perhaps with some aspects of state economic regulation and therefore be sneakingly attracted to unrepentant capitalism in some small way. Perhaps precisely that class least likely, in general, to allow authoritarian tendencies on law and order to decide its voting is going to be the one most likely to admit to seeing such a policy attractive in a party they have never supported. Certainly the lower class Labour supporters, people every bit as left-wing as their upper class brethren, demonstrate their position in the *lower* left-hand quadrant, the illiberal left quadrant, by listing trade union policy, law and order policy and race relations policy as reasons for liking the Conservatives, along with the specific lower class-interest housing policy.

Impressionistic though such data and its analysis must be, these three tables give a strong support for the overall characterization of the interaction between class, party and two-dimensional model of political orientation.

The Labour Party data is somewhat less interesting because it was inevitably more a matter of commenting on the track record of a recently defeated government. One or two points do arise that are worth brief comment. Starting with table 6.3a, those who are politically neutral are reported.

The first obvious point is the way in which the Labour Party's image as standing for the interests of the working class (or, often,

TABLE 6.3a Reasons for liking the Labour Party:
political neutrals

Upper class	Intermediate class	Lower class
Supports working class	Supports working class	Supports working class
Social services record	Pensions record	Pensions
Stands for socialism	General policy record	General policy record
General policy record	Record on inflation	Social services record
Leadership	Other social values	Record on inflation
		Leadership

for 'ordinary people') stands out. This is presumably by contrast with some feeling that the Conservatives remain a party of privilege. Not only the first table dealing with the political neutrals shows this; virtually every part of every table does, and usually as one of the one or two most important single issues. Just as unlikely people such as upper class Labour loyalists regarded capitalism as one of the reasons for liking the Conservative Party, Labour appeals as the party of socialism for the upper class neutrals. We also find again a preference for the concrete rather than for ideologies as one goes down the class ladder.

The equivalent table for Conservative supporters (table 6.3b) also shows some vague adherence to socialism present to some extent as a reason for liking the party. This goes along with a stress on the welfare side of socialism in the approval of Labour's record on social services and pensions. One must remember, however, the tendency of

TABLE 6.3b Reasons for liking the Labour Party:
Conservative supporters

Upper class	Intermediate class	Lower class
Leadership	Leadership	Supports working class
Social services record	Supports working class	General policy record
Pensions record	Stands for socialism	Leadership
Stands for socialism	Social services record	Social services record
Supports working class	Pensions record	Pensions record
Other social values		

the lower class also to approve of Conservative policy on the social services (Goldthorpe *et al.*, 1968; Robertson, 1976a, ch. 2). Again, also, there is a greater importance attached to a general simple support for the working class, which combines with an absence of any approval amongst the lower class Conservative loyalists for socialism as a general ethic. What does appear in both these tables is the approval of Labour leadership. Probably nothing much should be made of this, however, as it was, after all, a party that had been in office for some years, and the sheer impact of government publicity must have contributed. It is important only in the negative — overall it is the leadership of the party rather than almost any policy achievement, and at times more than any ideology, that attracts those who are not loyalists.

TABLE 6.3c Reasons for liking the Labour Party: Labour supporters

Upper class	Intermediate class	Lower class
Supports working class	Supports working class	Supports working class
Stands for socialism	General policy record	Record on inflation
General economic policy	Pensions record	General policy record
Other social values	Stands for people like us	Stands for people like us
Social services record	Stands for socialism	Pensions record
		Social services record

This overall impression is even further strengthened when we look at the reasons given for liking Labour by their own habitual supporters in table 6.3c. Leadership ceases to attract anyone, but that may well be natural when it is one's own party one is thinking about. Something slightly less natural is the way that socialism fails to get into the list of reasons given by the party's natural, or 'core', supporters, by which I mean Labour loyalists from the lower class. Not only is socialism an important reason to the upper class loyalists, but so is the party's general economic policy and record — both implying a more ideological support than any other group gives. But for the lower class three 'reasons for liking' dominate: pensions policy, social services generally, and the sheer fact of supporting the working class. Here, though, we must add another phenomenon, mentioned briefly when talking of the intermediary class Conservative supporters. There is a clear feeling amongst Labour loyalists in both the intermediate and lower classes that the party is a natural supporter for people in their position or social location, over and above those who state a similar idea in terms of supporting a particular class.

What one deduces from this mass of rather complicated data is very much up to the reader. A few things seem clear — the Labour Party is seen as operating in a rather simple world where its (traditional?) function of looking after 'ordinary people', 'people like me', 'the workers', and doing so especially by providing pensions and social services, is all important. There is very little trace of ideological support for Labour anywhere, except perhaps in the upper social classes where the ideology is somewhat quixotic. Nor does it appear to have a placing anywhere on the liberalism/illiberalism dimension. In terms of party competition, we get an oddly asymmetrical picture of the parties; the Conservative Party is approved of for a host of reasons, some none too creditable, maybe. But the Labour Party seems to depend still on a very narrow, if very powerful, message which makes it, in some ways, very hard to locate either in my own four-quadrant model, or indeed in any imaginable ideological model.

The open-ended data told us as much about the worries, and therefore the ideological placings, of voters as it did about the parties. But one does seem to have an image, or rather a set of images, about the Conservative Party, as well as a fairly clear class model of political attitudes and concerns from all voters, as demonstrated by their hopes from that party. Similar data on the Labour Party tells us much less. In part this may be an inevitable result for a recently defeated party of government for whom the perceived record rather than possible hopes may be most important. But it also suggests that in important ways the Labour Party has lost any clear-cut ideological image for the British electorate. Rather more will emerge from the next chapter where I pursue the opinions that have so far been aggregated into the quadrant model in separate detail. As almost a footnote to this chapter I can follow up insights into class and party concerns with a second set of data about the salience of issues and policies.

Many of the detailed policy attitude questions to be discussed in the next chapters were ones where a full assessment of responses really required a measure of how important the issues were anyway. It would, for example, be rather stupid to attach much importance to a huge difference in attitude on issue X between class–party groups were it the case that almost the whole sample thought the issue of only trivial importance. So most such attitude questions were followed by another, rather precise, question of this general form, 'When you were thinking about voting, how important was the question of "X": very important, fairly important, not very important?' Substitute, for example, 'the question of tougher laws to control the unions', or 'the question of nationalization' and so on. Averaging these answers over class–party categories gives us the relative salience to the voters of those issues the researchers thought to ask about. Perhaps the wrong issues were often mentioned. Certainly the data do not have the immediacy of the open-ended questions. But it is another way to put some more direct flesh on the quadrant model. The respondent cannot easily avoid answering any question put to him, and cannot at all stop me adding his answers to others to make up some scale I believe in, but which is totally foreign to him. But he can put in a corrective by effectively saying that some question refers to an issue he could not give a damn about. Collectively the sub-samples can force our attention to issues they care about a great deal, when I might have good theoretical reasons for leaving them out. So, briefly, we can consult again the respondents' own senses of what is vital in table 6.4.

Table 6.4 gives the rank ordering of nine major issues in terms of how respondents ranked them in importance inside the nine party-class families. Thus the upper class who are politically neutral, for example, regarded the problem of strikes as most important, followed, with equal importance, by the problem of law and order, and the question of the relative desirability of tax cuts versus public expenditure cuts. Equally least important for this upper class group

TABLE 6.4 Relative importance of major issues to nine class-party groups

Class: Party: Issue	Upper			Intermediate			Lower		
	N.	Con.	Lab.	N.	Con.	Lab.	N.	Con.	Lab.
Strikes	1	2	4	3	1=	4	4=	2	5=
Unemployment	6	6	2	4=	5=	2=	2=	7=	1
Law and order	2=	1	5=	1=	1=	1	1	1	2=
Social services	7=	8	3	6=	8=	7	6	5	5=
Taxes	2=	4=	1	1=	4	2=	2=	3=	2=
Nationalization	7=	4=	9	8=	5=	9	9	6	9
EEC	7=	9	7=	8=	8=	5=	7=	9	7
Wage controls	4=	7	5=	4=	7	5=	4=	7=	2=
Trade union laws	4=	3	7=	6=	3	8	7=	3=	8

were the issues of social service expenditure, nationalization, and membership of the European Community. As the precise scores are obviously subject to meaningless narrow fluctuations, it makes more sense to look at the most and least important few issues to each group.

One point of caution — the scorings indicate the importance of an issue, and not the policy preferred on it. Sometimes this is unimportant — no one who thinks 'law and order' is important (and eight of nine groups do) is anything but in favour of it! But other issues are clearly partisan. Obviously, however, the relatively high importance of social service expenditure to the upper class Labour family, and its unimportance to upper class Conservative loyalists combines with a directional effect. Those who think the question of expenditure on the social services is important want such expenditure, whilst those indifferent to it are also against expanding it.

Part of the message of any such table is usually the high consensus on relative importance or insignificance of issues that comes out. For example, 'law and order', as already mentioned, features amongst the first three areas for all but one group, whilst membership of the European Community is amongst the three least important issues for every group except intermediate Labour loyalists. Even near unanimity can indicate something of interest, however, in the deviant cases. The best example, and the most useful for my purpose, in this table is the question of nationalization of industry. Though to the layman, and some journalists, nationalization is almost definitional of 'left-wing' approaches to economics, it has not been highly regarded by the electorate for a generation. In this table nationalization is amongst the three least important issues for all but three groups. Even the two most 'left-wing' groups on matters of socio-economic radicalism, the upper and lower class Labour loyalists, put it ninth out of nine! But it is the fourth most important issue to the upper class Conservatives, and the fifth and sixth to the other two Conservative groups. Rather than support for nationalization characterizing 'left' views, opposition to such policies, even when hardly advocated by the Labour Party, is partially definitional of 'right-wing' views. Similarly 'law and order' features so strongly as a concern for the vast majority of the electorate as to be useless in telling us anything about group differences. But precisely this fact helps make still clearer the nature of the upper left-hand quadrant of our map, the 'liberal' and 'left' quadrant. There is only one group inhabiting that area, as I have shown, the upper class Labour family. They are the only group not to be highly concerned by the law and order issue. In both what does and what does not concern them one can see their overall ideology splendidly delineated. Their three strongest concerns are exactly those they will be least affected by in practice. Expansion of the social services does not rank better than sixth for any other non-lower class group, yet it is third for the upper class Socialists. Unemployment is mainly a concern only of Labour loyalist groups or lower class groups, for obvious reasons – and the Labour loyalty of the upper class Labour family leads to it being their second most important issue. Only on the issue of tax cuts versus public expenditure cuts does this family put an issue in the same perspective as most other groups and the rest of its class. Yet while upper and intermediate political neutrals, along with others, see the issue as equally important, they are in favour of cutting taxes, whilst the upper class Labour family wants to protect public expenditure at the cost of retaining high tax rates. The family is, in fact, more radical, in economic terms, than any other group, though also most liberal.

The two families most typical of the upper right quadrant, economically Conservative but socially liberal, have very similar profiles. These are the upper class neutrals and Conservatives, who combine, in their top few worries, many of the same things, but especially a concern about strikes (and law and order, which is partly the same thing in the historic context). Although only the Conservatives actually put the separate question of the need for stronger legal controls over trade unions into their top three issues, it is fourth in importance to political neutrals in the upper class. Yet this extreme concern about trade union control does not get out of the 'least important three' issues for any other non-Conservative group. The 'liberalism' of this quadrant does not show up in the particular data we have here, but its socio-economic conservatism most certainly does. Note, for example, that unemployment only ranks as a non-serious worry otherwise to Conservative loyalist groups.

The other patterns give similar support to what we have seen of the ideological positioning of the party–class families, whether from structured data as used to derive the four-quadrant exposition, or the 'open-ended' data from spontaneously given reasons for 'liking' the parties. The pragmatic aspects show, as they did with the 'likes' – lower class Conservatives may echo other Conservatives in their concern about strikes and trade union controls, which are not shared with other members of their class. But they also care greatly about the social services, which the other two class groups in their party relegate to eighth place. Amongst political neutrals 'unemployment' rises from sixth, to fourth, and then to second, place as one moves down the three rungs of the class ladder. At the same time concern over union activities, whether measured by the seriousness attached to strikes or to the need for legal controls over unions monotonically diminishes.

Finally, one group which ought, in a sense, to be typical of the overall population, those cut out of the forces that shape our politics by being outside a political family and ambivalent in class position, is the intermediate class political neutrals. Their salience ordering, allowing for ties, is exactly the same as the population total, putting tax cuts, law and order, and strikes as the first three issues, and social services, trade union laws, the EEC and nationalization as the four least important matters.

From three different sorts of evidence, then, we can see the ideological nature as the internal homogeneity of the nine possible class and family groupings, and especially the four corner-stone groups. We can see both class and partisanship working independently to structure the views, emotive reactions, and issue salience perceptions of these ideological entities in a complex, yet comprehensible way. Their views are disaggregated if looked at with a single-class model, and imperfectly homogenous inside purely partisan columns. But put these two forces together, accepting that many people do not have secure identities either in class or partisanship, and a much clearer picture emerges. The next chapter takes a series of specific issues and examines the interplay of class and partisanship along the two basic dimensions of socio-economic radicalism and social liberalism to detail this ideological topography further.

7

Class, Partisanship and Political Culture

Although the figures and graphs of the previous chapters have made it clear that the nine 'political families' or class-party groupings must be differentiated in terms of ideology, I have stuck, so far, to a rather abstract level. If we want to grasp what the political cultures, the general set of values and policy preferences are that go with such social groupings, we need to get below this abstract level, and to show with much more concreteness just what is believed. Or, to be more precise, if I want to argue that nine groups defined by two classes, two partisanships, and the intermediary positions on both of these dimensions represent real political entities, there are two tasks I must accomplish. I must first be able to give relatively detailed 'profiles' of the beliefs of the groups, especially in terms of how particular distributions of beliefs deviate from national attitude patterns. Secondly I must demonstrate that *both* social class and partisanship contribute to these characteristic profiles.

The best route to these twin aims is to examine a fairly large number of specific aspects of public opinion. In all, some 25 public opinion questions are used in this chapter, all drawn from the 1979 British Election Study survey. They range over a very wide area of public opinion. Some represent attitudes and policy preferences on highly concrete issues: Should council houses be sold to their tenants? Fairly consensual matters where party policies tend to be about only marginal differences: Should social services or the NHS have more money spent on them? And concrete policies which, although now largely settled, still occasion political heat: Should grammar schools be replaced by comprehensives?[1] They take in also very general, though very real, matters of long-term political aims still, arguably, unsettled in British politics (the desirability

159

of further wealth redistribution, the need for income systems that reward skill). They cover issues of a vital constitutional nature (the need for reform of the House of Lords, the proper government attitude to cooperation with the EEC). Finally a set of issues of great emotional importance, outside the usually agreed areas of party competition are included, touching on such matters as the return of the death penalty and the general imposition of tougher criminal law penalties, and attitudes to coloured immigration. Very little of what is important in British politics, whether in those areas approved of by the political elites or merely deeply felt by the population, are outside the coverage. With such a range, most important sub-cultural differences should be caught, at least crudely, and with so many, a roughly reliable outline of the cultures ought to be present.

It is very difficult, however, to canvass such a range of opinion questions without drowning the reader, and the author, in detail so repetitive as to risk losing all sense of any emerging picture. In addition, without some base line to guide us, it is impossible to know when a particular belief characteristic of a group, is important. So what, one might say, if 50 per cent of intermediate class 'non-aligned' voters are not opposed to repatriation of immigrants? Is this a lot or a little? The answer is that it is not a lot, when one knows that it almost exactly matches the figure for the population as a whole. Thus, for that particular group, the attitude to the repatriation of immigrants is not particularly useful as an ideological characterization. But does this argument work? The group may be so evenly spread that its members have a more or less equal chance of taking either view. This may be true of the population as a whole, and yet the fact that politically neutral members of the intermediate social class are in this position may make them stand out as very unusual compared with any other group. This is because the overall national attitude could be the result of sharply divergent views held by roughly equal proportions of the population. We need to keep in mind several different comparisons when considering what is both important and characteristic of a social group. For my purposes there are three main comparisons: first, how does one particular group compare with the population generally? This is especially important, as above, in determining whether a split in attitude preference is likely to mean indifference or great salience. The danger is that of thinking either that a 50:50 split in itself implies that the issue is pretty irrelevant, or that, say, a 90:10 split automatically means it is clearly an issue of great moment. Either, or neither, could be true.

If a social group is split 50:50 on an issue where the normal population split is very lopsided, the very fact of apparent indifference may
indicate something unusual about the politics of that group.[2]

The second and third comparisons I need to make are with opinion
distribution with other groups on the two dimensions I am using to
categorize the population. In this example, how do intermediary class
voters from Conservative and Labour partisanship groups react to
repatriation of immigrants? The answer here is, in a very similar way.
Throughout the intermediate class, attitudes are split fairly evenly.
Then, of equal importance, how do political neutrals in other classes
react? With this example, it is the latter comparison that pays off.
Surely it tells us a good deal about both the lower class neutrals
and the upper class neutrals if we know that, in the upper class,
political neutrals have odds of two to one against tolerating the idea
of repatriation, but it is even money what attitude is taken amongst
their political allies below them in the class order? The full analysis
of this single issue, in fact, helps not only to begin to characterize
each group, but to indicate a general position about class and politics
in the shaping of political cultures. I shall shortly run through the
issue in full detail as an example of how opinion attitude information
can be used in a task like the one set for this chapter.

I must first make clear one point of analytic perspective, and at the
same time explain a simplifying technique I use throughout this chapter to describe distributions of political attitudes. Saying that about
50 per cent of the members of the politically neutral intermediate
class are opposed to repatriation whilst 50 per cent are not, does not
mean that most members of that group take a moderate or indifferent position. I am talking, throughout this book of 'rates' of opinion
in a social aggregate, not about individuals. There is, in fact, no other
way one can go about social science research of this kind, but accepting the fact as also theoretically valid, even necessary, distinguishes
me as much nearer to the dominant *sociological* mode of thinking
than many political scientists. No statement I make can be taken to
represent a position about how any individual behaves, or what he
thinks. At the most I can only be read as talking about the probabilities of certain attitudes being held in a particular group. In fact,
opinion is spread quite widely on the repatriation issue amongst
intermediary neutrals. About 17 per cent think it is very important
that immigrants should be 'sent home', nearly a quarter think that it
is equally important that they should not, and 14 per cent even take
the improbable view that it does not matter either way.

The choice of cutting point to produce a 'for and against' distinction is mine. In this case I have lumped those who are indifferent with those who are in favour of repatriation. This is because of what seem to me good intuitive grounds regarding the likely consequence of holding such views. It might be that some other division is valid, but the overall impact would be much the same. Because, despite being concerned with 'rates' as to what can and should be analysed, I am no more indifferent to consequences, and no less involved in the impact of individuals, than would be any social scientist who took a different view. The easiest way to see this is to think in terms of the attitudinal impact on a member of the group who has not yet made up his mind on the issue. He may, for example, be an adolescent as yet too young to vote. If these groupings are sociologically real, the group attitude distribution will have a major impact on the individual's attitude formation. That is, in major part, what a social scientist means by talking about a group culture or peer group influence. Similarly someone inclined, perhaps, to change his social attitudes will be encouraged or discouraged in direct relationship to the group distribution. In this particular example the adolescent, or the politically unsure, will, on average, come across just as many people who wish to repatriate as he will those who are opposed to such policies. The likelihood of his forming one or other opinion because of peer group pressure (or parental influence, perhaps) is itself going to be about even. He may hold to whatever view he takes with greater or lesser passion, but his holding any one view on this issue is going to be a matter much less of his membership of the politically neutral intermediary class than would be the case with a much more lopsided attitude split. His opinion can neither increase any sense of identification, nor act to cut him off from a politically neutral stand, nor lead him to identify with the upper or lower class to anything like the same extent that holding a clearly deviant opinion, or accepting a strong group consensus, might.

For these and other reasons I proceed to analyse group rates, and do it entirely in terms of dichotomies, of groups tending towards one or other of two sides on an issue. With more space to spare, the sociological importance of binary opinion distributions could also be called into play in justification. Here there is a reason of expository convenience as well. Rather than quoting endless and complex percentages, I use, in describing an opinion distribution, the simplest and most intuitively plausible of mathematical tools, the idea of 'odds'. Where, as in the case I started from, roughly half of a group hold each of two opinions, the odds are 50:50, or 'evens'. (Arithmetically we can say the odds are $1:1$, or just 1.) Had 200 people believed in repatriation and only 50 been opposed, the 'odds on' supporting repatriation would have been 4:1 on (or, for simplicity, just 4). Given 130 people in favour, and 245 against, the odds on favouring repatriation would have been 130/245, or odds on of 0.53. The only reason this latter figure looks unusual is that, in ordinary gambling parlance, we would reverse the ratios and talk of the 'odds against'. These would be 245/130, or odds against repatriation of about 1.9:1 (that is, the odds against are roughly 2:1). This very simple and 'ordinary life' way of thinking about rates of opinion distribution allows for much more convenient description of sub-cultural opinions. To be told, for example, that an upper class Conservative has odds of 4:1 against supporting military cuts, 9:1 on thinking we have too many immigrants in Britain, and 3:1 on in favour of restoring the death penalty, gives an immediate picture, and one very quickly written and read, compared with looking at three tables of percentages. The less familiar looking odds should be equally plausible. The odds *against* thinking that more money should be spent on the NHS, for upper class Conservatives, are 1.5:1 (better than evens, not as strong as two to one against!). Wherever there is any doubt, remember that odds of greater than evens on some attitude are numbers bigger than 1, that 1 (which represents evens) is 1:1, and that numbers below 1 are odds against. (Usually the text will make it clear; but where confused, consult the Appendix on log-linear models at the end.) These simple measures are the basis for the much more complex-looking, and very powerful, statistical tests known as log-linear models which I have used already, and will use extensively in this chapter.[3]

I conclude this introductory section by giving a detailed analysis of attitudes to repatriation across all nine groups, relying on the idea of a group opinion 'rate', and using odds to explain what is happening. Table 7.1 gives the odds for or against supporting repatriation for the groups.

In this table, and for much of the chapter, I shall treat odds that deviate from evens only very slightly (that is, from odds against of 0.9 to odds on of 1.1) as though they were in fact evens, indicating that the group in question has no marked tendency, *as a group*, to take up any particular position. Given that, we can see immediately that the whole of the intermediate social class, of whatever or no political faith, is essentially neutral on the question of repatriation. In a general sense, any two members interviewed at random should produce one person in favour of each side. Thus it cannot have, as a class, any general predisposition towards or against this form of

TABLE 7.1 The odds on favouring repatriation of immigrants for nine class-party groups

| | Party | | |
Class	Conservative	Neutral	Labour
Upper	0.58 (1.7 : 1 against)	0.45 (2.2 : 1 against)	0.39 (2.6 : 1 against)
Intermediate	0.98 (1.1 : 1 against)	1 : 1	1 : 1
Lower	1.7 : 1	1.2 : 1	1.2 :

Notes:
1. For the whole sample: odds 'on' favouring repatriation were 0.90. This is equivalent to odds 'against' of 1.1 : 1, or, roughly, evens.
2. The relevant log-linear model with class and party effects fitted is easily significant, leaving only a residual chi square of 2.5, with 4 degrees of freedom. There is therefore no need to fit an interaction term, but both class and party variables are needed to get a significant fit.

racialism. The most obvious implication of the table is, in fact, that attitudes to repatriation are class related. No group in the upper class fails to be opposed to repatriating immigrants, with odds ranging from just below 2 : 1 against to well above that. Very roughly, of every three upper class voters, two should turn out to be opposed to this policy. The lower class is in general, though more marginally, in favour of the policy — odds on of 1.2 : 1 means roughly that about 55 per cent of the group would favour repatriation.

The second clear aspect in the table is that partisanship also plays a notable role in forming attitudes on the issue *outside* the intermediary class. Although upper class Conservatives have odds against favouring repatriation, this is by no means as clearly so as with upper class neutrals, and they in turn have less chance of being opposed than do the small minority of Labour loyalists in the upper class. Amongst the lower class, Conservatives are again rather more prone to favour repatriation than are either the politically neutral or the loyal Labour group.

Although the actual differences in the odds in this table are not stark (or anywhere near as great as in some areas to be analysed), the impression is that two separate effects, of class and partisanship, are at work. More rigorous testing of just these relationships, with the relevant log-linear model, confirms this. Both social class and partisanship show a statistically significant correlation with the pattern of odds, and, furthermore, both are needed to explain the table. In this case social class is considerably the more powerful in accounting for the pattern. Finally, the *only* model needed is the additive one. If one predicts the pattern on the assumption that there is a class effect, and a party effect, and that they are not intercorrelated themselves, the fit is so good as to leave no variation from the observed odds that could not arise from random error. Another way of putting this important, if obscure, fact is to say that the effect of class on attitude is of the same magnitude inside each of the three party orientations, and, *vice versa*, the effect of party is of the same size inside each class. This is by no means always so, and the presence or absence of interaction in these terms is an important difference in my interpretation of the political cultures. But that comes later. For the time being we can say that higher class and more 'left-wing' politics both lead to less desire to repatriate immigrants.

In itself this may not be a surprising fact. But remembering also the actual odds, I can go on to suggest that racialism is not, despite the party impact, a characteristic of upper class conservatism (the odds are against), but it is, if only marginally, an aspect of lower class socialism as a political culture. An alternative way of arguing much the same thing, which I develop with later examples, is this. On this particular issue, political and class impacts are opposed to each other. That is, given some basic assumption that 'right-wing' positions and 'higher' social location go together, there are cross pressures on the members of the two traditional groups in class-political models, the upper class Conservatives and the lower class left-wingers. The pressures partially counter each other. Upper class Conservatives are less keen on repatriation than their conservatism would predict, and more keen on it than their class position would imply. The opposite applies to lower class Labour loyalists. The consequence of this is to reduce the contrast between the two 'deviant' cases. For the conservatism and the lower class status of the 'deviant' lower class Tory, and the socialism and upper class position of its equivalent, the 'deviant' upper class, reinforce each other. This again is a common pattern contributing to the construction of party–class group cultures. Finally, as would be expected in a case where class was the major predisposing factor, the intermediate social class is exactly that — intermediate. They have 50:50 odds on the issue which seem also to reduce the partisan difference, for the odds in all three groups are the same. Again, this turns out to be characteristic of their culture. Thus the actual 'indifference' of their position may actually be part of the culture, as a result of cross pressures from class ambiguity being increased in impact from the latent cross pressures of the class and party forces in the model.

I have gone into greater detail on this single issue than I can in general to make clear the technique of analysis. As it happens, much of what the rest of this chapter argues is already partially visible in the data for this one issue.

7.2 THE TWO POLAR CULTURES AND ISSUES OF SOCIAL DISTRIBUTION

I start immediately by giving an overall characterization, again largely in the language of odds, of the two traditional components of the class politics model, the ones who should be maximally opposed, upper class Conservative loyalists and lower class loyal Labour followers. In the example in section 7.1 the opposition between the two was muted because of the cross pressuring of class and partisanship as predisposing factors. As we shall see, whilst this is not very unusual, it is not the normal case. The theory that leads us to assume that these two groups are maximally opposed is simple. If there is any single long-term ideological constant to political conflict between the Conservative and the Labour Parties it centres round equality. The Labour Party has always stood, historically, for increased equality in both economic and power terms, whilst the Conservative Party has championed the existing power and economic distributions in British society as being, at core, inevitable, desirable, or both. At the same time, social class positions produce natural reasons for finding one's self-interest involved in either maintaining or opposing such inequalities. Thus issues which touch on questions of distribution should be subject to reinforcing predisposing forces. To be either Conservative or upper class should lead towards pro-hierarchy attitudes, and to be both should lead to intensively inegalitarian views.

An easy way to see if there is anything in this thesis is to look over the issues and pick the ones with the sharpest skew of opinion for each group in which we are interested. Not all strongly-felt issues are immediately useful to us here, though. To make the most of the contrast between the two groups, we want to select issues on which upper class Conservatives and lower class Labour loyalists *both* experience odds a good way from 50:50. Secondly we need issues in which the odds are reversed, displaying the greatest amount of conflict. Arbitrarily I choose only issues in which upper Conservatives and lower Labour are seen to have odds of around two to one (or more) on the issue. There are five major examples of such a pattern amongst the 25 or so issues on which suitable data exists. These are: (1) social services should be reduced; (2) welfare expenditure has 'gone too far'; (3) the government should redistribute wealth; (4) comprehensive schools should replace grammar schools; (5) building land should be controlled by the government. There are others of great interest for the analysis of group ideologies which do not fit this restriction, and some will be analysed in detail later. In particular one question demonstrates how complex it may be to attribute *either* ideology *or* class interest unequivocally, namely the policy espoused in 1979 by the Conservative Party of selling council houses. But at this stage five issues of such importance are enough for my purpose.

It should be immediately apparent that all five issues most directly have to do with equality and social distribution. While this is implicit in the argument I have given for expecting reinforcement of class on party to produce polarity between upper class Conservative and lower class Labour groups, the substantive criterion was deliberately not built into the selection test of issues to look at. Rather, looking for the sharpest contrasts between the two groups immediately throws up precisely these issues. There is, sadly, no less laborious way to proceed now than discussing the detailed distribution of odds, and the statistical models needed to fit them, for each of these issues. Although my principal concern at this stage is with the two polar groups of orthodox class politics models, table 7.2 gives the details of odds for each of the nine groups on the first issue.

TABLE 7.2
Odds for or against the reduction of the social services

Class		Party	
	Neutral	Conservative	Labour
Upper	1.4	3.5	0.54
Intermediate	1.3	2.7	0.63
Lower	0.86	2.1	0.50

Note: The log-linear model to fit this data requires both class and party before an adequate fit is achieved. These two variables explain the data so that there only remains a chi square of 2.2, with 4 degrees of freedom. Consequently no interaction term is required, and the data can be treated as the result of the two additive effects.

I take the question of reducing the social services first, because it turns out to be one of the simplest to discuss. The immediate point about polarity between upper Conservatives and lower Labour is safely shown. The highest odds in favour of reduction are those of the upper Conservative group, which is well over three to one in favour of the proposal. The group most opposed to the policy is, indeed, lower Labour, whose odds of 0.5 are equivalent to odds of two to one against the issue. The reason for choosing this as the first example is that it is the characteristic of most of these sorts of issues in its *general* pattern. To start with, both class and party work well as predictors, in a way that shows up with the application of the log-linear significance test (brief comments on which are appended to each of these tables). As this test confirms, both party and class have significant correlations with attitude to social services, even when one is 'controlled' for the other. In fact, looking at the table would lead one to expect this. More or less (but neither exactly nor always), two patterns emerge. Not only are the two groups which are polarized by both class and party the furthest apart. But also this arises because: (1) inside each class, approval of reducing social services follows a clear left–right spectrum, with the Conservatives most keen, the neutrals second, and Labour least keen. (2) Inside each party, approval of this attitude follows a class dimension, with the higher class being more in favour of reducing social services than the one next below it. If it were generally true that British political sub-cultures followed exactly as the simple model would suggest, taking class and party to be well formed, polarizing, and mutually consistent forces, the cells in this and other tables would follow exactly this pattern. Equivalent data for a similar proposition in table 7.3, where the proposition that 'welfare expenditure has gone too far', almost replicates this table. The flaw in the perfect model is that the odds against cutting welfare or social services, *inside the Labour column*, do not neatly fit. To be sure, in both cases (and in virtually every example of an issue involving distribution), the lower Labour group have the position most in favour of redistribution; but not only are the differences amongst the three class groups for Labour seldom very great, but the group that might be expected regularly to be least in favour of redistribution, the upper Labour family, usually does not in fact take on that role.

Although this is anticipating somewhat, class turns out generally to be a poor, sometimes a useless, predictor of this sort of policy position amongst those committed to a Labour loyalty. To be more precise: if one tries to predict odds on questions of this nature only by knowing the class and not the party of the groups, most of the failure in prediction turns out to be caused in errors of predicting the three Labour class groups. Furthermore, the bulk of this is attributed to predicting the odds in the upper Labour group. Put in more direct language — upper class Labour loyalists are systematically too keen on redistribution-style policies for their class position. In this case, explaining attitudes to social service cuts, using only class, we find that 25 per cent of the total error in the model is attributed to the upper Labour group. Here, instead of the actual odds of around 1.9 *against* cuts, we would predict, on the strength of its class position alone, odds of 1.8 : 1 *in favour of* such reductions! The other two Labour groups together only account for a further 24 per cent of the error. There are mistakes in the predicted odds, of course, but much fewer. Thus the lower Labour group, which is actually 2 : 1 against the cuts, would be expected, taking notice only of class, to be only 1.2 : 1 against them.

Party remains a vital tool for predicting other cells in the table. Upper Conservatives are actually more opposed to social service cuts than one would expect from their class alone, for example. But almost invariably the ordering of the three class groups inside the Conservative faith is predicted to be what one would expect from the simple model, and politically neutral groups are usually exceedingly well fitted by considering class alone. Final errors of prediction, when party stance and class are used, are nearly entirely attributable to the six party loyalty groups. The general point is simple, and to be stressed continually: the political sub-culture of the upper class Labour group is far more 'left-wing' than the admixture of party and class would suggest. With this important exception, not only do the two predictably opposed groups occupy the polar positions, where class and party reinforce, but the general structure of the data fits the notion of a simple interplay between two forces. Thus, for example, lower class Conservatives are more in favour of redistribution than other class groups of their political column, but also less in favour than other party groups of their class row. For them, the two pressures meet head on, subduing either impact. For Labour upper class people, party overcomes class, at least on this sort of issue. These issues are the bread and butter of British politics, represented by questions on which, as empirical chance as well as theory would have it, the class–party reinforced groups are most polarized. A quicker look at a very similar, but not identical, issue, where the data represent odds on agreeing that 'welfare expenditure' has 'gone too far' is offered by table 7.3.

Alternative Model of Class

TABLE 7.3 Odds on believing that welfare expenditure has 'gone too far'

Class	Party	Odds on such belief	Error when predicting by class alone (%)	Error when predicting by party alone (%)	Error when predicting with class and party (%)
Upper	Neutral	1.3	3	25	**
	Con.	2.9	19	18	17
	Lab.	0.57	22	1	32
Intermediate	Neutral	1.0	**	**	3
	Con.	2.1	12	4	8
	Lab.	0.65	8	9	30
Lower	Neutral	0.87	1	15	3
	Con.	1.7	17	21	7
	Lab.	0.46	17	7	**

Notes:
** = Less than 1 per cent.
1. The percentage error attributable to party groups when explaining only with class, for neutral, Con. and Lab. respectively: 4%, 48%, 48%. When using both: 6%, 32%, 62%.
2. The percentage error attributable to class groups when explaining only with party, for upper, intermediate and lower respectively: 44%, 13%, 43%. When using both: 49%, 41%, 10%.
3. The log-linear model fitting both class and party effects is significant with a chi square of 1.65, and 4 degrees of freedom. There is no interaction effect, and both main effects are needed for significance.

The first column of this table shows the odds, in the same way as for the social service reduction issue. Exactly the same pattern emerges, with both the political neutrals and the Conservatives having the odds arranged in class order, those in the higher class being more prepared to accept that welfare expenditure is excessive. Furthermore, inside each class group, the expected left–right ordering is preserved. But again, although the lower Labour group is the least persuaded of excessive welfare expenditure (and although the two theoretical polar elements, upper Conservative and lower Labour are the highest and lowest odds), the ordering of the upper and intermediate Labour groups is reversed.

The other columns in this table tell us a good deal more about what is happening, about how class and political loyalty intersect to create these typical group ideological differences. When one uses log-linear modelling to test whether or not particular factors, in this case class or party loyalty, are significantly correlated with a third variable (attitudes to welfare expenditure), one is trying to predict the odds and related ratios first with one, and then with another, variable.

Thus at any stage the procedure gives one predicted odds, to compare against the known actual odds. The difference between predicted and actual data render a measure of the total error involved in assuming, for example, that class alone can predict attitudes. This error can be partitioned over the actual entries, so that we can see easily what groups are least well accounted for. This is what the other three columns display.

The results in the second column show that class alone is not a very good predictor (though it does well enough to achieve clear statistical significance). Where it goes wrong is in predicting the attitudes of those who do have partisan loyalty, and especially amongst the upper class. Although there is little difference in the amount of error caused by trying to predict upper Conservatives and Labour on the assumption that their partisanship is irrelevant, the difference in *direction* of mistake is crucial. Upper class Conservatives turn out not to be as right-wing, in the predicted data, as they actually are. But this we would expect, given that the theoretical model here is one in which party and class both act, 'cooperatively' as it were. The partisanship pulls Conservatives even more towards their 'natural' anti-welfare position. Upper Labour, however, the group with the biggest error, are mistakenly predicted not just in strength, but direction of effect. That it is these people especially who are out of tune is confirmed by the rather low error rate associated with the other 'misplaced' Labour category. This is the intermediate class group, who appear, looking at the odds, to be too 'right-wing'. They are, in fact, probably quite close to a theoretical position — were it not that upper Labour are far too 'left-wing', these class intermediates would actually fit into the middle of a class array, as with the intermediate Conservatives. The other most striking thing about the error data is just how very well predicted are the three class groups of the political neutrals. From the odds column one can see that they fall into the right ordering; far more impressive is the fact that they account for only about 4 per cent of the total error. Clearly, where someone has no strong party loyalty, class is of vital importance in determining his position on such attitudes. One group, in particular, stands out. The predictability of the central group in the array, those with neither political loyalty nor a polarized class location, the intermediate political neutrals, are so well predicted by class that they contribute less than 1 per cent of the total error.

This fact leads to the other conclusion: looking at the intermediate Labour group in the situation where one forgets class entirely and assumes that only partisanship affects attitude, one sees an exactly similar result. They are predicted almost perfectly. But party, as a predictor, works very much less well than class for those who are not in the Labour set of families! The three Labour class groups collectively account for only 17 per cent of all the error in this model. Nearly 80 per cent of the mistakes we would make if we tried actually to predict attitude to welfare expenditure by knowing only whether someone was a political neutral, or adhered strongly to either of the major parties comes from four groups. We would go badly wrong in predicting neutrals and Conservatives in the upper and lower classes. In other words, to know merely that they were either neutral or Conservative would lead us badly astray because, for them, the fact of their class location is crucially important. This whole analysis can be summed up in two propositions: (1) class location is relatively unimportant in determining the attitudes (and therefore the general political culture) of those committed to socialism, principally because upper class Socialists are unaffected by social status pressure against their ideology; (2) those who, being without political homes, have no partisan cue for attitudes, are very largely in the hands of Britain's class structure. Perhaps an obvious, but telling, corollary is that those without either cue, whose political neutrality connects with an intermediate class position, the ones with a minimum of structuring, are predictable to a very high degree by *either* politico-social criterion.[4]

The final stress on the difficulty of locating those who adhere to the Labour loyalty is given in the last column. As it happens, class and partisanship combined are such splendid predictors of attitudes to this issue that, put together, they leave very little room for error. But, of what error inevitably remains, over 60 per cent belongs to two areas of mistake. The upper and intermediate Labour groups each account for nearly one-third of the mistakes one would make in assuming that the group odds derived from the intersection of class and partisanship. Upper class Labour supporters are irreducibly more Socialist than patterns derived from the rest of the population can quite account for.

The canons of academic argument, sensibly, do not allow an author to rest his case on two examples. So I must, briefly, review the patterns thrown up by the other three issues selected to demonstrate the contrast between upper class Conservatives and lower class Labour supporters. Having done that, we can switch our attention to the sort of issue where the really opposed groups are the two 'deviant' political cultures – Socialists of the upper class and Conservatives from the lower. The remaining issues in this section of the chapter do, however, introduce a further complexity — one which increases our sense that political cultures of complexly defined subgroups shape British politics. This is, statistically, the concept of 'interaction', which I have discussed in earlier chapters. Already, in their failure quite to fit a model, the upper and intermediate class groups with Labour loyalty have given a hint of how political cultures transcend 'additive' modelling. To be an upper class Socialist (and, to a much lesser extent, being a member of the upper class with a generally Conservative disposition) is, somehow, more than just being both of a certain class, and of a certain partisanship. So far, though, this departure from the model has been sufficiently slight not to produce error rates above those that could arise from random factors.

In the following tables, the departures from random error are too great for the model to 'fit'. In table 7.4 I examine attitudes to the whole question of social distribution when it is expressed so precisely: 'How important is it that the government should redistribute wealth — "very important", "quite important" . . . "very important that it should not".'

TABLE 7.4
Odds on believing that the government should redistribute wealth

| | Party | | |
Class	Neutral	Conservative	Labour
Upper	0.65	0.25	3.5
Intermediate	1.1	0.73	3.1
Lower	2.1	0.94	3.9

Note: The log-linear model fitting party and class leaves a chi square of 13.2 with 4 degrees of freedom. Thus although each of the party and class effects is significant, the model still requires the interaction between the two fully to fit the data.

Any answer to the effect that the government should redistribute is treated as supporting the policy — indifference and a view that it was at all important not to redistribute is treated as opposition. The entries in the nine cells give, in order: the actual 'observed' odds on being in favour of the policy; the 'predicted' odds from the full model where both class and party are being used to predict the odds ratios; and finally the percentage of the final error that can be attributed to that cell. This latter figure is especially useful with these three variables because it helps us to see where the deviation from the simple additive model principally occurs.

TABLE 7.5
Odds on believing that comprehensive schools should be established

Class	Party		
	Neutral	Conservative	Labour
Upper	0.68	0.21	3.1
Intermediate	1.1	0.27	4.3
Lower	1.7	0.52	2.9

Note: The model fitting both party and class leaves a chi square of 16.8 with 4 degrees of freedom. Thus although both the party and class effects are significant, the model still requires the interaction between them fully to explain the data.

In the same way, table 7.5 reports on the issue of comprehensive education. This is particularly important. Although by 1979 there were few grammar schools remaining in England, the symbolism of the issue was still as vital as it had been in the sixties, when a desire to replace grammar schools with mixed ability comprehensives had been such a good prediction of voting. Indeed the class and partisan rivalry on this issue is shown in table 7.5 unusually clearly.

Finally table 7.6 gives observed and predicted 'odds' in favour of the proposition that the government should 'control all building land'. This questionnaire item may well be rather badly drafted; it can tap a variety of attitudes and understandings, from a general approval of environmental planning to a belief in nationalization of land. Whatever various detailed meanings respondents may have seen, it clearly works as a rough guide to preferences for government intervention and control, with both partisan and class effects at work.

TABLE 7.6 Odds on believing that the government
should control all building land

Class	Party		
	Neutral	Conservative	Labour
Upper	0.67	0.24	2.8
Intermediate	1.2	0.54	3.3
Lower	1.7	1.1	3.0

Note: The model fitting both party and class effects leaves a chi square of 12.3 with 4 degrees of freedom. Thus although both the party and class effects are significant, the model still requires the interaction between them fully to explain the data.

There are differences of detail in these three tables, but the general picture is clear and consistent. The partisan effect is obvious amongst the Conservatives and the political neutrals, where for all three attitudes there is a simple monotonic increase in the odds on favouring 'left-wing' parties as one looks down the social scale. The neutrals shift from odds against redistribution to odds of 2:1 in favour between the upper and lower classes; from being nearly three to one against comprehensives to evens; from odds against land control to moderate odds 'on' this policy. Upper class Conservatives are four to one against redistribution, nearly eight to one against comprehensives, and four to one against land control, but their working class counterparts are less than half as hostile to comprehensivization, are at 'evens' on government control of building land, and 2:1 'on' on wealth redistribution. To see such marked differences inside loyal supporters of the same party, on such clear-cut and 'practical' issues, is very strong evidence for a class-based set of ideologies, even more so than seeing the same pattern amongst the political neutrals. These latter could, plausibly, be expected to respond to class simply because of the absence of a partisan cue.

The crucial difference is that the class effect is vastly attenuated, if not totally missing inside the Labour columns of these tables. The lower class Labour family does, in fact, marginally more strongly prefer redistribution than their upper class brothers, but the difference is only between favourable odds of 3.5:1 and 3.9:1, and a similarly trivial difference applies to governmental control of building land. On the question of comprehensivization the marginal difference is actually the other way round, with the upper class more likely to favour the abolition of grammar schools. On two of the issues it is in fact the intermediate class Socialists who have the greater disposition to favour the policies. One of these, land control, may not be particularly significant except to help make the general point of the absence of a clear class impact on left-wing attitudes. The other, comprehensive education, is not likely to be a data artifact. Here intermediate Socialists are more than three to one in favour of the abolition of the grammar schools, when both other classes fall to just over a 2:1 ratio. But this is almost certainly a real, and highly rational, policy/ideology difference. More than any other sector, intermediate class voters with a socialist orientation are the products of social mobility (see the analysis in chapter 5), and are likely to believe that the old secondary education system was a barrier to such success for others. They are more than likely themselves in fact to have their mobility precisely because of the old system, but that is no reason for their not holding the more firmly to the orthodox Labour Party analysis. In contrast Conservatively oriented inter-mediate class voters, probably with extremely similar experiences, have a reverse pattern. This is the only attitude on which the socially intermediate Conservatives are not roughly halfway between the upper and lower class Conservatives. But their conviction that it was the grammar schools that enabled talent to 'get ahead' gives them odds against comprehensivization of 8.3 : 1, slightly stronger than upper class Conservatives. The issue is not unique in modern politics, though there is nothing quite like it in the available data. It is a splen-did example of my general thesis, that both class and partisanship work together to form ideologies, and that they do so in complex ways where the exact situations of socio-political families can pro-duce highly differentiated policy preferences. These are sometimes specific to one or two families, but operate inside a general class–partisanship framework.

Evidence for the specificity of a class interest that can occur is given by another issue where an overall class and party model works, but with this sort of 'special interest' alteration. This is the issue of whether or not the government should arrange for the sale of council houses to tenants. Not only was this an issue of supposed salience in the 1979 election, certainly one the Conservatives gave great prominence to, but it has a history, as an issue, of causing problems for the Labour Party. The problem is that as an issue in the abstract, Socialists have always been opposed to this diminution in public housing stock. Working class voters, however, can be seen to like the idea as an apparently easy way to improve their social and economic standing. There is, therefore, a potential for cross pressuring here, not, as usual on this sort of issue, of the working class right but of the working class left. The data certainly show this. The group most in favour of selling council houses are the lower class Conservative loyalists. Indeed in all three parties there is a steady increase in sup-port for the policy across the three class sectors, with a much more marked slope inside the Labour column than the other partisanships. Upper class Labour supporters are more than twice as hostile to the policy as those in the lower class, whilst opposition amongst upper class Tories, at odds of 1.5 : 1, is only slightly stronger than amongst lower class Conservatives, who are just on the favourable side of evens. Thus we have again an example of how the general 'class interest plus partisan ideology' model can be modified by details of specific class interests with apparently rational voters.

The impact of partisanship is equally clear, and simpler. In each row of each table there is a simple, firm, and significant pattern. For all three classes on all three variables the obvious left–right ordering holds, with the political neutrals between the Conservatives on the right and Labour on the left. In itself it is neither surprising nor enlightening: it should be remembered, though, that this partisan effect subsists after controlling for class, and *vice versa*. With all three variables one needs both class and partisanship in the explanatory model, and both are statistically significant predictors.

But they are not enough. The fit of predicted odds ratios to the actual ones is good in all three cases using just class and party. It is never quite good enough — the residuals, or 'errors' in prediction are always too great to be put down just to random factors or error in measurement. Something is missing in the simple additive model, because the patterns are too complex, the political ideologies of the class–party families do not follow a neat addition theory, giving so many increments of 'leftness' for each class or party step. An example has already been discussed, where intermediate class Conservatives and Labour supporters were more extreme than they 'should have been' on the topic of comprehensive education. There will, of course, always be special cases like this, and by itself the comprehensive versus grammar school example would not be an important exception to a general additivity thesis. Nor would several *ad hoc* examples matter, with one or two class–party families 'out of line' for special and 'local' reasons. What we actually have here is different and significant because of its systematic regularity. One class–party family is always 'out of line': the upper class Labour cell in each of the tables is always too left-wing, accounting sometimes for nearly 50 per cent of the residual error. In fact the pattern goes back to the one consistently found in this chapter, which is the lack of a class pattern amongst the Labour supporters. There probably is one. Taking all the variables that have to do with the socio-economic radicalism or 'egalitarianism' dimension of politics, both those analysed here and many others, the lower class Labour group is almost always more 'left' than the intermediates, and more or less as 'left' as the upper class. Taken by itself, it is in the 'right position' in the predictions. The odd man out is the class that finds ideology far more powerful than class interest, the upper class Socialists. These are the people who, in chapter 6, threw up spontaneous reasons for liking the Labour Party that had nothing to do with their own utility maximization. They are the group also in chapter 6 who gave salience orderings to policy issues that were unlike any other group, and consisted of a heavy concern for other classes' economic interests. It is as though a class and party model fitted eight of the nine cells, and just that for one family the class factor not only did not work in the expected way, but reversed direction. Upper class Socialists are not simply unaffected by class interest, their socialism is not reduced by their social location. There is a group for whom the analogy is true — the other 'deviant' class, the lower class Conservatives, have their conservatism reduced by cross pressure following from class interest. This does not, on the whole, stop them being well predicted by the additive model. For upper class Socialists, however, the cross pressure thesis does not just fail to work. If anything, it goes into reverse. These upper class left-wingers are not as left-wing as the working class despite their different class interests. They are, often, *more* left-wing, and always are more left than they would be if class and partisanship intersected in a rational utility maximizing way.

Other cells contribute in varying ways to the need for interaction effects to be fitted to the predicting variables, but none so systematically or with such theoretical importance. The most important is the tendency of the upper class Conservatives to be more right-wing than would be expected; this is theoretically less challenging, however, fitting simply into the reinforcing versus cross pressuring contrast already developed in this chapter. To be a loyal Conservative is to be attracted to 'right-wing' policies. To be upper class is to have an economic interest in pursuing such policies, so that the intersection of the two not surprisingly pushes such voters slightly further than can be explained just by adding the two pressures together in a political parallelogram of force. This is not necessarily a very strong impact, however. On the issue of comprehensive education, for example, the simpler additive model predicts upper class Conservatives so well that there is no difference between observed and predicted odds — the cell makes a zero contribution to the residual error.

Basically the models deviate from the simple thesis according to a fairly simple pattern. Taking only the four 'core' cells, for people of clear-cut class and partisanship, two cells are more 'right-wing' than they would be were the world simply additive. Upper class Conservatives are pulled even more firmly in a rightwards direction. Their natural opposites, lower class Labour supporters, follow in this direction for different reasons — they are prevented from appearing in their own 'natural' position as the most left-wing party–class group because of the unnatural 'leftness' of the upper class Socialists. The other two cells are the deviant cases. For the upper class Socialists, social location — perhaps out of some guilt complex — actually intensifies the leftward pull of ideology rather than minimizing it. The lower class Conservatives suffer a perfectly natural cross pressuring from a clash between class interest and partisan polarity. The results are simple enough to understand, and the data are eloquent. Nonetheless we get four different patterns, four different effects and at least three different explanations for only four political families, and only two different structuring variables.

Vastly more data could be cited to back up this thesis, but the five policy questions studied are representative enough. The pattern is clear in each case, though the deviations are strong enough to require a statistical interaction term only in the last three. The socio-economic radicalism dimension, the dimension that takes egalitarianism and distribution of wealth and power as crucial to the meaning of 'left and right' is clearly affected by class.

The way in which this primary dimension is coloured by attitudes to the redistribution of power as well as wealth can be seen by considering the odds on favouring reform of the House of Lords, and on supporting the idea that 'workers should be given more say'. In the former, for example, the pattern of ratios is very much like the ones we have just considered. Not only does the class ordering inside the parties monotonically rise in favour of reform of the Lords as the respondent's class declines, not only is the expected left–right ordering across parties inside each class there, but so is the interaction effect. Again the upper class Conservatives are pulled even more to the right than one would expect, the working class Conservatives are cross pressured into being less supportive of the Lords, the upper class left is further left than it should be. Here, even though lower class Labour supporters are the keenest of all on Lords reform, they are still less keen than the additive model would suggest. So we can safely accept the idea that there is a general 'radicalism' dimension, and that the class and party effects are fairly uniform on all the issues that make it up.

We can see both how and why class and party structure ideologies, separately and together, and why there is, despite the parsimony of the explanatory variables, a richness of effect which can hide the bases of political orientation which still lie in the simplicity of the double dichotomy of social location and partisan identity.

7.3 ISSUES OF SOCIAL LIBERALISM

The sorts of policy or attitude questions to which I turn now, characteristic of the second dimension of politics — the social liberalism continuum —present a more diffuse picture. To be sure, the basic idea that class and partisanship are both important predictors is still valid. Indeed the way these two structuring factors intersect to create identifiably different ideologies for the political families is, if anything, more obvious. Class, for example, is if anything more important in determining belief in this rather more psychological dimension than it was for the more obviously rational self-interest variables discussed above. Although the class factor was a necessary and statistically significant part of each predictive model in the previous section, it was never the more important of the two. To take the measure with which I started this chapter — the attitudes of voters on the question of repatriating immigrants were so heavily affected by class that over 90 per cent of the variance in the relevant table is accounted for by the class variable alone. But taking seven of the sorts of issues characterizing the socio-economic radicalism dimension gives an average reduction in this error measure of only 30 per cent if class alone is used to predict. The policy of industrial democracy, for example, shows class accounting for only 21 per cent of the variance, though the full model, where class and partisanship are put together additively reduces the error of prediction by 97 per cent. The principal reason for the increased predictive capacity of class on issues of social liberalism is that all three partisanships, neutrality and conservatism and socialism, produce usually a simple class ordering. On questions of egalitarianism, however, the Labour column in the tables destroyed this fit, because, as I pointed out repeatedly, the upper class Labour loyalists were systematically too keen on redistribution to fit their class position. On most, though by no means all, issues of this second domain the upper class is more 'liberal' than the other classes for all issues. Furthermore the important family of lower class Conservatives were pulled in two opposing directions on the first domain, their conservatism contradicting their class interest. When we shift to issues less obviously or clearly of a class interest nature, this cross pressuring dies off. If it is, for some reason, a psychological attribute of a lower class position to be 'reactionary', then the right-wing ideology of lower class Conservatives reinforces the class position.[5] Similarly the 'liberalism' of the upper class is not incompatible with a Socialist perspective, so upper class Socialists are better fitted to the expectations of the 'partisanship plus class' predictive model. If anything, the cross pressuring reverses, so that the two groups one might expect to have their position 'moderated' by a conflict between social location and partisanship are the upper class Conservatives and the lower class Labour supporters. There is some evidence for this, but no such simplified model works.

Indeed the surprise should really be that class is more powerful here, precisely because, in the absence of class interests, there is no obvious connection between social location and political attitude. In fact we are forced to recognize that class interests and partisanship are related in a subtler way than this crude thesis would suggest. For where there is a greater element of egalitarianism about a questionnaire item in the battery used to create the 'liberalism' dimension, it is exactly there that party starts to become important again, as we shall shortly see. It is not so much that any individual issue causes difficulty in interpretation in this domain; most are fairly easily susceptible to explanation — but the patterns are varied, and leave one more impressed with the differences between class–party families than with any generalized impact of the two separate variables. This, of course, is exactly what I mean and expect by talking of the nine ideological groupings represented by the class–party families, and is the principal reason why crude expectations of what class politics should look like are unsatisfactory. Nonetheless there is a difficulty, if only of exposition, when tidy patterns refuse to emerge.

One problem is that many of the intuitive expectations one might have do indeed show up, but they are so many, so ill documented and less well verified standard intuitions. One can be seen as validated by the first opinion area analysed, portrayed in figure 7.1.

I use a graphical method of presenting the data here partly for convenience of summary and equally because a visual representation brings out clearly many of the points. Figure 7.1 shows the relative positions of the class groups inside each partisanship on two measures typical of the ideas of a 'civilized' or 'permissive' society. These are attitudes to abortion, and to the easy availability of pornographic material. In both cases the question format invites respondents to say whether they think the move towards easier abortions or more available pornography has 'gone too far', or 'not gone far enough', via an intermediate position of seeing the trends as 'about right'. Dichotomizing into those who do see the trends as having 'gone too far' and those who do not, produces the graph lines in figure 7.1 for the two issues. In both of these, and the following six issues the graphs can be standardized on a central line representing the 'evens' position. As each has been standardized to give odds in favour of the 'reactionary' position above the line and odds against below, all eight issues can easily be compared. Thus both relative differences between class–party groups, and absolute positions on the various issues can be read off, providing a rich portrait of second-dimension ideology in Britain

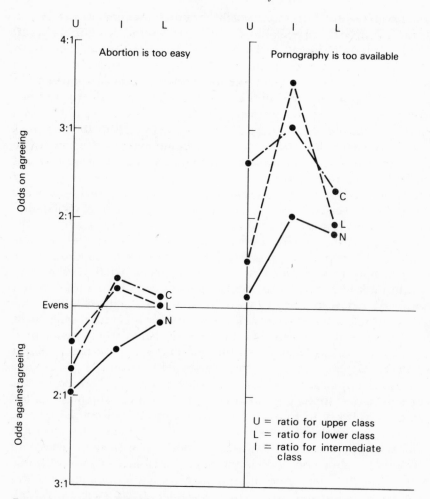

Figure 7.1 Relative positions of nine class-party groups on two selected issues

at the end of the seventies. It is worth repeating here that on all eight of these issues both class and party are statistically significant as attitude predictors, that each has a significant effect controlling for the other, that both are needed to explain the variance on each issue, and that all the models are additive, with no significant interaction terms.

The tracks of the lines representing odds ratios of the three partisanships over the three classes are complicated, and no absolute generalization applies properly across all eight issues. As far as the two sexual permissiveness issues go, the obvious point is that there is a class difference — for each party a very rough tendency exists for attitudes to be more permissive in the upper class. It is not, however, a monotonic relationship. With one exception it is not the lower class, but the intermediate, which takes the least permissive line, with the strongest odds on agreeing that trends towards availability of pornography or the legality of abortion have been excessive. The one exception, those of neutral partisanship on the question of abortion still shows, by the slight kink in the line connecting the three class positions, that the intermediate class are less permissive than a simple linear relationship between social location and permissiveness would imply. On the pornography issue linearity is still less present, and for the Conservatives it is not even true that the upper class are the most permissive — they are actually more prone to think pornography is too easily available than are the lower class Conservatives. Generally, though, the striking thing is the combination of upper class permissiveness with the extreme lack of such permissive attitudes amongst those of intermediary social status in all three partisan groupings. The patterns certainly fit a stereotype of 'lower middle class' morality, a rigidity in attitude and social conservatism often held to be characteristic of those socially cross pressured and unsure. Remembering how much of this social class is occupationally mobile, one can hardly be surprised at an attitude profile that might well be characteristic of those seeking a reassuring identity by conforming to what they may see as 'traditional' values.[6] It is notable that the 'neutral' group, many of whom have, of course, voted Liberal at least once in the seventies, is consistently more 'liberal' or permissive and that partisan differences are relatively slight.

The 'odds' for the other eight issues are presented in table form (table 7.7), but can still best be thought of as being coordinates for graphs.

Very much the same pattern emerges on a second pair of variables. These attitudes to criminal punishment touch another familiar area where the lower middle class moral reaction would popularly be expected to show, and it does. Both on the question of whether it is important that the government should or should not restore the death penalty, or the more general idea that they should lengthen prison sentences, the gap between a relatively liberal upper class and the rest of the population inside each partisanship is stark. Upper class Labour supporters are evens on the question of restoring the death penalty, lower class Labour more than 2 : 1 in favour; amongst neutrals, the upper class is slightly more than evens in favour, the lower class three to one on. But in both cases the real enthusiasm for

TABLE 7.7 Odds 'on' and 'against' eight 'social conservatism' issues

Proposition	Class	Neutral U.	I.	L.	Conservative U.	I.	L.	Labour U.	I.	L.
Sexual equality has 'gone too far'		1.8	2.3	2.5	4.6	4.3	2.8	1.5	2.3	2.5
Racial equality has 'gone too far'		1.7	2.7	2.0	3.0	4.5	3.4	1.7	3.3	2.6
Restore death penalty		1.3	3.5	3.0	3.3	4.8	5.3	1.0	2.8	2.2
Increase sentences for criminals		1.3	2.6	2.5	2.1	4.3	4.2	1.1	3.0	2.4
Respect for authority has declined too much		1.5	1.9	1.3	5.5	4.0	3.3	1.1	1.3	1.6
Modern methods of teaching have 'gone too far'		1.9	1.0	-1.4	2.6	2.6	1.6	-1.2	-1.7	-1.8
Prevent communist influence		2.1	4.1	3.3	5.0	5.0	6.2	1.3	3.7	2.5
Do NOT increase foreign aid payments		1.0	1.8	2.0	1.8	2.6	2.4	-1.7	2.6	1.7

Note: The symbolism has been chaged slightly here. In this table I use a negative number, for example, -1.2, to indicate odds of 1.2 *against* the proposition. This is to enable the odds to be used in a graphical sense. Accordingly, odds of 1.0 represent a state of even balance, where the group has a 50:50 chance of assenting to the proposition.

killing people is in the intermediary class, who show much stronger odds in favour of this policy. Though less sharp, the same pattern appears on the general issue of stiff sentences. Conservatives are less clearly of this pattern. Though there is no doubt of elite liberalism, the lower class is at least as retributive and, on the death penalty, more bloodthirsty than the intermediary class. In this specific case, however, the slope of a line connecting the three Conservative classes would show the intermediate class to be more illiberal on the issue than any linear progression from a liberal elite to a reactionary lower class would provide.

So far certainly a recognizable set of stereotypes of socially liberal elitism combined with especially morally stern people of intermediate class position sustains. The remaining four issues, while not destroying this impression, complicate it considerably, showing how differentiated are the class-party families on this second dimension of ideology.

The next two issues combine one aspect of the liberalism versus traditional morality or social conservatism with a flavour of the first, socio-economic radicalism, dimension. They relate to social equality, hence introducing some aspects of the orthodox left-right dimension; but the equality in question is sexual or racial, and hence arouses a separate set of prejudices and fears. In both cases the question is whether moves towards equality, between sexes or races, have 'gone too far'. It should immediately be said, because otherwise the data make the British population look uncomfortably reactionary, that the cutting points on these attitudes are set high. Thus both thinking that equality has gone either 'much too far' or 'a little too far', and thinking that matters are more or less right count as agreeing with the inegalitarian position. Only those who definitely regard progress towards sexual or racial equality as having not yet gone far enough are counted as against the statement. Even with that proviso it is striking that not a single one of the nine class–party families have, overall, odds against the propositions that sexual or racial equality has gone, at least, 'far enough'!

Of the two issues, the question of racial equality most clearly fits the pattern of the four 'traditional morality' attitudes. The fit is perfect for the model suggested there. In each partisan group the upper class is the most liberal (or, in this specific context, 'egalitarian'), followed by the lowest class. Indeed the differences in odds between the upper and lower class, though significant, are not great. Upper class Conservatives have odds of 3.1:1 on agreeing that racial equality has 'gone far enough', but the lower class is only slightly more complacent, with odds of 3.4:1. In all three cases, however, the intermediate social class is very clearly less in favour of racial equality, providing yet more support for the thesis, which might have been taken from any classic study of fascism, that it is a social location peculiarly prone to illiberal attitudes. The strength of the class factor is shown, as earlier, by the very fact that the liberal oriented political neutrals demonstrate the same class effects.

Sexual equality is clearly an issue where partisan groups behave differently. Conservative loyalists show a very different pattern from others, and from Conservatives themselves on other issues. Here the egalitarianism seems linked in a purely monotonic way to class location. Rather than having a liberal elite and a reactionary mass, upper class Conservatives are very much more likely to feel that sexual equality has, at the least, gone far enough than are lower class Conservatives. The intermediate class again shows a slight tendency to the reactionary position, but just by being more like the upper class than the lower class, than a linear progression would predict. There is no obvious reason why, for Conservatives alone, there should be such a reversion to a first dimension type class progression, though it may very well be a highly pragmatic matter, arising perhaps from a tendency for women in working class Conservative households in fact to have benefited less than their sisters of other partisanships from actual progress in this matter. For the other two groups the by now standard liberal elite and less liberal mass pattern sustains again. Furthermore, though much attenuated, the general tendency for the intermediate class to be out of line exists. Amongst political neutrals this class is actually the least egalitarian, whilst amongst Labour supporters they are merely nearer than they 'ought to be' (in a mathematical sense) to the inegalitarian position.

The final two issues are chosen mainly to follow through on this special sense of egalitarianism, one that arises in a non-economic context, where one can expect class position to have more of a direct and less of a purely socio-psychological impact. The first of these examines the odds on agreeing to the general proposition that 'respect for authority has declined too much' in Britain. It clearly taps very much the same strain as the earlier question of sexual equality, suggesting that the Conservative class interrelationship on that may reflect an ideological curiosity of class-based deference attitudes as much as pragmatic experience. But, if this is so, it is a pattern of deference expectations that runs contrary to many previous assumptions about the role of working class deference in supporting Conservatism (see McKenzie, 1968; Nordlinger, 1967). The political neutrals and the Labour supporters are, in all classes, much nearer an evens situation than any Conservative class sector. The group most prone to agree that there has been too great a decline in respect for authority amongst the non-Conservatives is the intermediate class political neutrals. But they reach odds of only slightly less than 2 : 1 on agreeing. In contrast the least authoritarian Conservative group has odds of 3.3 : 1, and the most has odds in excess of 6 : 1. The more important aspect, though, is the relative positions of the three Conservative classes, with a clear monotonic decrease in authoritarianism as one goes down the social ladder. If regrets about the trend to sexual equality can be seen, as they surely can, as associated with such a notion of authority, especially in the family, we can suggest that the considerably greater salience of concern for traditional authority amongst Conservatives none the less follows a clear pattern congruent with the usual distribution of authority. This would certainly fit with the Dahrendorfian lines of my definition of social class in part II of this book (see Dahrendorf, 1967). More pertinently, it throws light on the familiar assumption that working class Conservatives are those unusually deferential to authority. This would now appear to be a result of a general ideological concern for authority that lies at the heart of conservatism *per se*, rather than a peculiar, perhaps ego-defensive, psychological characteristic of working class Tories. Instead such lower class Conservatives, less endued with authority and benefiting less from it, quite rationally regret its decline only half as forcefully as do upper class Conservatives. This Tory pattern of congruence between social location and concern over the diminution of authority is also shown on the final issue. This is chosen to offer evidence of the impact of such second-dimension ideological reactions on apparently pragmatic issues. The questionnaire item, again part of the battery of 'has a trend gone too far' questions, asks whether 'modern methods of teaching in schools' have 'gone too far'. Technically it is, of course, a somewhat ambiguous question, because the modern methods of teaching referred to have not been made specific. But in the popular culture a set of stereotypes about changes in teaching style towards informality, less rote learning and memory drill, more stress on creative expression and less rigid discipline go together. There is also a general concern, from time to time breaking through into the media or even into politicians' rhetoric, about declining educational standards attendant on this change in educational philosophy. The issue is politically important, albeit in a largely symbolic way. It is the sort of issue, apparently practical but actually largely emotional, on which many people have views, but few any information. The patterns on the issue are fascinating, presenting the concern as very much a matter of elitist reaction versus a lower class acceptance of the supposed trend, across all three party groupings. The position of the intermediate class depends notably, however, on partisanship. For Conservatives, the gap lies between the intermediate and the lower class, with the intermediate, largely socially mobile, regretting the decline of traditional education as much as the elite. Labour shows the mirror image — only the elite regret the change at all. The intermediate class welcomes it as much as the lower class, both getting on towards odds of two to one in favour of increasing informality and lack of authoritarianism. To see class as so firmly affecting opinion distribution, along with partisanship on an issue like this, demonstrates very powerfully the impact and nature of class–party ideologies in modern Britain. One summary, even if the prose is barbarous, may make the point. The intermediate class amongst those who are politically intermediate is intermediate in opinion between the elite and the mass.

No useful purpose can be served by endless further comment on the evidence. Other issues show much the same patterns. Asked about the need to curb 'communism' in Britain, elites are much more moderate than masses, and the intermediate usually least moderate. Elites favour Britain increasing aid to the Third World, the lower class does not, and the intermediate class usually likes it even less. And so on.

The general thesis of two dimensions of ideology, with equally important but very different class and party effects on both, stands out clearly. It only stands out clearly with a class model more subtle than the standard dichotomy. It only shows in all its detailed fascination when one looks at ideology, at belief systems, rather than the vote. But Britain's class system is rapidly becoming more and more complex and refined. So is the choice of partisanship. What are the implications for the future of the class impact on the British electorate and therefore on British politics? To a large extent that is a question for the future. The final chapter, entitled for more than one reason the 'Afterword', can offer no more than a cautious guess.

8

Afterword: Policy, Attitudes and Voting

8.1 THE IMPORTANCE OF ISSUES –
SOME EVIDENCE FROM 1975

A good deal of this book has been spent examining the distribution
of issue opinion inside partisan groupings and social classes. I have
attached considerable importance to a particular way of characterizing public opinion in terms of two different sorts of ideological
dimension, and the four quadrants of ideological space they delimit.
Other measures of public concern have been discussed, and in an
earlier chapter I spent some time on a description of social consciousness of class. Yet all of this is open not only to potential criticisms of
detail or of methodology, but to a much more powerful objection.
The objection would be that, true or not, nothing I say about class,
partisanship, and opinion or consciousness matters at all because issue
attitudes do not significantly influence voting decisions. No-one,
perhaps, would make quite so strong a claim today. Certainly, though,
such a rejection of the importance of policy preferences in deciding
elections was once orthodox, and is still latent in the approach of
many electoral sociologists. Butler and Stokes (1974) in *Political
Change in Britain*, and Angus Campbell and his colleagues (1960)
in *The American Voter*, profess a theory of socio-psychological
voting determination through party identification that leaves very
little room for the genuine rather than spurious correlation between
political ideology and electoral choice. Furthermore, not only does
their theory 'explain away' any evidence of vote and preference
congruence, but they amass evidence and analytic power to destroy
even the semblance of stability or coherence to what beliefs the
public do hold. Thus the existence at all of formulated ideologies
amongst the population was dismissed – only 2.5 per cent of voters
were seen as having sufficient articulation of belief to qualify as

189

ideologues (Butler and Stokes, 1974, ch. 15; Campbell, 1960, ch. 9). Elsewhere it was held that 'mass belief systems' lacked internal logical or substantive connections and could not be seen as sufficiently consistent to serve as political guides (Converse, 1964). Even on single issues attitudes were seen as so unstable as to be of no conceivable long-term use in structuring electoral orientations. Overall, questionnaire data on public attitudes seemed to have little value in predicting voting.

Of America, the professional consensus has been forced to change, especially with the analysis of new data from the more politically turbulent sixties. But Britain has had no equivalent of *The Changing American Voter*[1] to set off against the issue-less politics described by Butler and Stokes. Of course there have been counter-arguments, and some counter-data. The most important, though severely restricted in scope, was the recently published longitudinal study by Himmelweit and others (1981), *How Voters Decide*. This work, which reports the changing political views and voting behaviour of a cohort of males from boyhood to mature adulthood, looks at a variety of explanations for their voting, including — obviously — class. In the end the only conclusion the authors can come to is that ideology is the long-term dominant influence. Whilst I happily accept their conclusions, the study is enormously limited in its utility for extrapolation, because its initially small, localized, and all-male sample gets progressively even further unrepresentative as the cohort ages. Still it is valuable as a counter to the dominant stress on party identification and social background, and the particular descriptive model of ideology that the authors use is similar in many respects to mine.

Some other evidence has accumulated from studies of the 1974 election and re-analyses of data originally collected by Butler and Stokes between 1963 and 1970. Prominent here are articles by Ivor Crewe and James Alt. Crewe *et al.*'s work (1977) is important to the extent that it tends to show a diminishing predictive power of party identification. Alt's articles (1975, 1976) demonstrate a considerably greater congruence between partisan preference, policy as attributed by voters to parties, and their vote than would previously have been accepted. Crewe and Sarlvik in their study of the 1979 election use the same data that this book is principally based on. Although their conceptual framework, class operationalization and aims are radically different, the relevant chapters in their study tend also to show the importance of issue attitudes (Sarlvik and Crewe, 1983).

Much of the reason for the perception of voting as predominantly a matter of social structure, and then of psychological identity ties to parties, rather than as a quasi ratiocinative process of policy choice mediated by ideological position — itself a result of class and partisanship — may lie in the simple fact that social scientists tend to find what they are looking for. It must also in part be the fact that the political world was once simpler and the issues missing or irrelevant. This is less and less true, however, and as a result one would expect it to be easier to find evidence of voter rationality and issue relevance as these 'cues', as Budge and Farlie (1977) have called them, come to be more necessary. Certainly the greater part of the difference between the portraits drawn of American voters in the 1960 publication *The American Voter* and the 1976 *The Changing American Voter* is directly due, precisely, to change in those voters. Greater education and decreasing faith in the parties combine to produce more and more political independents and greater cohesion and importance of policy and issue preference amongst both independents and identifiers.[2] Above all, the brutal importance of the actual issues — war and race riots — in the sixties in America, forced people who quite genuinely had not needed to base partisanship on policy in the tranquil Eisenhower fifties to think, calculate, and rely on ideologies.

The standard analysis, especially presented by Crewe *et al.* (1977) in their seminal 'Partisan Dealignment in Britain 1964–1974', suggests, if less dramatically and for less violent reasons, a similarly increasing necessary role for ideology in modern Britain. The obvious strains, and potential break-up in the established post-war party system, exacerbated by the leftward shift of the Labour Party and the consequent emergence of the SDP, simply make voting from inherited and intellectually contentless psychological identification impossible. I have already shown very simple evidence, highly indicative of this, in an earlier chapter, where a strong correlation was displayed between the size of the rightward ideological shift of socio-economic groups and the degree of swing towards Conservative voting between 1974 and 1979.

There is available evidence of the role of ideology, and the non-random shift of issue attitude in an earlier case where strains inside the standard two-party system made party-identification voting very difficult, if not impossible. This was the 1975 referendum on continued membership of the European Community.

A restricted set of extra data about relevant attitudes and perceptions, as well as referendum vote, was collected by the Essex-based British Election Study and integrated with the 1974 general election survey. I use it here to show a little about the role of ideology and attitude in a voting context other than an ordinary election. The main reason for this is that we see the referendum campaign as analogous to elections as they may be in the future, and may have started to become already in the seventies. That is, an election in which previous partisanship does not, perhaps logically or empirically cannot, present adequate cues for electoral choice. The point is that, in the referendum, both major parties were severely split; the leadership of both the Labour and Conservative Parties were both in favour of Britain remaining in the European Community, and, to that extent, a 'yes' vote was the official policy of both major parties (and, indeed, the Liberal Party). In addition, 'yes' was the official advice of the (Labour) Cabinet. On the other hand large minorities, arguably indeed a majority in the Labour case, of the parliamentary contingents of the major parties were opposed to continued membership. The 'no' campaign, partially financed by the government (as was the 'yes' campaign), included senior members of the Cabinet, because the doctrine of collective Cabinet responsibility had been suspended. The Labour Party's extra-parliamentary leadership in the shape of Conference was officially on record as advocating a 'no', as was the TUC. To make matters worse, there was a clear left–right correlation inside each party between ideological position and 'yes-no' preference. But it was a counter-acting correlation. It was the left of the Labour Party who were then, as now, opposed to the EEC on the grounds that it was a capitalist institution antagonistic to the interests of the working class. But it was the nationalistic right-wing of the Conservatives who campaigned, as they always had, against a treaty they saw as a serious breach of British national sovereignty. The 'no' campaign, indeed, was led by Mr Enoch Powell and Mr Wedgwood Benn, two otherwise totally antagonistic politicians. Public opinion had, in the long term, been opposed, first to joining, and then to continued membership. But some months before the referendum the government had emerged, at least by its own description, triumphant from an EEC summit in Dublin with terms of membership supposedly altered considerably to Britain's interest. From then onwards up to and through the campaign public opinion seemed to move steadily in favour of membership. The first use to which we can put this data is to provide a contrast with the usual presentation of attitude stability. The classic example of attitude stability over a time in Britain is a much discussed figure in *Political Change in Britain* (Butler and Stokes, 1971; Robertson, 1976a, p.179). Here Butler and Stokes took attitudes to nationalization of industry; they had used exactly the same question wording during several successive interviews of the same group of respondents.

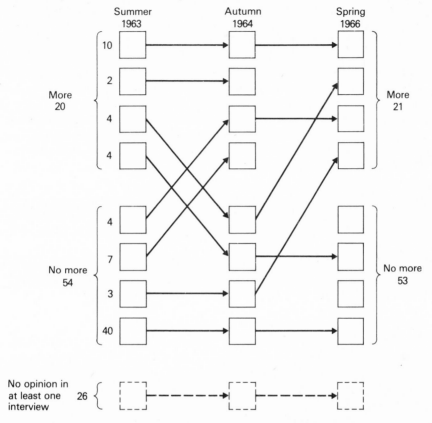

Figure 8.1a Pathways of opinion towards nationalization 1963-6 (%)

Despite nationalization being, in that period of our political history, almost definitional of Labour Party membership (at least in the eyes of academics), and despite the apparent relative stability of opinion on the issue, they found enormous instability in terms of actual individual responses between any pair of interviews. Furthermore, the instability was almost random – it was not a process of steady conversion, as must surely be allowed and indeed expected as an electorate changes its mind on an issue in response to empirical changes. Rather attitudes swapped back and forth for no apparent reason. Thus the data, as given in figure 8.1a, was seen as evidence for the shallowness and irrelevance of policy preferences amongst

the electorate. Indeed it was. But was it typical? Was nationalization
in fact a sufficiently real and important issue on which to test consistency of electoral opinion? We know after all, from 1979 data
discussed in chapter 6, that it no longer counts as an important issue
to anyone except the Conservative elite. What happens if we take an
issue that could not but be important, and on which there were not
only good reasons for respondents to hold a particular opinion at any
one time, but sensible reasons for them to change. Will they be consistent from time to time? And, when not stable, will the attitudes
change in a way consistent with a process of conversion and rational
change rather than randomly? Because the people whose referendum
vote we know had been interviewed in both 1974 elections, and had
been asked exactly the same question about staying in or coming out
of the EEC, we can look at a directly analogous figure (figure 8.1b).
In this case we see a very different set of attitude change pathways,
one to give very much more confidence in the intelligence of democracy, one that suggests policy preferences in the mass electorate are
fully capable of functioning to inform rational electoral decision.

The real evidence of the nature of the conversion process of attitudes to the EEC comes from a consideration of the consistent
change paths, numbered 2, 4, 5 and 7 in the figure.

In our sample these account for 22 per cent of the population,
compared with only 13 per cent in the Butler and Stokes figure.
Furthermore, while the nationalization change is very nearly balanced
between the two response categories (6 per cent going from more to
less, 7 per cent from less to more), ours is clearly unbalanced in a
ratio of nearly three to one in favour of the 'yes' vote. The balance
of change in Butler and Stokes' data, combined with the fact that
nearly 50 per cent of those who did not retain a constant attitude
changed in an inconsistent manner, is typical of most attitude change
data, suggesting fluctuations that do not correspond to any serious
process of attitude conversion occasioned by social forces. This they
themselves clearly explain in the chapter from which the data are
taken. In our case, however, only a little under a quarter of all change
is *prima facie* inconsistent, and the rest is heavily biased towards one
side.

From both figures one can garner several other indications of the
one-sided net pressure that must have existed to convert so many
from an initial position of hostility to one of either active support or
at least apathy. Of the 51 per cent of the sample that, in February,
indicated a positive inclination towards Europe, 74 per cent actually
ended up voting 'yes', and they were joined to 42 per cent of those

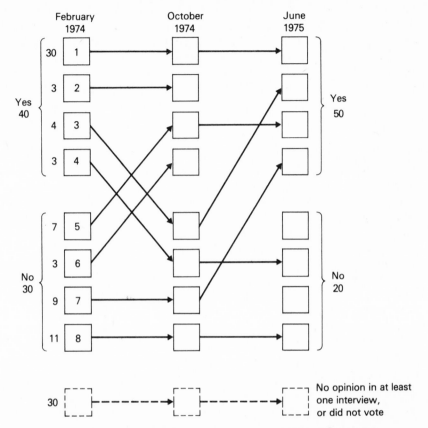

Figure 8.1b Pathways of opinion towards the EEC, 1974–5 (%)

Paths 3 and 6 are inconsistent, and account for 7 per cent of the sample; the corresponding paths in Butler and Stokes account for 11 per cent.

Paths 2, 4, 5 and 7 demonstrate one-way change: they account for 22 per cent of the sample in the ratio of nearly 3:1 in favour of a change to 'yes'. The corresponding paths for Butler and Stokes account for only 13 per cent of the sample, in a ratio of almost exactly 1:1.

who in February had been inclined against the EEC. Only 38 per cent of those initially against continued membership voted 'no'. Of those who changed from pro- to anti-European attitude between February and October, 49 per cent still voted 'yes' and 20 per cent ended up not voting. But of the converts that the 'yes' camp made between February and October, only 26 per cent returned to the negative fold and indeed only 16 per cent even abstained.

So attitudes to retaining EEC membership, and vote on the question, are capable of having been intelligently linked. But were those previous attitudes in fact important? And what of more general political ideology which ought to have informed the referendum vote? What of perceptions of the views of important reference groups like MPs, the CBI, the TUC? How important were these informations and views in the voters' minds, compared with socio-economic background and party loyalty? Did the actual results of the referendum fit the issue-salience model well enough so that, granted the analogy between referendum and an election in a stressed and decaying party system, we can believe the class-party ideological cultures described earlier are going to be significant for the future of British party politics?

I can best suggest the answer to these questions is definitely 'yes' by briefly presenting the evidence from a series of regression based causal models (or 'path analyses' for those who shy away from the implications of 'causal' in the standard name for the technique).[3] For those unfamiliar with this use of regression techniques, the statistical descriptions in the Appendix offer a brief guide.

The best reason for answering all these questions in the positive is that, on the three separate occasions between February 1974 and June 1975 that opinion on the EEC was tested, it was invariably the case that highly specific attitude questions were always the most important predictors of attitudes. The two possibly relevant 'background' variables that were measured and available for use in such predictions, were social class, and partisan identification. If anything like the orthodox model of the uninformed and unratiocinative voter simply responding to cues from his social background and his empty psychological tie to a party were true, these two variables should have been highly important. Further, if the instability and essential emptiness of attitude opinion, as assumed in the 'mass-belief system' literature was a truth about voters, previously held opinions should have little impact on the voting decision. Yet in October 1974 and at the vote in June 1975 the initial view held in February 1974 about whether or not voters were glad we had ever joined the EEC turned out to be an important predictor of the current opinion.

The data reported in table 8.1 show what variables are chosen, in what order, by an automatic data analysis technique known as 'stepwise' regression. No great understanding of this technique is needed here. It suffices to say that a whole clutch of variables are fed into the computer, and it is set to pick out all the ones that can usefully predict the target variable, in this case attitude to leaving or staying in the EEC. Further, it selects them in order of importance. Note, therefore, the social background variables are simply virtually

TABLE 8.1

Regression models for predicting attitudes to EEC membership

(A) Attitude in February 1974

Predicting variable	*Beta*
Initial approval of joining	−0.413
Estimate of effect of staying in	0.213
Importance attached to the issue	0.115
Party identification	−0.099
Perception of own party being in favour	−0.103
Estimate of impact of leaving on inflation	−0.079
General degree of interest in politics	−0.074
Educational level	0.072

Overall model: R^2 = 0.446, significant at 0.01 level

(B) Attitude in October 1974

Predicting variable	
Estimate of the effect of leaving	−0.371
*Initial approval of joining	−0.150
Party identification	−0.118
Estimate of the effect of staying in	0.118
Perception of own party being in favour	−0.093
Educational level	0.072
*Estimate of effect of staying − February	0.071

Overall model: R^2 = 0.448, significant at 0.01 level

*These variables were measured not in October, but 10 months earlier during interviews in February, thereby demonstrating the real permanence of attitude effects.

ignored, but policy questions come very much to the fore. Data are reported for predicting the EEC attitude in both February and October 1974. The really telling results are those in figures 8.2a, 8.2b and 8.2c. These concentrate on the actual EEC vote, in June 1975, and divide the population up, as I have done throughout part II of the book, into three party families. The three figures here represent full 'causal' or 'path' models of influence, both direct and 'indirect', on the final decision to vote on continued membership of the EEC.[4]

Separating the sample into the three partisan groupings is necessary for this analysis, as it has been in the last few chapters, precisely because the interactions between variables are quite different given the partisanships. In this sense party is vital, not because it determines

198

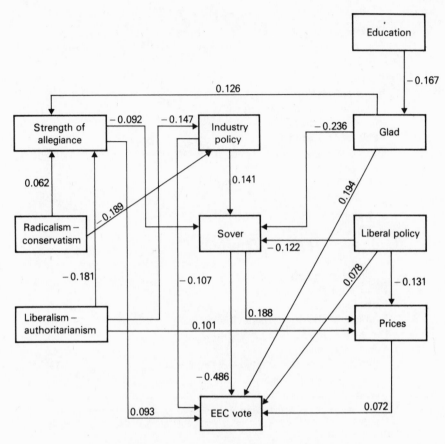

Figure 8.2a Conservative supporters and the EEC vote
$R^2 = 0.445$, significant at 5 per cent level

Key to variable names in figure 8.2a–c

Union/Industry/Labour/Liberal, etc. (with or without 'policy') — these are measures of whether the voter thought the elite in question was in favour of retaining membership.
Sover/Sovereignty — is a measure of whether or not it was felt that loss of sovereignty entailed would be a 'bad thing'.
Prices — measures the expected impact on inflation of continued membership.
Glad — is the measurement (taken in February 1974) of whether the respondent was initially pleased that Britain had joined the EEC.
Radicalism–Conservatism and Liberalism–Authoritarianism — are ideological measures very similar to the ones used throughout part II of this book.

attitude but because it shapes the connections between attitudes, acting again as a sub-culture. Consistently with the unimportance of class both in table 8.1 and figure 8.2 is shown the importance instead of educational level.[5] (Other logically similar measures take on importance too – the amount of information about the EEC as measured by the number of official leaflets read is a good predictor of attitude.) The long-term importance of policy opinion, measured by the variable called 'glad', shows up. The slight but definite importance of generalized ideology, measured in a way closely akin to the definitions of the two dimensions of ideology used for most of this book, is there in the background. Party loyalty counts, but much more important is the question of the actual perceptions of the policy preference of one's party. Nor are party elites the only ones to count. Significant reference groups, sensibly regarded as having specialist knowledge, like business leaders and union leaders, are shown to have an important influence. But, above all else, the decision on voting in the referendum was dominated by one single policy opinion. This, for shorthand called an attitude to loss of sovereignty, was predictively crucial, accounting for more of the variance in the results than all the other variables combined. It was not in the slightest tautological. The question itself was as follows:

Being in the Common Market means that Britain will have to accept that many decisions must be taken with the approval of other countries. How do you think this will affect Britain's best interests?

The possible answers were:

(1) On the whole it will be a good thing   (48 per cent)
(2) On the whole it will be a bad thing   (23 per cent)
(3) It will not matter much either way   (29 per cent)

                                            (N = 2071)

(These were coded, respectively, +1, -1, and 0, to produce a three-point scale.)

Not only was this single opinion vitally important, but it was much more important than a more pragmatic or short-term bread and butter issue, the likely impact of membership on inflation, which had been the major talking point of the campaign itself. The referendum campaign, and the three wave panel data on it, are rich in evidence to back this quick demonstration of the importance, even the primacy,

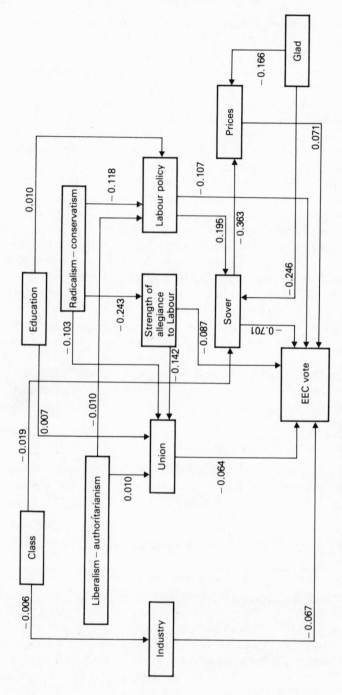

Figure 8.2b Labour supporters and the EEC vote. $R^2 = 0.568$, significant at 5 per cent level.

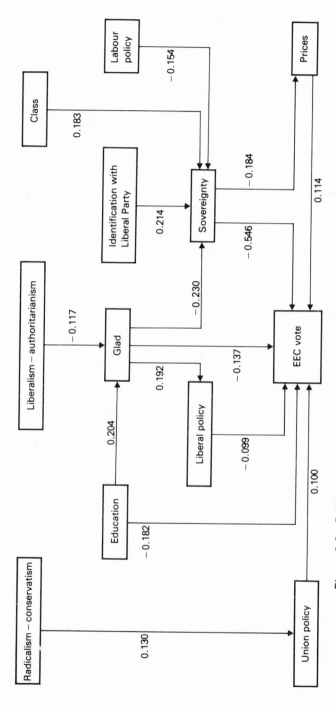

Figure 8.2c Political neutrals and the EEC vote. $R^2 = 0.580$, significant at 5 per cent level.

of attitudes and evaluations in electoral decision making. The two dimensions of political ideology discussed in chapter 6, for example, can be shown to operate with great importance in moulding opinion and opinion change at different times during the February 1974 to June 1975 period; attitudes to the market can indeed be shown significantly to affect the strength of partisan loyalty itself. There is no space here to discuss it further. The importance, to re-iterate, is to show, with data from an electoral situation where normal party cues are irrelevant, how little social background, and how much thought and opinion, matter. For my thesis here is that the old party cues have vanished, or are at least decaying in general now, and partisan-class sub-cultural ideologies can only be of increasing importance.

We can now turn to evidence from the 1979 election itself about the connection between issue opinion and electoral choice.

8.2 THE IMPORTANCE OF ISSUES —
SOME EVIDENCE FROM 1979

If the less structured situation of the 1975 referendum shows policy preferences and ideology to be vital (while still giving class a major role), we should be able to see some signs of such importance in the 1979 election, perhaps the last ever election of the post-war party system we are so familiar with.[6] The causal modelling/path-analysis technique can be used to effect again. Figure 8.3 first presents evidence for the relative importance of general ideology, along with structural variables, in predicting 1979 voting.

The aim of this figure, which represents in full detail a particular causal model of voting is to show not only the relative impact of different sorts of variables on voting, but to trace also the indirect impacts. Thus, for example, we can expect not only that a voter's educational attainment will partially constrain his voting choice, but will affect other characteristics of him which also affect voting. Education, in this example, partially determines a person's class, which in turn determines his vote: thus education has a second, or 'indirect', effect on vote. In its own turn, education is partly affected by the class of the voter's father; thus parental class has three or more ways of affecting vote. It has its own direct effect, it has indirect effect on education, and thus, through the mediation of education, on anything that education affects. A full account of the impact of a variable, therefore, requires consideration of at least its major indirect impacts. Path analysis is not, could not be, automatic. The

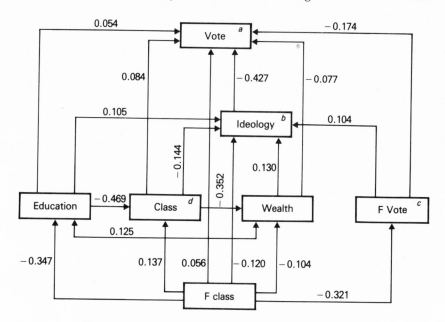

Figure 8.3 A path analysis of 1979 voting. R^2 = 0.573.

a Vote: 1 = Conservative, 2 = Liberal, 3 = Labour   *b* Ideology: hi scores are right wing
c F Vote: 1 = Conservative, Ø else   *d* Class: hi = lower

computer cannot tell one what pathways there may be. They have
to be tested for. If a theoretically possible effect does not exist in
practice, the estimating equations will produce a statistically insignificant 'path coefficient' (the figures attached to each of the arrowed
paths in the model), and we will know to leave it out. But if a path
that is in fact significant is not thought of and tested for, it cannot
present itself. These causal or path models are, in fact, encapsulated
social theories, turned into regression equations and tested against
data – they rely for their meaning on the social theory. This is true in
a second vital sense: though we call them, sometimes, 'causal' models,
the causality implied cannot be proven, but has to be assumed. Thus
we cannot show, statistically, that a person's father's class 'causes' his
class, rather than the other way round. In this case, because of the
time sequence, our assumption is not likely to be challenged, but not
all such assumptions are equally safe, and some pathways even in this
rather unexceptional model might be argued about.

In this case my main interest is to compare the strengths, which
might be equated with causal weights, of the different paths, as

by the path coefficients. The model was specified on these ~~~ptions: that voting is a function both of a person's ideology, and of background facts about him, which include not only his own wealth, class, education, but his father's economic and political circumstances. To measure these latter, I use the reported social class of his father, and the report of his father's usual voting choice. Ideology is measured by using the economic radicalism, ideological dimension discussed in earlier chapters, which was also shown to have had some impact on voting in the 1975 referendum. The other variables are all measured as they have been described in earlier parts of this book. The 'vote' variable is a three-point scale constructed by attaching 1 point to a Conservative vote, 2 to a Liberal vote, and 3 to voting Labour. The signs on the path coefficients simply indicate the direction of causation. So, for example, because ideology is measured in such a way that 'right-wing' responses get higher scores than 'left-wing' responses, there is a negative correlation between ideology and vote—high ideology scores go with voting Conservative, and thus with low scores on the voting variable. As class is typically given a scale with 1 for the upper social grade, rising to 7 for unskilled manual workers, the correlation with voting is predictably positive.

The extent to which the theory as a whole fits the data is given by the overall multiple regression coefficient associated with using the six predictors to account for vote. At 0.573, this shows that the model explains over 50 per cent of the variance, which is rather high for a model tested on survey research data. All of the variables in the model have a significant direct effect on voting, and most have one or more indirect effects. For our purposes there is one crucial finding — ideology is more than twice as powerful a predictor than any other single variable, even when one takes the indirect effects into account. (Given the way this model is set up, an individual's ideology does not itself have an indirect effect through any other mediating variable.) To back up this importance of ideological causation, it is notable that the second most important variable is the respondent's father's vote which is used as a measure of the general ideological background in which he grew up. That there is a significant direct effect of educational attainment adds to this impression of the importance of the mental and, at that, thoughtful world. For education is not here standing as a surrogate for current or past social status or wealth. Educational attainment is associated with high social class, both for oneself and one's parents, of course, and, independently, with one's wealth. This makes it especially interesting that it should be associated with, or partially determine, a left-wing vote. In fact, it has a two-edged impact – it actually tends to make people more right-wing in general ideology, but, once this is controlled for, the remaining impact of education is leftwards. There is no mystery, though – the more highly educated tend to be 'liberal' on the second dimension of ideology, the social liberalism dimension, which pushes people towards Liberal Party or even Labour partisanship. For simplicity in the model this ideological dimension has been left out. What is important for us is the sheer fact of education having an impact, not the complexities of its impact, though this explains why simple bivariate checks on the effect of education on voting tend to show little connection. The connections are there. They must be for thoughtful voting because education facilitates the development of analysis, the holding and stability of opinions, and the gathering of information, but it contains no homogenous effect on voting, so less careful controlling of other variables does not disclose this. Its presence is shown, as is the impact of sheer information levels, also in the referendum study.

Though of independent interest, there is no point here in considering the details of other pathways in the model. Its significance here is to demonstrate the combined importance of the two general sorts of variable I have concentrated on in this book – social class and generalized ideology – and especially to show that ideological matters are vital even when more directly proximate measures such as wealth and social inheritance are examined at the same time. I turn now to examine in more precise detail how particular policy preferences were important in shaping the vote in the last election for which we yet have powerful evidence, the 1979 election.

The first thing to establish is very simply that the easiest possible explanation for the Conservative victory in 1979 is given by the most obvious one for democratic theory. By this I mean that, on the most important issues in that election, it was simply true that the electorate nearly always preferred the policies of the Conservative Party to those of the Labour Party. But in itself this raises difficult questions, one of theory, one of measurement. First, theoretically, what connection should there be between attitude opinion and electoral choice? What exactly should the logic of this connection be? Secondly, what do we mean by policy preference, and how do we measure policy preferences of voters, and their perceptions of the party policy? It is crucial to deal with their perceptions. No study will find a connection between what voters think and how they vote if the analyst insists on using his own perceptions of party policy offering, however perceptive he may be, unless his perceptions match those of the voters. If a

voter systematically believes the Conservative Party favours nationalization, and votes because of this perception, he is still voting out of
policy considerations, though a test which asserted that Conservatives
were opposed to nationalization would judge him an example of
the irrelevance of attitudes. In this case, the example is chosen
deliberately, the voter might have very good reason for holding an
apparently odd view of party policy. Within the lifetimes of most
youngish voters, the Conservative Party has nationalized quite a lot,
and denationalized very little. We absolutely must, therefore, have
data which shows both what a voter wants, and what he thinks he is
offered by whom. Yet the question of measuring policy is not solved
so simply. There is a difference, acknowledged sometimes in the
technical literature but not given a systematic labelling, between
holding general attitudes on matters in some policy area, and specifically having a preference for one or other solution to a specific policy
problem. Up to this point I have tended to use such language loosely,
because the distinction has not mattered. Now it does, and the truth
is that little survey research in the past has actually measured what I
need to know here, namely which of a set of policies voters prefer as
solutions to specified problems. With my co-researchers of the 1979
British Election Study I designed a set of questions, in a standard
format, which could provide data of this precision in the relevant
format, both for voters' preferences, and for their perception of
party policy.

Six of the seven questions in this battery were on highly salient
issues of the 1979 election campaign: legal control over trade unions;
unemployment and job creation; public expenditure and taxation
levels; incomes policy; policy towards the EEC; and race relations. In
each case respondents were presented with a polar choice between
rival policies, instead of simply being asked how much or little they
favoured one specific end or value. They were asked whether there
should or should not be legal controls over trade union activities;
whether the best way to create jobs was for government to invest
money raised by taxes, or to allow companies to keep their profits;
whether they would prefer to reduce taxes and therefore reduce
public expenditure, or to keep up expenditure even if this meant
higher taxes; whether incomes should be decided by a policy of
government guidelines or left to free collective bargaining; whether
the government should be more prepared to cooperate in EEC economic policy, or should be more prepared to oppose it in the UK's
national interest. Finally they were asked an unusual question about
race relations, in that they were asked to choose between two policies

to improve race relations, rather than being asked simply about attitudes to immigration. They were asked whether the first priority
should be to improve housing and other conditions to improve relations, or just to reduce immigration. Each of these oppositions was
set in terms of a seven-point scale running from being very strongly
in favour of one policy, fairly strongly in its favour, moderately for
it, via an intermediate position, usually that 'it would not matter
either way', or that 'there was no need for change', to being very
strongly in favour of the opposite policy. Thus, unlike many such
measuring instruments, a precise meaning could be given, and taken
by the respondent, to each point, and both ends actually represented
concrete and opposed policies. Each respondent was asked not only
to opt for a preferred position himself, but also to say which position
he thought the Conservative and Labour Parties advocated. As each
of the six issues were measured in precisely the same way, they can
be used in an easily comparable manner to chart a spatial location of
voters and parties. The seventh question, though not about a concrete policy choice arising from the campaign, is similarly precise. It
investigates a general attitude to democracy, setting up an opposition
between changing the political system to give leaders more control,
or to give 'ordinary people' more say in politics, and similarly located
both respondents and parties on a seven-point scale.

All these variables in one way or another turn out to be very
significantly related to the vote, but I have not as yet discussed the
problem of the logic of the connection between policy preference
and party choice. At this stage it is more instructive just to see what
the distribution both of opinion and perceived party positions is.
Figures 8.4 to 8.7 chart these for four of the issues that turn out to
have the highest correlations with vote: legal control over unions, job
creation, taxes and services, and wage controls.

The first three of these issues have an important characteristic
from the viewpoint of electoral decision — they are all cases where
parties are seen to be clearly different. In each case at least three
points on what is only a seven-point scale separate the average positions attributed to them by our respondents. Secondly, and equally
important, these issues all show a clear preference on the part of the
electorate for one party over its rival. On two issues (trade union
control and job creation) the distance between the average position
of the Conservative Party, and the average respondent preference
is less than one unit on this scale. On the third, the question of
preferring tax cuts to maintaining levels of public expenditure, the
Labour Party is similarly close to the voters' preference point. A third

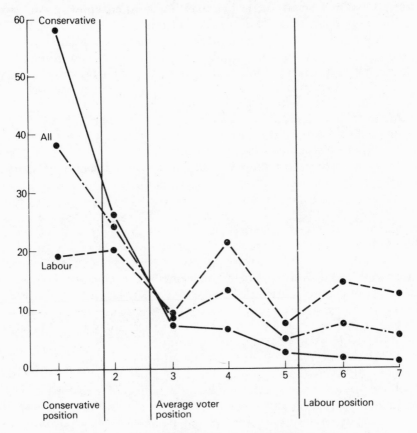

Figure 8.4 Preferences and perceived party positions on issue 1:
the need for laws to control trade union behaviour.

A score of 1 = very much need such laws   A score of 7 = very much against such laws
——— = preferences of Conservative voters   ——— = preferences of Labour voters
— · — = preferences of all respondents, including non-voters

characteristic is worth noting. This is that the opinion distribution
is sharply 'skewed', meaning that the bulk of voters are found near
one end of the spectrum, rather than being either evenly distributed,
or concentrated round the mid-point. Sixty per cent of the whole
sample are either very strongly or fairly strongly of the view that
stricter controls are needed over trade unions; 56 per cent are in the
same part of the spectrum supporting the idea that jobs will best be
created by allowing private firms to keep their profits; the third is
less dramatically skewed, but one still finds over 50 per cent feeling

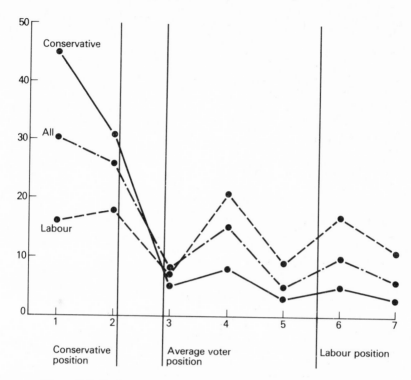

Figure 8.5 Preferences and perceived party positions in issue 2:
solutions to unemployment

1 = let companies keep profits.
7 = government to tax companies and invest profits themselves.

very or fairly strongly that public expenditure levels must be main-
tained, even if this means keeping up tax rates at the same time.

Opinion distributions, and party relative placements, can take
many forms, not all of which are conducive to ease of electoral
choice, and thus not all of which can be expected to work well in
predictive models. These three at least are ideals, as often discussed
in the abstract theoretical literature on voting, but not that often
met in data. The fourth, the issue of government guidance of pay
norms versus unrestricted private collective bargaining, is much less
well adapted. And, indeed, it is only the fifth of my seven predictive
variables in importance in the actual data analysis. The fourth in
actual ordering is the more general question of attitudes to democracy. Here we have a flatter, less skewed, distribution, and a much

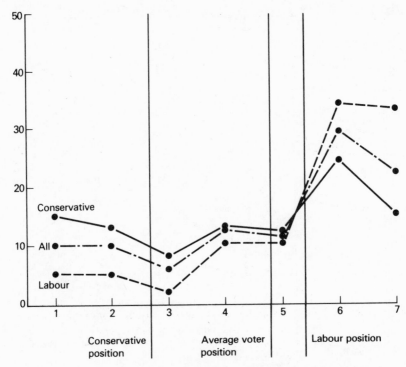

Figure 8.6 Preferences and perceived party positions on issue 3:
tax cuts versus cuts in services

1 = very strongly in favour of cutting taxes even at the cost of a reduction in services.
7 = in favour of increasing expenditure on services, even if taxes have to rise.
4 = 'things should stay as they are'.

narrower gap in the voters' relative placing of the parties' own preferences. The Labour and Conservative Parties are only 1.2 units apart,
very probably because voters are much less clear about just where
they do fit on the issue. This is borne out by the fact that the standard deviations, which measure how much spread there is around the
average, are notably higher for estimates of Conservative and Labour
policy for this dimension (respectively 2.1 and 2.0) than for the
equivalent estimates of average positions on the trade union law issue
(1.2 and 1.6).[7] It is hardly surprising: a purported ability to cooperate
with the unions in a 'social contract' had been the highlight of the
Labour government claims in its campaign, whilst an insistence that
the unions would be made to see who was master was the point of
the Tory campaign. In contrast, anyone could be forgiven for being

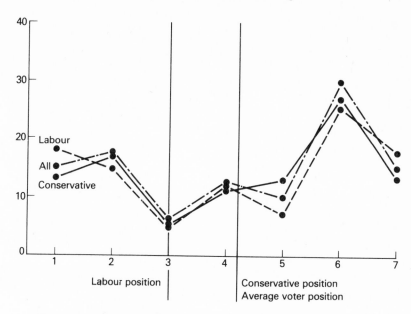

Figure 8.7 Preferences and perceived party positions on issue 4:
method for dealing with wage negotiation

1 = very strongly in favour of government guidelines.
7 = very strongly in favour of free collective bargaining.
4 = 'leave things as they are'.

In this figure, the average voter preference, and the average perception of the Conservative
Party position are identical, at a score of 4.2.

vague about which party took what line on a wages policy. The
Conservatives, with their new-found faith in the free market, insisted
they were against wage controls, but any government, through its
control over public sector wages, in fact must operate one, and the
ensuing Conservative government certainly did so. At the same time,
the Labour Party necessarily had to stress the voluntary nature of its
guidelines (precisely because of the 'social contract'). In addition the
actual phrase 'free collective bargaining' had for long been a cry of
the Labour Party supporting unions. This impression is made stronger
by the fact that the actual position given by the average of respondents' estimates for the Conservative Party is the non-committal
middle position. Scored at 4.2, the party is only a fifth of a unit off
the position marked in the interview schedules as meaning 'leave
things as they are'. As this was exactly the average position of the

voters themselves, the Conservatives gained on this issue simply by being fuzzier than their only mildly more determinate opponents. But this is also much in keeping with the theoretical literature on electoral choice, where the advisability of being vague where the electorate is not strongly of one opinion is well tested. To take the median position on what was, if anything, a flattened but bi-modal distribution (there are slight peaks of voter preferences at point 2 and point 6 on the scale) is what the Conservatives appear to have done, and is exactly what is predicted by the best established of the abstract theories.

A further point needs to be made about all four opinion distributions. The graphs show the preference distribution of Labour and Conservative voters as well as for the whole sample. At a glance it can be seen that there is very little party differential. One might have expected the graphs to be opposites, with the bulk of opinion in each party distributed around opposite ends. Though the graph lines for the two parties are always different, they are not vastly so. Basically, the distribution of opinion on these specific issues is very similar, regardless of the party of the voters. Table 8.2 makes this point more clear. It gives the average preferences on each of the four issues for adherents of both the major parties, the Liberal Party, and even for those who did not vote at all. Thus on the four issues that seem to have had the greatest impact on the country we see a considerably narrower gap between the preferences of the partisans than between at least their own perceptions of party policy. On all four of these

TABLE 8.2

Average positions of Conservative, Labour, Liberal and non-voters on four issues

Group average	Trade unions	Jobs	Taxes and services	Wage controls
Conservatives	1.7	2.1	4.2	4.2
Labour	3.6	3.8	5.4	4.2
Liberals	2.6	3.1	5.0	3.9
Non-voters	2.7	3.1	4.6	4.2
Party gap	3.4	3.5	2.7	1.2
Conservative-Labour gap	1.9	1.7	1.2	0.0

Note:
Party gap is the difference between the average perceived positions of the two major parties. Conservative–Labour gap is the difference between rows 1 and 2, i.e. between the average preferences of the supporters of the two parties.

issues, to varying degrees, we have the stuff of competitive democracy. Clearly seen and quite strongly opposed alternatives, a relatively consensual electorate with a well-shaped preference distribution and positions in each case clearly nearer to one party than another.[8]

On one issue, that of tax and expenditure cuts, an issue that ranked as a major one in the campaign, the Labour Party had a clear advantage over its opponents. That issue cannot have helped the Conservatives win the election, although at the time they certainly felt it would. On the others, and this applies also to the three not shown here, the Conservatives had a clear advantage. The party that had this cumulative advantage won a definite electoral victory, and one that took many working class voters away from their assumed class loyalty, as we have seen. In one sense, that is the whole story, and easily backs up the notion of the importance of the issue domain in electoral sociology.

There is something more to be said, however. The whole point of the analysis so far has been to stress not the absolute positions of parties, or the simple preferences of voters, but the interaction between them. The mere fact that a voter is at point X on a spectrum does not tell us how he is likely to vote; after all, a good many voters are a long way away from any party. Forty-five per cent of voters have scores of 6 or 7 points on the wage control issue. This puts them further away from either party than either party is from its rival. Absolute positions cannot logically determine a vote. Yet relative distances between parties rest heavily on the voters' ability to tell reliably where a party does stand, and this can be no easy matter, as I have already suggested with reference to this very issue. One school of thought, those influenced by the early Michigan researchers who made popular the idea of party identification, goes much further, and suggests that voters do not in fact have, let alone use, independent policy preferences in deciding between parties. Instead, it is argued, voters inherit or otherwise develop for psychological reasons, a predisposition to one party or another. They cannot easily understand the political issues, however, and they use the party as the leader, adopting as their own preference whatever policy the party itself supports. There is, therefore, at best a spurious correlation, and not a causal link, between a voter's avowed policy preference and his vote — both are caused by a prior attraction to a party. This model cannot, in fact, ever be logically or empirically falsified fully, but we can suggest some evidence to doubt it. One reason is simply that there is a high consensus on where parties stand, both amongst opponents and adherents. Table 8.3 gives the average estimates of

TABLE 8.3 Estimates of party positions on four issues by 1979 vote

| | | Estimates by: | | | |
| | | Conservatives | | Labour voters | |
Issue	Estimates of:	Con.	Lab.	Con.	Lab.
Union controls		1.6	5.6	1.8	4.8
Jobs		1.8	5.8	1.9	5.4
Taxes and services		2.9	5.4	2.5	5.5
Wage controls		4.3	3.0	4.2	3.0

Conservative and Labour Party policy on the four issues separately for Conservative and Labour Party voters.

This table does not disprove the thesis that preferences are learned simply by adopting what one's own party says it believes in. But it throws doubt on any thesis that makes the voter's opinion independent of his own autonomous reflection. To fit this table, two things would have to be true. First, the parties would have to be very good indeed at getting over their message, because of the very high consensus, in aggregate, of where they stand. Second, they would have to be able to get over where their opponents stood. It is rather difficult to imagine that someone so puzzled by politics that he had no real view of his own should so accurately internalize not only what was believed by the party to which he does feel a psychological attachment, but also (and from what source?) pick up an equally consensual image of the opponent to which he is not psychologically linked.

In fact table 8.3 somewhat oversimplifies the situation, and gives too strong a picture of the *non*-partisan nature of voters' perceptions. One would actually expect that a good deal of rationalization goes on in deciding where one thinks one's own and one's opponent party stand. All evidence has been to suggest a good deal of selective misperception of party stands, sometimes known as cognitive dissonance (Berelson and Lazarsfeld, 1965). In the referendum, already picked out as a nearer approximation to current elections than past elections before the decline of partisanship, this certainly went on. Then, in 1975, voters whose own preference was against their own party policy (Labour supporters of the Common Market, Conservative opponents), were quite likely to misperceive both their own party position and that of the other party. Thus Conservative anti-marketeers often reported that the Conservative Party was against retaining membership (it was not), that the Labour Party was in favour (it was not), and even that the TUC wanted to retain membership (it was unambiguously for coming out of Europe). In contrast Labour pro-market voters would invert in the other way. In other words, perceptions of where opinion leaders stand are often filtered through one's own preferences to produce an inner harmony that would not, given unbiased perception, actually be there.

It is easy to show that a similar mechanism is at work in the current data. Two examples should suffice. Though the distribution of preferences on tax cuts and expenditure levels was clearly skewed towards the Labour Party end, many Conservatives did indeed strongly prefer the low tax–low expenditure end. These people, with scores of one or two on the scale, were very much more prone to think their own party was near their end of the spectrum than were Conservatives who themselves sat at the far end of the spectrum. Conservatives gaining scores of six or seven gave an average position to their own party of 3.8, much nearer than the overall sample average of 2.7, and the 'right-wing' Conservatives brought their party to their end, with an average position of 1.8. Put another way, as in table 8.4, 89 per cent of 'right-wing' Conservatives gave the Conservative Party a right-wing position, but only 44 per cent of 'left-wing' Conservative voters did so. Symmetrically, nearly 40 per cent of Conservatives who were in favour of retaining public expenditure levels thought that was Conservative Party policy, but only 3 per cent of their fellow Conservatives who wanted cuts agreed with them.

As in the referendum campaign, such selective perception does not belong to one's own party. As the data in the table show, the Labour Party was 'mis'-perceived, systematically being pushed away from the Conservative voter's own preference. Thus 'left-wing' Conservatives saw the Labour Party as less near their own (deviant) end of the spectrum than did the overall sample. Only 4 per cent of right-wing Conservatives managed to get the Labour Party so far wrong as to think it favoured tax cuts, but 11 per cent of Conservatives who themselves wanted to keep up tax and public expenditure attributed such a position to their enemy. If one takes instead an issue on which Labour has a clear electoral disadvantage, and a wide spread of preference within its own ranks, the question of the proper policy for job creation, the situation applies in reverse. They too alternate the perceived positions of the Conservatives. In fact on both issues the supporters of both parties see both of them according to a very simple formula. 'Pull your own party towards your own end of the spectrum, push the opponents away towards the other end. Do this however odd the results, and however deviant, in terms of your party loyalty, your own position may be.'

TABLE 8.4 Selective perceptions of party positions on two issues (%)

Conservative voters and attitudes on tax and expenditure cuts

	Voter's preference	
	1/2 (cut taxes)	6/7 (keep up expenditure)
Perceives Conservative position as:		
1/2	89	44
3/4/5	8	18
6/7	3	38
	100	100
Perceives Labour position as:		
1/2	4	11
3/4/5	23	31
6/7	73	58
	100	100

Labour voters and attitudes to job creation policy

	Voter's preference	
	1/2 (companies keep profits)	6/7 (government to tax and invest)
Perceives Labour position as:		
1/2	21	6
3/4/5	26	11
6/7	53	83
	100	100
Perceives Conservative position as:		
1/2	65	75
3/4/5	24	13
6/7	11	11
	100	100

The full details are given in table 8.4. Now this result does indeed suggest a connection between partisanship and private policy preference, and a most plausible one. It suggests that absolute truth in placing parties is hard to come by, if not indeed a figment of theory. It suggests that a prior partisan disposition, which no one would deny, partially informs voting. This prior loyalty interacts with one's own preference in filtering information, and, as a result, the policy one attributes to each party is a function of one's own view on an issue and one's feelings towards that party. The world is made more comfortably consistent, but not by adopting as one's own what one sees the party thinking. Instead the model must be much more complicated, involving, autonomously, a generalized party predisposition and a set of policy preferences in a complex pay-off assessment. Were the Michigan school right, there would be no need to dissolve a conflict between preference and loyalty. The problem arises because there is a conflict, because policy preferences *are* prior to perception of party policy, and probably simultaneous with generalized party loyalty.

The data make it more than ever important to grasp that issue-related voting is a matter of subjective relative distances to each party, not of absolute positions on policy dimensions. Each voter, as it were, inhabits a set of dimensions of his own, between which any mapping would be most difficult. It is worth stressing, though, that we are talking of rather marginal misperceptions — very few voters get the parties badly out of line. Even those in extreme difficulties rarely produce a total distortion. Yet the actual logic of issue voting is now clear. What we must measure is the relative advantage a party has over the other to each voter on an issue. This can be put neatly, and conveniently, into a simple formula. If we let V stand for a voter's own preference on an issue, and L and C for his perception of where the Labour and Conservative Parties stand, the relative advantage to the Labour Party of any set of preferences and perceived positions is given by:

$$\text{Absolute Value } (C - V) - \text{Absolute Value } (L - V).$$

For example, if there is a large gap between a voter and the Conservative Party, and a small gap between him and Labour, the result will be a positive number, a positive relative advantage to the Labour Party. But if he is near the Conservative Party, and distant from Labour, the figure on the left-hand side of the formula will be small, a large number will be taken from it, and the result, a negative number, will indicate a negative relative advantage to Labour, a positive advantage for the Conservatives. The beauty of this way of looking at the matter is that the results are the same regardless of whether or not the voter is to the left or right of the party, and regardless of whether he sees the Conservatives as left or right of the Labour Party. Furthermore the same result will emerge for any two voters who are a similar relative distance from the two parties, quite regardless of what they actually prefer and where they put the parties. It serves to measure only what is important, the interaction between the voter and how he sees the parties, in his own perception space, and yet allows any two spaces to be compared.

This is the only intelligent way of measuring the impact of an issue on a voter's choice. We can now quickly demonstrate how important these issues were, by using such relative advantage measures for each voter on each issue in a simple regression equation, and its associated path diagram. Table 8.5 gives the results of a regression analysis in which all seven attitudes, expressed as the Conservative relative advantage, are combined with two measures of social class to predict the actual vote in 1979. These class measures, one of objective socio-economic status using the seven-point scale discussed in chapter 5, and one of subjective class identity as discussed in chapter 4, were included as general 'background' variables. Clearly political attitudes do not come from nowhere, and indeed the work of the whole of part II of the book is addressed to the way in which classes and parties form political sub-cultures. But what I need to demonstrate at this point is a model in which, whilst class can be seen to have a formative impact on political policy preferences, and a direct impact on the voting choice, those preferences also have their own direct impact, after controlling for social location. It is, additionally, of considerable interest to find out how important issues are, compared with social location and subjective class status, in influencing voting, and, indeed, how relatively important different issues are, given these controls. Hence the use of a full path analysis to establish the simple point that what people want from government influences which party they support in an election.

The detailed complexity of the model I have in mind is shown when one remembers that not only the direct effects of class and policy preference on voting, but the effects of the class measures on the policy preferences are important. It should be remembered that for the full effects of the two background variables their indirect effect via the attitudes should also be taken into account.

So, for example, the direct effect of objective class on voting is −0.100. This means that, as the class score goes up (which, unfortunately, means, counter-intuitively, that social status declines), the voting score is reduced (made more Labour) by just over a tenth of a standardized unit. As this happens, the probability of the respondent having a pro-Labour proximity score increases. (The path from objective class to TU law is 0.122.) Having such a score decreases the voting score, i.e. moves it more towards Labour. Thus the full effect

TABLE 8.5 Regression analysis using policy preferences
and class indicators to predict 1979 vote

(A) To predict vote:

Variable	Beta weight
Trade union laws	−0.298
Jobs	−0.190
Taxes and services	−0.172
Democracy	−0.139
Subjective class	−0.114
Wage controls	−0.106
EEC policy	−0.095
Objective class	−0.106
Race relations	−0.058

R^2 (adjusted) = 0.564

(B) Using objective and subjective class to predict each attitude:

Variable	Beta weight from subjective class	Beta weight from objective class
Trade union laws	0.183	0.122
Jobs	0.162	0.122
Taxes and services	0.119	0.050
Democracy	0.123	0.115
Subjective class	—	0.162
Wage controls	0.088	0.028
EEC policy	0.133	0.041
Objective class	—	—
Race relations	0.055	−0.089

Note: Both objective and subjective class measures are coded so that a high score = low social class. Vote is coded so that 1 = Conservative, 0 = Labour. (Other votes are excluded.) All preference variables are coded so that a high positive score is an advantage to the Labour Party.

of objective class, taking account only of this one extra pathway, is −0.110 + (0.122 × −0.298) = −0.146. Properly we should consider all the indirect pathways; as this model allows for a causative effect on objective 'on' subjective class as well, the number is very large. Leaving out these three paths, the total effect of class still rises to be −0.217, making it the second biggest variable. Even then, and this perhaps is the most important part of the analysis, one proximity variable by itself, the one measuring attitudes to legal controls of the unions, is still more important, even though it can work only through its own influence with no indirect pathways.

No comment is really needed on the second half of the model, present most clearly in table 8.5, where these path coefficients (or Beta weights) are shown for the impact of class on the attitudes themselves. It must continually be remembered, though, that these are complicated theoretical measures. The data in table 8.5(B) do not say anything about how class brings people to take a particular view about a policy, which we have already seen at length in earlier chapters. Nor do they reflect the impact of class on causing people to see political parties in certain ways. Instead they show something more remarkable — the impact of class on the results of the equation overleaf which has three variables in it — the voter's own preference, and his perceptions of both parties.

It is a clear mark of the overall sub-cultural influence of social class that such a second order measure as the relative proximity advantage of the Labour Party over the Conservative Party in a voter's perceptions should be significantly correlated to both objective and subjective social class. Given the way this must be a sub-cultural impact, a product of a full class ideology as described in the last three chapters, it is not surprising that subjective class perceptions are usually more important than objective social location, though the latter never loses its significance completely. The direction is also the same. The one exception is very much to be expected, given the sub-cultural portraits discussed already, especially in the second half of chapter 7. This is on the one issue that clearly comes from the 'social-liberalism' domain — attitudes to race relations. Where subjective class identity is more working class than would be expected from actual objective social location (which is what we mean by talking about 'controlling' the impact of objective class in estimating the impact of subjective class), people are led to a preference for the 'liberal' policy of improving race relations by improving social conditions. This is the 'Labour' end of that spectrum, and gives a proximity measuring leading to a Labour vote. But then, these, more subjectively than objectively lower class, are precisely those who inhabit the upper left-hand quadrant of chapter 6, the theoretically conscious Socialists. For the others the ordinary working class culture, which is authoritarian rather than liberal, leads them towards the Conservative end of the dimension, to want to solve race relations by cutting immigration.

I discuss that one relatively trivial result as a good way of pointing out the intricacies of considering attitudes and social background as joint influences on political action. The actual impact of race relations policy proximities is by far the weakest in the model. The really crucial finding from the whole analysis is that these theoretically derived relative proximity measures work very well indeed. The overall package of variables account for 56 per cent of the variance in the vote, which is a surprisingly high score for data of this sort, and over 90 per cent of this is accounted for by the attitude and not the social background variables. It is notable, in addition, that these policy proximity variables are invariably more highly correlated with vote choice than they are with the socio-psychological concept of party-identification — they actually lead to choice in a complex situation, rather than just to a non-action psychological affinity. (Both objective and subjective class are also more highly correlated with vote than with party identification, a concept that might well be on its way out from political sociology, having contributed almost nothing after 30 years of plaguing researchers.[9]

The first four variables in importance are all proximity measures, one being the general attitude to democracy. That even so abstract an attitude should rank easily above subjective social class as an influence on vote may be even more remarkable than the vastly greater impact of the first two variables compared with all others. The degree to which one was relatively nearer the Conservative Party than the Labour Party, in one's own private political universe, on policies towards trade unions and to job creation, issues which were seen by all journalists as vital in the campaign, alone account for 45 per cent of the total variance in this model. Proximity to a party on the trade union issue was nearly three times more important than one's subjective sense of class. None of this emphasis is meant to deny the continued vital role of social class: both from evidence in this very model, from other points in this chapter, and, above all, from the preceding three chapters, the vital importance of our modern disaggregated class sub-cultures is clear. The point of this last chapter has been to show, however, that class (and doubtless other background factors) has its primary importance in circumscribing and shaping policy preferences and general ideology. It is the ideology, and the beliefs about how a society should be governed, that have the ultimate role in directing political action. It has also been a prime argument in this chapter that the conditions for attitudinal and ideological impact on voting are more and more ripe. By looking at the referendum campaign, during which ordinary partisanship was a much weaker cue than ever before, and now at voting in the election where the traditional and oversimplified class model broke down, and where the 'dealignment' in terms of classic psychological identification continued to decline, one can show how elections of the future must go. Class certainly remains crucial, though it is now a more complicated class model, with subtler connections to self-interest, and a more general ideological disaggregation. Self-interest itself has certainly not declined, but, as I showed earlier, fits ill with previous orthodox assumptions about class interest. The old classes have ceased to be cultural communities, witness the decline in class consciousness and class loyalty. Partisanship, not only increasingly weak in the electorate, is increasingly not inherited. Social mobility, especially if one admits of more than two classes, means that very few people in any case have a pure class inheritance from which to adopt a parental vote.

The ideologies of the class and party communities seldom fit elite perceptions of how opinions ought to fit together. Above all, a newly open electorate, ready and able to respond to opinion and policy cues, is spread out over a two-dimensional ideological map, the most populated quadrant of which combines a redistributive radicalism with a social conservatism and authoritarianism that can only be regarded as populist. Britain does not have a populist party, at least as yet. But to some extent in 1979, and then to all appearances massively in 1983, the floodgates began to open. Deprived of its ability, one that can surely never return, to rely on a solid working class loyalty, a radical Labour Party performed disastrously. The Conservative Party had already shown in 1979 (see my discussion of class consciousness in chapter 4) that it did not require people positively to think of themselves as middle class to vote out of class self-interest for the Conservatives. In 1979 the Labour Party could only do well amongst those who both were, and thought they were, working class. That is already a tiny proportion of the population. The Labour Party, to its credit perhaps, has always asked its supporters to be loyal despite the fact that, on the second, social liberalism, dimension, a brand of conservatism is nearer to their class ideology. Mrs Thatcher's party in 1983, partly without intent, relied heavily on the symbols that could attract such voters – the chauvinism of the Falklands, the emotion surrounding law and order, the national security aspect of nuclear disarmament, a coolness towards welcoming immigrants, an evocation of (literally) Victorian beliefs about family relations and morality, could have been predicted to be potent. In the past a class loyalty could still have overcome them, still have got out the vote for a disunited and, within the context, extreme Labour Party. But the source of that class loyalty is no longer.

For more than a decade now analysts have been commenting on

what they have rather patronizingly referred to as the 'volatility' of the electorate. The 'volatility' appears, from my analysis, to be simply a willingness to vote from a mixture of a very complex self-interest calculus, and a highly differentiated class–partisan ideology, which has been of increasing importance. To have stuck with the same party in 1983 that it had elected in 1979 despite a massive increase in unemployment and the arrival of a new political party trying hard to capitalize on a somewhat vague 'middle ground' is not volatility. What happens in the future is, as ever, problematic. Perhaps a party will break the mould of British politics. That would involve a degree of redistribution of power and social honour as well as income that we have not seen since the post-war government. But it would have to be accompanied by a chauvinism, brutality, and moral and social repression that we have not seen this century. There seem to be two parties that might take off in the hope of building a new coalition in British politics. The Conservative Party may continue its current trend which has, perhaps rightly, been seen as in the interests of the 'haves'. This is a perfectly good electoral strategy, because the haves, in the absence of the old class communities, essentially means not just the upper class right, but nearly any youngish person in employ-ment and not particularly concerned with publicly provided goods. If this continues to be combined with social conservatism, it should be able to win elections quite often. The popular press rejoiced at the hope that, in the new House of Commons, the Conservative victory had brought the return of the death penalty nearer. Over 80 per cent of the population now wish for that. Though in the end it was not given by the 1983 House, there were enough Tories who voted for it. If unemployment gets no worse, and expenditure cuts continue largely to hit the middle class left who care for education and cannot afford to buy it privately, why should there not be a Conservative victory?

Alternatively the Labour Party might at least drop issues like uni-lateralism that risk its working class authoritarian support, might drop Socialist rhetoric, and simply concentrate on its real appeal of soaking the rich in the interests not of society's really needy, but the direct material interests of those same employed or once-employed mass of workers. Remembering the analysis of the open-ended ques-tions in chapter 6, it might go simply for 'pensions' and, this time, for unemployment benefit. It might note that it is Labour voters who live in council houses and want to buy them. There is no reason why the Labour Party cannot orient itself so that it gets on the right side of the self-interest of a large enough plurality of voters, as long as it does not offend them by being socially liberal, and does not expect them to vote out of a Socialist-oriented and no longer existent class interest.

But is there any way in which the *soi-disant* 'mould-breakers', the Social Democratic Party and their Alliance partners, the Liberals, can hope to do the same? Nothing in this book has been meant to suggest for one moment that real class interest, class perceptions, and self-interest have ceased to be the fundamental building blocks of political action. It is true that the three class/three partisanship model in chapters 5–7 leaves five out of nine cells, accounting for a lot of the population outside the double dichotomy of the old Con/Lab middle/working construct. There are a lot of people who are intermediate in class or 'neutral' in partisanship. These, as is fully shown, tend towards their own sub-cultural ideologies. And they, above all, may ratiocinate, may opt for the party which minimizes relative distance between voter's desire and his perception of party policy. But this does require policies, and it requires policies that relate to the interests and the actual beliefs of those people. It is very dubious that the policies, to the extent that they were manifest at all, of the Alliance in 1983 were well designed actually to pick up the interests of these voters. Certainly they were not designed to fit the ideologies of these groups. The Alliance suffers, as did the old Liberal Party, from being (see chapter 2) terribly well representative of all sectors of society. It is well placed to practise the politics of compromise, to avoid the politics of confrontation so hated by political analysts of the seventies. Like the Liberals, it probably appeals to those cut free from class locations, those who are relatively well educated, those who genuinely espouse the 'civilized society', in the long-ago words of one of their leaders when he was a Labour Home Secretary. Were Britain becoming classless in the true sense, as a simple approach to crude data has suggested to some, they might well win an election. But Britain is not becoming classless; it just has a more subtle class structure than we are used to thinking of; it is not more 'civilized', and it is certainly not less motivated by self-interest. There may well be room for a party that will represent the interests of the intermediate class — in a three-class society why not have three class parties? But that does not mean a 'classless' party can make that appeal. Instead, and as my analysis of 1979 would suggest, with two class parties, those in the middle decide which class interest is nearer their own and vote for it, unworried that they do not mentally attribute a class home there.

It is too soon after one election, in a book written primarily from data about the previous one, to be sure of anything. But although my argument throughout this book would suggest an unfreezing of the simple class-party electorate, a great possibility for new results and for the reflection more precisely of what voters feel and want, the constraints are deeply laid and the changes are changes inside the clay round which the mould fits. The clay is what it always has been, and modifications to the Conservative and Labour Parties ought to suffice them as moulders for a long time to come.

Appendix: Statistical Techniques

Although this book does not rely very heavily on esoteric statistical analysis, there are places where I have felt it necessary to go beyond the usual simple percentage tables to which general works in political sociology normally restrict themselves. Usually it is still possible for the reader essentially to ignore the graphs, tables and equations, trusting that any improprieties I may have committed will be caught quite soon enough by technical experts. The exception is the heavy use I make in chapters 5-7 of a technique known as 'log-linear' analysis. This I have tried to describe as much as possible in lay language where first introduced. Indeed one of the main reasons for using it is that the constituent element of log-linear analysis, the idea of 'odds', and the comparison between odds by 'odds ratios' is itself more readily grasped by the statistical layman than are many of the more commonly encountered ways of dealing with tables in which several variables are interconnected.

However it seems useful to describe very briefly the four main techniques I have used. These fall into two natural groups. Two, factor analysis and multi-dimensional scaling, are used to explore the structure of a data set, seeking for simplicity in the multivariate universe. The other two, regression analysis (and its derivative, path analysis or causal modelling) and the log-linear approach are used to discover how well a dependent variable can be explained by a set of other variables.

FACTOR ANALYSIS AND MULTI-DIMENSIONAL SCALING

Factor analysis has been used in this book to create dimensional scales from a set of attitude questions. As such, particularly in chapter 6, but throughout much of the book, the results play a crucial

226

role. The model underlying factor analysis rests on the idea that, where variables are inter-correlated, part of the correlation arises from the fact that both variables are measuring the same phenomenon. In this sense the two main dimensions of ideology I use to define the four 'quadrants' of British political culture — the economic radicalism dimension and the social liberalism dimension — are to be thought of as underlying structures each of which is partially measured by each of a series of separate attitude questions. By mathematical techniques it is possible to deduce the 'scores' of individuals as they would be were it possible to measure these dimensions directly. The easiest analogy is that of measuring general intelligence, a hypothesized general intellectual capacity which underlies the directly observable scores on a whole series of more precise tests of mathematical reasoning, verbal fluency, spatial acuteness and so on. Indeed it was the pioneering work of original IQ researchers that started the development of factor analysis.

Whilst there is no reason to doubt the purely mathematical results of any factor analysis of a correlation matrix, the meaning to be given to the derived factors, and sometimes even the decision as to how many underlying factors there are is more subjective. The two principal factors used from the analysis of the attitude questions in chapter 6 were interpreted, as is usual, by considering the relative 'loadings' of each original attitude variable on the underlying and mathematically derived factors. The details of the analysis from which this interpretation was made are given in table A.1. These 'factor loadings' are the correlation between the original variable and the underlying factor, so that the higher loadings indicate a closer measurement of this basic phenomenon, and carry more weight in its interpretation.

Multi-dimensional scaling (henceforth MD scaling for short) is in part an equivalent technique to factor analysis for use on data at a different measurement level. Theoretically only variables which can be measured in a fully metric or 'interval level' manner, such as heights of respondents or their ages should be used with factor analysis (or, for that matter, with regression. The fact that the attitude question data on which I use both these techniques do not fully justify the application is technically a statistical sin. However it is a sin I commit in extremely good company — it is widely accepted now that well-constructed attitude scales are near enough to real metrics to permit of such techniques.)

MD scaling works on what are known as 'similarity' matrixes. These give a numerical score for the relative similarity of any pair of

TABLE A.1 Basic factor analysis used to create ideological scales

Variable	Factor one	Factor two
Increase NHS expenditure	0.244	0.012
Establish comprehensives	*0.573*	−0.017
Repatriate immigrants	0.030	*0.538*
Control building land	*0.530*	0.037
Increase foreign aid	0.211	*−0.386*
Restore capital punishment	−0.079	*0.593*
Increase worker participation	*0.430*	−0.129
Get rid of poverty	*0.467*	0.032
Redistribute wealth	*0.713*	0.047
Give stiffer criminal sentences	−0.035	*0.473*
Withdraw troops from Ulster	0.251	*0.328*
Reduce power of House of Lords	*0.452*	0.089
Eigenvalue and percentage of variance explained	2.553 21.3	1.857 15.5

Notes:

This analysis was carried out on a battery of 12 questions, of the 'How important is it that the government should do. . .' format discussed in chapter 7. A simple principle components analysis was carried out, which yielded three factors with Eigenvalues greater than unity, accounting altogether for 47 per cent of the variance. Only the first two were used in subsequent analyses.

Eigenvalues refer to the percentage of variance explained and are conventionally used as a form of significance testing. One is not expected to extract factors whose Eigenvalues are below 1.00.

The Eigenvalue and percentage for the third, unused, factor were: 1,167 and 9.7; no variable had a loading higher than 0.302 on this factor.

The reasons for the interpretations of the meanings of the factors are obvious given the loading pattern. Following the usual rule of thumb, only loadings of 0.3 or greater were considered. These are shown in italics. Only the first variable failed to load on either factor.

Because of the direction of coding of the variables, and the signs of the loadings it works out such that High Scores on F1 indicate a 'right-wing' and on F2 a 'liberal' position.

elements. Thus one might, for example, produce a similarity matrix for a bench of judges, by counting the proportion of times each pair of judges agree with each other out of all the cases they hear jointly. The higher the agreement score, the more 'similar' the pair of judges. The scaling technique uses these as though they were measures of physical distance in a many dimensional universe. The aim is to reduce the total number of dimensions to the smallest number which can portray the original elements in such a way as to preserve the shape of the relationships and the relative distances between them, in a much more economical portrayal. It is, deliberately, directly analogous to drawing a two-dimensional map of a three-dimensional reality. For many purposes the whole of the important distances and relationships between a set of towns (the elements referred to above) can be represented with no important loss two-dimensionally, relative height not being sufficiently salient. It provides social science data analysts with the ability to produce a spatial mapping of the similarities between a large set of points in two or three dimensions, so that natural groupings can be observed. I have used this technique on socio-economic categories twice in this book to find natural groupings of classes and display them. Once I used a similarity matrix based on the voting profiles of age/sex/class groups, once on a matrix based on attitude scales measured across the seven social grades I identified in chapter 5 so as to come up with the three-class model. In both cases the two-dimensional results were very good representations of the original similarity-distances in the complete matrix, as tested by the relevant coefficient, known as the 'stress' coefficient, which checks that no pair of similarities is being forced out of true to get the reduced-dimension model.

REGRESSION AND LOG-LINEAR MODELLING

Both regression and log-linear modelling are variants on what is increasingly being seen as one general data analysis technique, nowadays often referred to as the 'general linear model', and they bear much the same data-type relationship as do factor analysis and multi-dimensional scaling. Thus regression can technically only be used on interval level data, as opposed to variables that represent only an ordering rather than a precise set of measurements. Log-linear modelling is used to ask much the same questions about data which is only categorical or 'qualitative' in nature. Such data, coding someone's sex or race, for example, cannot be seen as measurement in the same sense as recording his age or her income. Yet by taking certain assumptions, mathematically too complex to go into here, the logarithms of the ratios between such qualitative measures can be treated by the general linear model.

This model assumes that relationships between variables can be caught by an equation of the general form:

$$Y = b1(X1) + b2(X2) \ldots \ldots + bn(Xn) + e$$

This apparently horrific piece of maths is code for a very simple idea.

Y is the variable one is trying to explain. X1, X2, to Xn are the variables one is using to explain it. The b1 etc. are coefficients which multiply the values of the X variables to give their exact impact on the Y. To find out the actual value of Y for any set of X1–Xn, one puts the actual X values into the equation, multiplies by the bs (they are usually called beta weights, or 'regression coefficients'), and adds up the scores. The key to the technique comes in grasping what is meant by 'explaining' a Y variable in this context. Effectively one is predicting Y from the equation. But as one knows, in fact, what the Y value actually is, one can see how good the prediction is, and how each particular X variable contributes to the prediction. When I assert that some variable explains Y well, I am saying that it predicts well the way in which each Y value deviates from the overall average for Y values. When I say that one X variable is more powerful as an explanation than another, I am comparing the beta weights. If b1 is higher than b2, more weight is being given in the regression equation to X1 than to X2, hence it is a more powerful predictor, and by analogy, a more important explanatory factor. The overall regression model can also be tested for its total predictive/explanatory power, by asking how much of the way the actual Y values differ from the average Y value is predicted by the whole package of X variables. In the sort of data I deal with here, there is always a large amount of error in the measurement. The final term in the model equation above, 'e', is the error term. The equation as a whole is saying that the actual recorded income for a respondent, Y, is found by adding together his age (X1) multiplied by the beta weight for that variable (b1) and his educational achievement score (X2) multiplied by that beta (b2) plus an error factor e. The larger the e, the less good the fit. The error can arise from two sources. It may be that all three variables, Y, X1, X2, are perfectly accurately measured, but that income actually mainly depends on something else (class, say), which we do not have in the model. Or it may be that we have very bad measures of one or more of three variables, and the exact fit ought to be perfect, were we only able to measure properly. It is impossible to know which form of error we have, but survey research is notoriously bad at getting good measures even of precise quantities like income or age, let alone those metaphysical entities we know as attitudes and try to measure by questionnaire items. Thus e is usually large, and correlations, or equivalent coefficients to judge explanatory power usually very low. In the cases that regression and log-linear models are used throughout this book, the results are nearly always surprisingly good for data of this type.

BIBLIOGRAPHY

Anyone wishing to understand more fully the techniques used here can consult any one of a thousand statistical textbooks. Simple and well-written accounts of the four techniques are to be found in the SPSS Manual (1977), 2nd edn (N. Nie *et al.*, 1974) and in references given in the various notes. H. M. Blalock *Social Statistics* is used by more social scientists, probably, than any other textbook.

PROGRAMMES AND DATA SOURCES

Unless specified elsewhere, all the data are drawn from the three surveys taken by the British Election Study at the University of Essex for the general elections of October 1974, May 1979, and the EEC Referendum Survey of 1975. Full technical details of sampling and questionnaires can be obtained from them, or from the SSRC Survey Archive, University of Essex, Colchester, Essex. The programmes used are: for all basic tables, and for regression and factor analysis – SPSS Version 7, implemented by the University of Essex and the University of Oxford Computing Services. For multi-dimensional scaling – MINISSAN (V.3) – MDS(X) as developed by Professor A. Coxon, University College, Cardiff and implemented by the Oxford University Computing Service. For log-linear analysis – the general linear model programme GLIM, Version 3, Royal Statistical Society, implemented by the Oxford University Computing Service. I am particularly grateful to Mr Clive Payne, of the University's Social Studies Faculty for help with these programmes, and to both him and Mr Eric Roughley of the University of Essex for help in implementing the data set in Oxford.

Notes

CHAPTER 1

1. One measure of just how low 'spontaneous' class identification has become is that, in 1979, considerably more people were prepared to offer a spontaneous party identification than a class identity. Yet 1979 came at the end of a decade of steady decline in party loyalty.

2. This is not meant to imply that the term 'middle class', or its derivatives like 'lower middle class' had not been used by historians and novelists before. From at least Dickens onwards one finds such references. But the recognition of the political force of this element, and anything like a seriously rigorous definition, are as new as Bonham argues. Until about 1945, English class sense might have included the middle class as a social grade, but with very little sense of what the term covered. Certainly in newspaper terms, the references Bonham quotes before 1945 do not cover what we have come to think of as the middle class.

3. Bonham quotes (p. 27) from *The Economist* after by-election results in 1946 where that journal appears to have discovered a direct economic voting interest in something like the modern 'middle class' for the first time.

4. M. Abrams *et al.* (1960). A similar argument is found in C. A. R. Crosland (1962). This latter is especially important because it was Crosland's holding the thesis described that led him to his famous revisionist version of socialism, *The Future of Socialism*. D. E. Butler and R. Rose (1959) was the last of the Nuffield Election Studies to be written before reliable survey evidence from academic studies could be used to check such theses.

5. David Butler and Donald Stokes (1974) *Political Change in Britain* (2nd edn), especially ch. 10. More generally, this book, and the first edition (Penguin, 1971, Macmillan, 1969) is *the* indispensable and nearly unique authoritative source for survey based data and analysis of the British electorate. Part I of my book, and Sarlvik and Crewe's (1983) book are in part deliberately written to replicate and compare with Butler and Stokes. However out of date their work may now be (the second edition takes in data only up to 1970), the entire professional understanding of electoral

232

sociology in this country is grounded on their seminal work. I shall very frequently refer to it from now on. It is worth readers noting that the second edition is *not* just an updating of the first — they differ in substantial respects and in emphasis, and both should be read.

6. In chapter 2, where I break the usual class coding up into more refined detail, one can see some glimmer of traditional marxist 'owners and controllers', who are indeed almost purely Tory in voting behaviour, but account for a very small proportion of the electorate. I am grateful to Patrick Dunleavy for giving me this idea.

7. The best work on class structures in North America has been in the social mobility field, the leading work of which is P. M. Blau and O. D. Duncan (1967).

8. A good study of nationalism at its height is W. L. Miller (1981). But despite the rise in Welsh and Scottish nationalism in the sixties and seventies, the general pattern has been for all non-class dimensions to decline. This is particularly true of religion. Compare the religious denomination voting figures given in table 1.6 with the data reported by Butler and Stokes. Their discussion in chapter 7 of the second edition is still correct, though the situation is even more clear.

9. It used to be commonly argued that inflation really hurt only the middle class because their incomes were much less geared to price changes than those of manual workers, and because they might well depend on investment income. On the other hand, unemployment was supposed really only to worry the working class because of middle class job security. However much truth there may ever have been in this, it is no longer plausible. The thesis in any case dates from the days when it was commonly supposed, even by professional economists, that inflation and unemployment were opposite evils, and that one had a pay-off relationship between them. In the last 15 years we have been used to both at the same time. It may be that the policies of the Thatcher governments, which have indeed reduced inflation and raised unemployment, will bring back into fashion both theories.

10. This can be seen both by looking at the voting profiles of those educated in and out of comprehensives, and the attitudes of party groups to the systems in all surveys taken by Butler and Stokes and the British Election Study. The change to comprehensive schooling was perhaps the earliest 'new' policy the Labour Party adopted after its electoral defeat in 1951. Until then it had accepted the consensus of the 1944 Butler Education Act.

11. My discussion throughout part II of this book of upper class socialism, especially prevalent amongst academics, is germane. The worst offenders in the technical work have been the American authors of the Michigan school, perhaps especially the extreme efforts of Philip Converse (1964) to deny any stability to public opinion. Like all such work, it is dependent on correlations existing between attitudes as measured in surveys, and on the researchers' own sense of what ought to be correlated with what.

12. The idea of a 'catch-all' party probably derives from M. Duverger's (1966) classic. The first much written of catch-all party was the Gaulliste party in

France after 1958, and both the Adenauer CSU–CDU in Germany and the Italian DC have long been seen as examples. The Italian case at least is still true. See H. Penniman (1978).

13. One can produce widely different levels of class identity by asking the question with a more or less forceful prompt buried in the language. Split half samples in 1964, for example, produced 60 per cent admitting to thinking of themselves with a class identity with one wording, and only 40 per cent with another. I have been careful only to use identical wording data. In general the British Election Study questionnaires used the same wording throughout the seventies, and used a lesser rather than stronger prompt form than did Butler and Stokes.

14. For the generation thesis, see Butler and Stokes (1971) ch. 5, and for a very powerful attack on it, see I. Crewe (1974). As all those born between 1969 and perhaps 1992 will have spent their formative years under Tory dominance, the generation thesis ought to produce a very stable Conservative electorate well into the next century.

15. Not only is living in a council house an extremely good predictor of Labour voting, but there is a powerful theory to explain why this should be so; see F. Parkin (1967). Parkin's argument is, roughly, that Britain has, overall, a Conservative culture, and only those insulated from these major cultural cues by working class sub-cultural factors, especially like living in a large council estate, are free to follow a natural interest and vote Labour. Crosland's concern to remove a social stigma he felt attached to council housing may be a reverse version of this theory.

CHAPTER 2

1. A problem arises throughout this book about class location of women. I have taken a married woman as having the same social grade as her husband. In one sense there is no excuse for this, and arguments against the process can be found in, *inter alia*, J. Lovenduski (1981). Butler and Stokes also took this approach, as have most survey researchers. The huge sample in the Nuffield Social Mobility survey, for example, was restricted to men only. Ideally one would allot class status to all of the sample, but none of the existing occupational status coding schemes, and none of the existing developed theories of social status allow this.

2. There may be relatively simple underlying explanations. One is that manual public sector jobs tend to be more highly unionized. However, even if this is the case, one should not overlook the fact that such details are simply part and parcel of a general difference in work experience and nature between the two sectors. Being able to offer specialized explanations for each datum is irrelevant against the general argument here that it is important what sector one works in, and that this transcends the mere class location.

CHAPTER 3

1. One reason for a lack of marked voting tendency amongst the lower categories of table 3.1 is that disposable income is not restricted to wages, though political orientation probably is. Thus weekly income may be roughly similar between a large family whose breadwinner has a low income but qualifies for many benefits, and a single highly paid affluent worker. It is sensible to expect the latter to be interested in a low tax Tory policy, and the former to be attracted to a high welfare benefit Labour policy. They would cancel each other out in table 3.1. There are other problems like this. For example, manual workers tend to have reduced income as they get older, but older voters are more Conservative. For all these reasons it is sometimes more surprising that income variables show any political trend, rather than that they do not show more pronounced trends.
2. The definition here is not restricted to unions affiliated to the TUC.
3. The data is from Butler and Stokes. Note that they use the 'party preference' of the 1963 respondents, rather than their vote. This is equivalent to my 'party identification'. The main reason for this is that the earliest wave of their surveys was in 1963, which was not an election year, hence there could be no vote reported. In comparing my analyses with theirs it must be remembered that I am treating their report of 'party preference' (they sometimes refer to partisan self-image) as a surrogate for vote. I could have used my equivalent measure, party identification, but prefer to use the more behavioural measure of the respondents' actual reported vote. As 'party preference' and vote are very highly correlated it is unlikely that any serious lack of comparability emerges.
4. There is an extensive literature on the way in which middle class aspirations, views and so on hang on amongst those who are socially mobile. For an entertaining and still extremely careful and interesting study, with excellent references, see K. I. Macdonald (1974).

CHAPTER 5

1. It should be realized that I refer only to books intended for general readers in saying that model fitting is rare. The professional journals are rife with models. But I see no reason why ordinary readers should be patronized and not offered the full scope of the discipline.
2. By membership here I am referring to voting loyalty or social and psychological ties. In a formal sense, membership of a political party is extremely rare in the UK.
3. It may seem that this is over strict, as it automatically precludes those too young to vote in 1974 from a party family. This is intentional – it is well known that the first vote cast in a voter's lifetime is more probable to be changed subsequently than any pair of later votes are to be different.

1979 was unusual in that, for the first time in a long time, Labour did not get a majority of first time voters. It is therefore far safer to treat first time voters like vote changers than like stable voters, whatever other evidence — say from their party identification scores — might suggest.

CHAPTER 6

1. Eysenck (1951). Similar results have been achieved by co-workers of his, especially in the investigation of the psychological dimension of conservatism; this tends to unite in one the two separate factors I use.
2. The particular attraction of the unilateralist position on nuclear weaponry not only to the Labour Party, but to important segments of the Liberal Party, and their surprise at its rejection by the electorate in the 1983 election, is typical of this misconception of the mass electorate.
3. These were television comedies running in the early seventies in both Britain and America. The (original) British version was called 'Till Death Do Us Part', and the very good American imitation 'Those Were the Days'.
4. It is a great pity that an alternative tradition of political science study of mass ideology, the depth interview with a small sample, as brilliantly demonstrated in R. E. Lane (1962), has almost entirely died out in favour of the apparently more 'scientific' large-scale survey with fixed format questionnaires. To some extent the tradition is still kept up in the socialization studies, especially by American writers like Richard Merelman. During the Second World War, the British government monitored public morale by using a survey form, Mass Observation, to get researchers just to write down what they heard people talking about in pubs and shops. Such an approach would be invaluable as an additional way of researching election campaigns, but it is very unlikely that any grant giving body would be prepared to finance it, so complete is the orthodoxy about 'scientific' sampling.
5. The fully detailed coding scheme for these open-ended questions is lengthy and complex. The version used in 1979 was my modification of an even more complex one developed by J. E. Alt, then Senior Research Officer on the British Election Study in 1974. The details can be got from the SSRC Survey Archive, University of Essex.

CHAPTER 7

1. Although there were very few grammar schools left in England and Wales by 1979, the issue of comprehensivization was both symbolically, and practically, both alive and intense. An example of how politically important the issue still was as late as 1976 is the court case, going all the way to the House of Lords between the Secretary of State for Education and the Borough of Tameside. It is exceptionally rare for political issues to turn into litigation in Britain, and this case, along with the GLC public transport case

in 1981 were overwhelmingly the most 'political' cases in the last 20 years.

2. A good example is the distribution of opinion on trade union power. Roughly 70 per cent of the population think they are too powerful. This means that there would be odds of about 2.3 : 1 in favour of such a statement. It is thus a 'skewed' issue, and on that count a candidate for a useful way of categorizing group attitudes. However this odds figure is constant across all groups of the population. Thus the opinion does not serve to differentiate any group from the others. Yet again, the fact that union members themselves have the same ratio is theoretically interesting, precisely because they *ought* to be different. Thus when an opinion distribution is 'useful' depends entirely on the theoretical purpose in question.

3. Log-linear modelling is actually based on comparing 'relative odds', or 'odds ratios'. Suppose the odds against believing X in group A is 2 : 1, and in group B it is 4 : 1. The ratio between these two odds, 2 : 4, is itself 2. One might have another two groups, with respective odds against of 3 : 1 and 6 : 1. Again the ratio of these odds, 3 : 6, is 2. Thus the relationship between A and B and C and D is the same. It was the discovery that the logarithms of these odds ratios behave mathematically in certain ways like ordinary averages that made it possible to convert the odds measured over purely 'nominal' data of the form found in cross-tabulated data into an equivalent of analysis of variance or regression type statistical modelling. See Upton (1978) for a proper explanation.

4. One way of looking at the very high predictability of the completely intermediate group, those with middle locations in class and party, is to say that they are so completely without opinion-distorting cues that they represent the cancelling out of all forces. They are, in a way, as a group a 'null' group, about whom we actually know nothing at all.

5. It can be argued that these apparently authoritarian and reactionary views are not psychological orientations, but perfectly concrete class interests. It is, after all, the case that the vast majority of victims of violent crime are actually very poor. Whilst there may be very little evidence that coloured immigrants take away jobs that white working class people might otherwise get, it is certainly more likely that an unskilled worker will have to compete with a 'New Commonwealth' immigrant in the job market than that any member of the upper class will have to do so. There are powerful semi-marxist explanations for racial prejudice and lower class illiberalism, which I have no particular wish to deny. But they must compete against another powerful (and originally marxist inspired) research tradition, as represented by such works as T. Adorno *et al.* (1950). Here the emphasis is much more on the socializing process, and especially the family/peer group influences in the working class culture.

6. There is a well known argument to explain a similar rigidity of attitudes and unexpected conservatism amongst some sectors of the American electorate who are of first or second generation immigrant stock. The thesis, sometimes called the 'status anxiety' thesis, is that in pursuit of a sense of belonging such marginal groups over-stress what they take to be the dominant and

traditional value set. See R. Hofstadter in D. Bell *et al.* (1955) for the probable start of this thesis. In the UK there is an additional probable explanation, in that the nonconformist churches, traditionally morally more rigid, have always been more popular amongst the lower middle classes than the solidly establishment Anglicans or the originally (but no longer) Labour inclined and working class Catholic Church.

CHAPTER 8

1. N. Nie *et al.* (1974). This book both re-analyses the data covered by Campbell *et al.* (1960) and adds new data from a later period, radically altering the old view of the American electorate. A good recent collection that continues the updating, though being perhaps more on the Campbell side than Nie's, is *Trends in American Electoral Behaviour* (1980) by D. Hill and N. Luttbeg, Itasca, Illinois: F. E. Peacock.

2. See N. Nie *et al.* (1974). In 1978 the polls show 39 per cent Democrat identifiers, 21 per cent Republicans, and 37 per cent Independent. However surveys in the UK have never offered respondents the chance of saying they are independent — rather, if a voter does not immediately offer an identification he is prompted to offer one. It would be interesting to speculate what our data and anlyses would look like had the American question been asked fully right from its first use here by Butler and Stokes in 1963. Even from the beginning there were powerful dissenters from the model proposed by Michigan researchers. See V. O. Key (1966).

3. There are innumerable treatments of causal modelling in social science data. I follow the line developed by O. D. Duncan (1966) 'Path analysis: sociological examples' in *American Journal of Sociology*, rather than the partial correlation approach favoured by H. M. Blalock (ed.) (1970) *Causal Models in the Social Sciences*, Chicago: Aldine.

4. Naturally the division of the population into three partisan groupings is not the same as the one I construct from 1974 and 1979 data. In this case I take strong or moderately strong identifiers with the Conservative and Labour Parties, as reported in 1974, as the two partisan groups, and all others, principally Liberals, as the 'neutrals'.

5. The variable measuring education is different in construction from the one used in 1979. The 1974 data provide only for a crude scale of type of school attended and age when leaving full-time education. 1979 data gives an 'educational attainment' scale. The impact of class might well, of course, have shown more strongly had the measures I use for 1974 and 1979, taking certain groups out of the skilled manual categories into a category of their own, been then available.

6. Whatever happens to the SDP–Liberal Alliance in the next few years it is hard to imagine that the old solid loyalty to the Labour Party can ever regain its pre-1974 level. But this, as I argue at the end of this chapter, does not necessarily mean that the Labour and Conservative Parties will cease to

be the only important parties in the system. It is a matter of the difference between an instrumental support for Labour and an instinctive one.

7. Not being precise, as well as being precise but selective in your audience is a standard both of actual politics and the predictive rational choice literature. For a good summary see P. Ordeshook in Budge *et al.* (1976).

8. The implications for electoral democracy of this sort of policy preference distribution are argued at great length in S. E. Finer (ed.) (1975). For a more detailed discussion of the implications, see my forthcoming article (1984).

9. The inutility of party identification in most other countries has in fact been shown several times, as early as the 1966 study of Norway in Campbell *et al.* (1966) and in several country studies reported in Budge *et al.* (1976), especially in West Germany. See also A. Mughan *Political Studies* 1983.

References

Abrams, M. *et al.* (1960) *Must Labour Lose?*, London: Penguin.

Adorno, T. *et al.* (1950) *The Authoritarian Personality*, New York: Harper.

Aitken, D. and Kahan, M. (1974) 'Australia: class politics in the New World', in R. Rose (ed.) (1974) *Electoral Behaviour: A Comparative Handbook*, New York: Free Press.

Alford, R. R. (1963) *Party and Society*, New York: Rand McNally.

Alt, J. E. (1975) 'Angels in plastic', *Political Studies*, vol. 22.

Alt, J. E. (1976) 'Partisanship and policy choice', *British Journal of Political Science*, vol. 6.

Alt, J. E. and Turner, J. (1982) 'The case of the silk stocking socialists and the calculating children of the middle class', *British Journal of Political Science*, vol. 12.

Apter, D. E. (1964) *Ideology and Discontent*, New York: Free Press.

Barry, Brian (1970) *Sociologists, Economists and Democracy*, London: Macmillan.

Berelson, B. and Lazarsfeld, P. (1965) *The People's Choice*, New York: Columbia University Press.

Blalock, Hubert M. (1972) *Social Statistics*, Tokyo: McGraw Hill.

Blau, P. M. and Duncan, O. D. (1967) *The American Occupational Structure*, New York: John Wiley.

Bonham, J. (1954) *The Middle Class Vote*, London: Faber and Faber.

Budge, I. and Farlie, D. (1977) *Voting and Party Competition*, London: John Wiley.

Budge, I., Farlie, D. and Crewe, I. M. (eds) (1976) *Party Identification and Beyond*, London: John Wiley.

Butler, D. E. and Rose, R. (1959) *The British General Election of 1959*, London: Macmillan.

Butler, D. E. and Stokes, D. E. (1971) *Political Change in Britain* (1st edn), London: Penguin.

Campbell, A. *et al.* (1960) *The American Voter*, New York: John Wiley.

Campbell, A. *et al.* (1966) *Elections and the Political Order*, New York: John Wiley.

Childs, D. (1970) *The Essentials of Factor Analysis*, London: Reinhart.

Converse, P. E. (1964) 'The nature of belief systems in mass publics', in D. E. Apter (1964) *Ideology and Discontent*, New York: Free Press.

Crewe, I. M. (1973) 'The politics of "affluent" and "traditional" workers in Britain', *British Journal of Political Science*, Jan.

Crewe, I. M. (1974) 'Do Butler and Stokes really explain political change in Britain?', *European Journal of Political Research*, vol. 7.

Crewe, I. M., Sarlvik, B. and Alt, J. E. (1977) 'Partisan dealignment in Britain, 1964–1974', *British Journal of Political Science*, vol. 7.

Crosland, C. A. R. (1959) *The Future of Socialism*, London: Cape.

Dahrendorf, R. (1959) *Class and Class Conflict in Industrial Society*, London: Routledge & Kegan Paul.

Dahrendorf, R. (1967) *Society and Democracy in Germany*, New York: Doubleday.

Downs, A. (1957) *An Economic Theory of Democracy*, New York: Harper.

Dunleavy, P. (1980) 'The political implications of sectoral cleavages and the growth of public employment', *Political Studies*, vol. 28 (two part article).

Duverger, M. (1966) *Political Parties*, London: English University Library.

Eysenck, H. J. (1951) *The Psychology of Politics*, London: Routledge & Kegan Paul.

Finer, S. E. *et al.* (1975) *Adversary Politics and Electoral Reform*, London: Anthony Wigram.

Gerth, H. H. and Wright Mills, C. (1963) *From Max Weber*, London: Routledge.

Giddens, A. (1973) *The Class Structure of the Advanced Societies*, London: Hutchinson.

Goldberg, A. S. (1969) 'Social determinism and rationality as bases for party identification', *American Political Science Review*, vol. 63.

Goldthorpe, J. H. (1980) *Social Mobility and Class Structure in Modern Britain*, Oxford: Oxford University Press.

Goldthorpe, J. H. *et al.* (1968) *The Affluent Worker: Political Attitudes and Behaviour*, Cambridge: Cambridge University Press.

Goodhart, C. and Bhansali, R. J. (1970) 'Political economy', *Political Studies*, vol. 18.

Halsey, A. H. *et al.* (1980) *Origins and Destinations*, Oxford: Oxford University Press.

Harmon, H. (1967) *Modern Factor Analysis*, Chicago: Chicago University Press.

Heath, A. (1981) *Social Mobility*, London: Fontana.

Hildebrandt, K. and Dalton, R. (1978) 'The new politics' in M. Kaase and K. von Beyme (1978) *Elections and Parties*, London: Sage.

Hill, D. B. and Luttbeg, N. R. (1980) *Trends in American Electoral Behaviour*, Itasca, Illinois: F. E. Peacock.

Himmelweit, H. *et al.* (1981) *How Voters Decide*, London: Academic Press.

Hofstadter, R. in D. Bell *et al.* (1955) *The New American Right*, New York: Criterion Books.

Hope, K. (ed.) (1972) *The Analysis of Social Mobility*, Oxford: Oxford University Press.

Kaase, M. and Beyme, K. von (1978) *Elections and Parties*, London, Sage.

Kavanagh, D. (1984) *Essays in Honour of S. E. Finer*, London.

Key, V. O. (1966) *The Responsible Electorate*, Cambridge, Mass.: Belknap Press.

Lane, R. E. (1962) *Political Ideology*, New York: Free Press.

Lockwood, D. (1959) *The Black Coated Worker*, London: Allen & Unwin.

Lovenduski, J. and Hills, J. (eds) (1981) *The Second Electorate*, London: Routledge.

Macdonald, K. I. (1974) 'Downwardly mobile mothers and other interaction effects' in K. I. Macdonald and J. M. Ridge (1974) *Mobility in Britain Reconsidered*, Oxford: Oxford University Press.

Macdonald, K. I. and Ridge, J. M. (1974) *Mobility in Britain Reconsidered*, Oxford: Oxford University Press.

McKenzie, R. T. and Silver, A. (1968) *Angels in Marble*, London: Heinemann.

Marwick, A. (1980) *Class: Image and Reality*, London: Collins.

Miliband, R. (1969) *The State in Capitalist Society*, London: Weidenfeld.

Miller, W. L. (1981) *The End of British Politics?*, Oxford: Oxford University Press.

Mughan, A. (1983) 'The cross-national validity of party identification', *Political Studies*, vol. 31.

Nie, N. *et al.* (1974) *The Changing American Voter*, Cambridge, Mass.: Harvard University Press.

Nordlinger, A. E. (1967) *The Working Class Tories*, London: MacGibbon & Kee.

Parkin, F. (1967) 'Working class consciousness: a theory of political deviance', *British Journal of Sociology*, vol. 18.

Parkin, F. (1971) *Class Inequality and Political Order*, London: MacGibbon & Kee.

Peele, G. R. and Francis, J. G. (1978) 'Is there a shared political perspective?', *Political Studies*, vol. 26.

Penniman, H. (ed.) (1978) *Italy at the Polls*, Washington DC: American Enterprise Institute.

Poulantzas, N. (1973) *Political Power and Social Class*, London: New Left Books.

Rawlings, C. (1979) 'The lower middle class vote', Ph.D. thesis, Essex University.

Robertson, D. (1976a) *A Theory of Party Competition*, London: John Wiley.

Robertson, D. (1976b) 'Surrogates for party identification in the rational choice perspective', in I. Budge *et al.* (1976) *Party Identification and Beyond*, London: John Wiley.

Robertson, D. (1984) 'Adversary politics, public opinion, and electoral cleavages', in D. Kavanagh (1984) *Essays in Honour of S. E. Finer*, London.

Rose, R. (ed.) (1974) *Electoral Behaviour: A Comparative Handbook*, New York: Free Press.

Sarlvik, B. and Crewe, I. M. (1983) *Decade of Dealignment*, Cambridge: Cambridge University Press.

Schoen, D. (1977) *Powell and the Powellites*, London: Macmillan.

Statistical Package for the Social Sciences (SPSS) (1977), Chicago: McGraw Hill.

Thorburn, P. (1977) 'Political generations: the case of class and party in Britain', *European Journal of Political Research*, vol. 5.

Upton, J. G. (1978) *The Analysis of Cross-Tabulated Data*, London: John Wiley.

Weber, M. (1947) *The Theory of Social and Economic Organisation*, New York: Free Press.

Index